PRAISE FOR *VIOLENCE: HUMANS IN DARK TIMES*

"Many of us live today with a pervasive sense of unease, worried that our own safety is at risk, or that of our loved ones, or that of people whose bad circumstances appear to us through networked media. Violence feels ever-present. Natasha Lennard and Brad Evans help us to analyze those feelings, talking with a wide range of thinkers in order to gain insight into the worst of what humans do, and challenging us to imagine a world in which violence is no longer a given. Their book is full of surprising insights and intelligent compassion."

—S─── L──────, co-editor of *Th─ ─uture We Want: ──── ──── ──── ──he New Century*

"In *Violence*, ─── ──── ──── ──── ──── ─ have created, alongside the ─── ──── ──── ──── ──── ─ic exploration of the conce─ ──── ──── ──── ──── expected and not, in prose taut and unexpectedly gorgeous. Their philosophical rigor provides the reader with an intellectual arsenal against the violence of the current moment."

—Molly Crabapple, author of *Drawing Blood*

"This is a book that will make everyone feel clever. Reflections on violence, both actual, and the possibility of, mediating so much of social interaction, also makes for critical reading. The range of interviews with leading academics, to filmmakers and artists, is impressive, at once immediate and relevant, but also profoundly philosophical. More essentially, though, the conversations underline the need and suggest ways to resist and organize in a visionary way, in the extraordinary times we live in."

—Razia Iqbal, BBC News

"Standing on their own, the interview subjects featured in *Violence: Humans In Dark Times* might be identified as the foremost intellectuals, artists, and activists engaged with questions of how violence moves, acts, and is witnessed in the world. But summoned together in this collection by two political thinkers distinguished by both their unmatched intellects and their willingness to deploy those intellects in acts of service rather than performance, their voices materialize as a creative space large and fertile enough to lay the groundwork for an actionable hope. The result is a groundbreaking testament to the vital role of the abstract and the theoretical for understanding the depth to which violence is entrenched in human experience and consciousness and to the necessity of empathetic intellectual stewards like Lennard and Evans to direct such understanding into transformative action. We would be wise to read this collection with a similar eye toward service, and in so doing, open ourselves up to the rare mercy of no longer having to stand on our own."

—Alana Massey, author of *All The Lives I Want*

VIOLENCE
Humans in Dark Times

Brad Evans & Natasha Lennard

City Lights Books | Open Media Series

Open Media Series Editor: Greg Ruggiero

Cover art: detail from Being Open and Empty. Copyright © 2005 by Wang Dongling. Hanging scroll; ink on paper. 88 x 57 in. (223.5 x 114.8 cm). Gift of the artist, 2013.
(2013.188.2)
The Metropolitan Museum of Art. Image source: Art Resource, NY

Library of Congress Cataloging-in-Publication Data
Names: Evans, Brad, 1968- author. | Lennard, Natasha, author.
Title: Violence : humans in dark times / Brad Evans & Natasha Lennard.
Description: San Francisco, CA : City Lights Books, 2018.
Identifiers: LCCN 2018002365 (print) | LCCN 2018019869 (ebook) | ISBN   9780872867802 | ISBN 9780872867543
Subjects: LCSH: Violence. | Violence--Social aspects. | Social media.
Classification: LCC HM886 (ebook) | LCC HM886 .E936 2018 (print) | DDC
 303.6--dc23
LC record available at https://lccn.loc.gov/2018002365

ISBN: 978-0-87286-754-3
eISBN: 978-0-8728-6780-2

City Lights Books are published at the City Lights Bookstore
261 Columbus Avenue, San Francisco, CA 94133
www.citylights.com

Brad Evans dedicates this book to his loving and caring parents, Steven and Wendy. Without their support and guidance nothing in his world would have been possible.

Natasha Lennard dedicates this book to her mother, Sindy, sine qua non, and to Lukas, her partner in counter-violence.

CONTENTS

HUMANS IN DARK TIMES

Writing in the late 1960s, Hannah Arendt conjured the term "dark times" to address the legacies of war and human suffering. Arendt was not simply concerned with mapping out the totalitarian conditions into which humanity had descended. She was also acutely aware of the importance of individuals who challenge with integrity the abuses of power in all their oppressive forms. Countering violence, she understood, demands sustained intellectual engagement: we are all watchpersons, guided by the lessons and cautions of centuries of unnecessary devastation.

Mindful of the importance of Arendt in terms of thinking about violence, we deploy the phrase "humans in dark times" not as a description of something definitive but as a provocation. Just as we recognize that there are varying degrees of pain and suffering when it comes to the saturating capacities of oppressive power, so we also recognize every age has contingent problems that often reveal the worst of the human condition. As a result, we do not subscribe to the conceit that our times might be quantitatively deemed "lighter" on account of some triumph of liberal reason or its veritable retreat. Instead, we pursue the ways in which new and old forms of violence appear in the contemporary moment, what this means in terms of emphasizing the political urgency and demands of the times, and how we might develop the necessary intellectual tools to resist what is patently intolerable.

Across the world today, it is possible to witness the liberation of prejudice, galvanized by the emergence of a politics of hate and division, that plays directly into the everyday fears of those seduced by new forms of fascism. Such a condition demands purposeful and considered historical reflection. But here we immediately encounter a problem: if fighting violence and oppression demands new forms of ethical thinking that can be developed only with the luxury of time, what does this mean for the present moment when history is being steered in a more dangerous direction and seems to constantly accelerate?

Just as humans are not naturally violent, peace is not impossible. But in order for us to ethically develop styles of living that are suited to the twenty-first century, echoing the challenge set by Walter Benjamin, it is imperative that we develop a critique of violence that does ethical justice to the subject. To bring out the best in us, we have to confront the worst of what humans are capable of doing to one another. In short, there is a need to confront the intolerable realities of violence perpetrated in this world.

So we need to begin by recognizing that violence is not some abstract concept or theoretical problem. It represents a violation in the very conditions that constitute what it means to be human as such. Violence is always an attack upon a person's dignity, sense of selfhood, and future. It is nothing less than the desecration of one's position in the world. And it is a denial and outright assault on the very qualities that we claim make us considered members of this social fellowship and shared union called "civilization." In this regard, we might say violence is both an ontological crime, insomuch as it seeks to destroy the image we give to ourselves as valued individuals, and a form of political ruination that stabs at the heart of a human togetherness that emerges from the ethical desire for worldly belonging.

Victimization is but one part of the human condition. We also have the capacity to think and imagine better worlds. To accept violence is to normalize forms of coercion and domination that violate the bodies of the living. Through the subtle intimacy of its performance, it brings everything into its orbit such that the future can only appear to us as something that is violently fated. Every trauma left upon the body or psyche of the individual is another cut into the flesh of the earth.

In order for violence to be accepted there is a need for normalization. Such normalization depends upon immunization, like a surgical strike penetrating the body with such ruthless efficiency we no longer see it as being violence. While we might see cruelty as painful, we can reason beyond this, hence beyond the violence itself, for some greater political good. The violence in this regard is overlaid with a certain metaphysical cloak whose mask of mastery covers the desecrated body with a virtuous blood-soaked robe. That is to say, violence is also an intellectual and pedagogical force, underwritten by formidable schools of thought whose very purpose is to hide things in plain sight.

We also know that violence is always mediated by expressed dichotomies of permissible and impermissible actions. Some forms of violence can be fully reasoned and excused, while others clearly go beyond the tolerance threshold. Let's connect this directly to the intimate realities of violence today. What we have witnessed since 9/11 has been a notable public shift in the modalities of violence from spectacular attacks (in which humans were often removed from representations of the crimes) toward violence that is more intimate and individualizing. Such violence seems to actually be more intolerable for us as the intimacy addresses a different register. While both are abhorrent, images of exploding towers are arguably easier to deal with than the more focused types of suffering we now witness, from unarmed black men being killed by white police, to civilians—including children and the elderly—being slaughtered during "imprecise" U.S. military operations in places like Syria, Yemen, and Afghanistan, to courtroom testimonies of more than 160 women who were assaulted by a doctor. There is something about the raw realities of intimate suffering which affects us on an all too human level.

Such intimacy has also fed into and in many ways been driven by the pornographic violence of popular culture. Movie franchises, children's cartoons, and video games in particular seemingly excel in commercializing—and thus normalizing—the intimate possibilities of violence. Violence should be intolerable. Instead, it is mass-marketed, promoted, and sold as entertainment.

Yet it would be far too reductive to say that people have become inured to violence. The fact that people may turn away from violence or try to switch it off is arguably an all too natural reaction to its forced witnessing. The challenge is how to find meaningful solutions to the raw realities of violence that don't simply end up creating more anger, hatred, and division. People are certainly frustrated that the seemingly daily exposure to violence doesn't become a catalyst to steer history in a more peaceful direction.

It was with this shared appreciation for the importance of rethinking violence that, in September 2015, we began the project leading to this book. Following an initial meeting in New York City, Natasha proposed an interview with Brad for the *New York Times* philosophy forum "The Stone." The resulting conversation, "Thinking Against Violence, ran in the *Times* in mid-December 2015 and appears as chapter 1 in this collection.

The interview's success in the *Times* made the public appetite for a broader discussion about violence urgently clear. We were also acutely aware that there was no point in discussing violence unless something could be done about it. If violence undoes any idea of humanity we might want to sustain and develop, we need to learn how to undo violence—even if that means interrogating what we mean by "humanity." But such undoing is not going to come about from the voice of a single individual. Violence demands a conversation with somber and honest reflection.

And it was with this conversational ethos in mind that we envisaged a series of conversations as a truly trans-disciplinary mediation with artists, writers, and cultural producers that would bring critical thought to bear on violence. Violence cannot be countered by retreating back into academic enclaves that privilege certain vantage points. Nor can the idea of the so-called "aesthetic turn" in politics be undertaken if the work of artists is merely appropriated to make a theoretical point. A conversation on violence demands creating an ethical platform based upon reciprocity, where the voice of the contributor is recognized as being a genuine and viable form of political intervention. Just as we don't think that politics can be reduced to electoral procedures, so the call for more compassion, dignity, and love in the sphere of the political demands seeing art itself as integral to the political field. Hence, while the *New York Times* series (which successfully ran throughout 2016) largely featured renowned critical scholars, the ongoing *Los Angeles Review of Books* series continues to develop the conversation in more artistic but no less important directions.

"Humanity is in crisis," Zygmunt Bauman told us in one of his last interviews before passing away, "and there is no exit from that crisis other than the solidarity of humans." We hope this collection offers the critique—and the solidarity—adequate to our dark times.

—Brad Evans and Natasha Lennard

ONE

THINKING AGAINST VIOLENCE

We are immersed in a relentless stream of real and virtual violence. How can we break the cycle?

Natasha Lennard interviews Brad Evans

December 16, 2015

Brad Evans is a political philosopher, critical theorist, and writer whose work specializes on the problem of violence. The author of ten books and edited volumes, and over fifty articles, he serves as a Reader in Political Violence at the School of Sociology, Politics and International Studies, the University of Bristol, UK. He is the founder and director of the Histories of Violence Project.

Natasha Lennard: The premise of your book Disposable Futures *is that "violence is ubiquitous" in the media today. There seems to be plenty of evidence to support this claim—just look at the home page of this news site for a start. But the media has always been interested in violence—"if it bleeds, it leads" isn't exactly new. And the notion that there is just more violence in the world today—more*

*violent material for the media to cover—doesn't seem tenable. So
what do you think is specific about the ubiquity of violence today,
and the way it is mediated?*

Brad Evans: It is certainly right to suggest the connections
between violence and media communications have been a
recurring feature of human relations. We only need to open
the first pages of Aeschylus's *Oresteia* to witness tales of victory in battle and its communicative strategies—on this
occasion the medium of communication was the burning
beacon. But there are a number of ways in which violence
is different today, in terms of its logics intended, forced witnessing, and ubiquitous nature.

We certainly seem to be entering into a new moment,
where the encounter with violence (real or imagined) is becoming more ubiquitous and its presence ever felt. Certainly
this has something to do with our awareness of global tragedies as technologies redefine our exposure to such catastrophic events. But it also has to do with the raw realities
of violence and people's genuine sense of insecurity, which,
even if it is manufactured or illusionary, feels no less real.

One of the key arguments I make throughout my work
is that violence has now become the defining organizational
principle for contemporary societies. It mediates all social
relations. It matters less if we are actual victims of violence.
It is the possibility that we could face some form of violent
encounter that shapes the logics of power in liberal societies today. Our political imagination as such has become
dominated by multiple potential catastrophes that appear

on the horizon. The closing of the entire Los Angeles city school system after a reported terrorist threat yesterday is an unsettling reminder of this. From terror to weather and everything in between, insecurity has become the new normal. We see this played out at global and local levels, as the effective blurring between older notions of homeland/battlefields, friends/enemies, and peace/war has led to the widespread militarization of many everyday behaviors—especially in communities of color.

None of this can be divorced from the age of new media technologies, which quite literally puts a catastrophic world in our hands. Indeed, not only have we become forced witnesses to many tragic events that seem to be beyond our control (the source of our shared anxieties), but also accessible smart technologies are now redefining the producer and audience relationships in ways that challenge the dominance of older medias.

A notable outcome of this has been the shift toward humanized violence. I am not only talking about the ways in which wars have been aligned with humanitarian principles. If forms of dehumanization hallmarked the previous Century of Violence, in which the victim was often removed from the scene of the crime, groups such as ISIS foreground the human as a disposable category. Whether it is the progressive liberal, the journalist, the aid worker, or the homosexual, ISIS put the human qualities of the victims on full broadcast.

One could argue that by focusing on "humanity" when considering acts of violence—the human face of victims—we assert that the human is in fact indispensable (we might think of, say, newspaper paeans to victims after massacres). But you argue that this does the reverse and that violence-as-humanized and human disposability go together. Can you explain this a little further?

What we are engaging with here are two distinct types of violence, which, although appearing separate, often link and connect in subtle yet complex ways. On the one hand, we can point to the widespread disposability of human populations, those countless, nameless, and faceless victims, who experience violence often. Such populations live out a wide range of human insecurities, indignities, oppressions, and hardships. Yet these "disposable" populations, which are often contained, at times overspill their confinement to reveal the violence of the hidden order of politics. This is true whether we are talking about the Black Lives Matter movement, which has been galvanized by the spectacle of police brutality, or the bodies of refugee children like Aylan Kurdi, whose body washed up on the shores of a Turkish beach.

On the other hand, we have more orchestrated spectacles of violence, from real events to cultural and entertainment productions, which prove to be deeply significant in the normalization of violence and in producing the conditions for violence to come. We can explain this in terms of the interplay between disposable lives and sacrificial violence, onto claims for militaristic forms of justice. A number of philosophers have attended to the relationship between violence and the sacred. What concerns me are the ways in which sacrificial victims become loaded with symbolic meaning to sanction further violence and destruction. That is to say, how the spectacle of a truly intolerable moment is politically appropriated to sanction further violence in the name of the victims.

We have seen a terrifying example following the recent attacks in Paris and in San Bernardino. As the Islamic State, or ISIS, continues to push the spectacle of violence to the nth degree, it brings together the sacrificial and the disposable in challenging ways. ISIS has a clear strategy that seeks to maximize its exposure through the most intimate forms of sacrificial violence. There is, however, a further outcome to its violence; it creates the very conditions in which a violent response becomes inevitable. Its violence seeks to create disposable futures. By focusing precisely on populations which are actually most likely to resist the calls for further war and violence, what is effectively witnessed is an assault on the imagination and the ability to steer history in a different direction.

Faced with such spectacles, our complex range of emotions—sadness, horror, fear, anger, and concerns for the safety of families, friends, and loved ones—are consistently mobilized to justify a violent and militaristic response. Or as President François Hollande of France recently remarked, what's now needed is the purest form of justice, a "pitiless war," as if the previous age of violence was somehow marked by compassion. This raises serious questions about how we might even think about breaking the cycle of violence, as the future already appears to be violently fated.

It seems that the media only access the humanity and struggle of oppressed populations once we have had (literal, visual) exposure to spectacular violence enacted on their bodies. I think of the example you cite—of the child Aylan Kurdi dead on the Turkish beach or of the unarmed teen Michael Brown's body seen lying in the Ferguson street for three and a half hours. And that the corpses of privileged white people are often not used as a media spectacle in the West (indeed, publications and social media platforms scramble to ban ISIS execution videos). Does part of our world being "violently fated," as you say, relate to the fact that we often only find empathy and solidarity after we've seen people as victims of violence?

There is also a need to be mindful here of the power relationships invested in what we might term the mediation of suffering. How we encounter and narrate the spectacle of violence today is subjected to overt politicization, which prioritizes certain forms of suffering, and, in doing so, concentrates our attentions on those deaths that appear to matter more than others. Politics in fact continues to be fraught with claims over the true victims of historical forces. Part of our task then remains to reveal those persecuted figures subjected to history's erasure. But we need to go further. Indeed, while much has already been written about the recurring motif of the victim in terms of developing forms of solidarity and togetherness, there is also a need to be mindful today of the appropriation of the humanitarian victim—who is now a well-established political figure—for the furtherance of violence and destruction in the name of global justice.

In his book The Better Angels of Our Nature, *Steven Pinker argues that there is objectively less violence in the world, but it is not clear to me how we could or whether we should quantify the history of violence in this way. It makes no sense, to me, to say there is more or less violence now than ever. Or at least I would challenge any attempt to do so as problematically historicist—privileging our current notions of what violence even is as something timeless and unchanged throughout history. But we can talk about a spreading spectacle and its qualities. How do you respond to efforts and findings of Pinker, which are being popularly accepted?*

There are a number of issues to address here. We shouldn't lose sight of the fact that many dedicated organizations and individuals are doing tremendously important work documenting the casualties of war and conflict. Whether we are talking about the meticulous research involved in revealing the forgotten testimonies of victims, or efforts to record and detail the "collateral damages" of more recent campaigns, these measures are crucial in holding power to account. No life should be collateral. This requires recording and continued vigilance.

Yet, as you intimate, there is a need to avoid falling into the methodological trap set by the likes of Pinker. Not only does his work lead to the most remiss historicism as violence can be judged in terms of various scales of annihilation, it is ethically and politically compromised in the extreme. These attempts to offer quantitative reflections on violence in fact lead precisely to the forms of utilitarian calculations through which some forms of violence are continually justified or presented as the "least worse." As a result, the human dimensions to the violence—for example, the qualitative aspects of it—are often written out of the script.

Such approaches are in fact incapable of answering the ethical question "when is too much killing enough?" Just as there is no clear line to be drawn concerning levels of tolerable casualties, can we justify the acceptance of 1,000 deaths but declare 1,001 too many? Each form of violence needs to critiqued and condemned on its own terms. Only then can we think of breaking the cycle of violence by moving beyond overtly politicized dichotomies as good and bad, just and unjust, tolerable and intolerable, that rely upon such quantifiable derivatives.

Pinker's specific claims are historically dubious in respect to the relationship between liberalism and violence. What is more, the classifications he uses conveniently fit his preexisting normative positions and worldviews. Yet, as we know, what actually constitutes an act of political violence is intellectually fraught and deeply contested. The recent mass shootings in the United States, for example, illustrate how both the naming and quantification of violence remain loaded with political determinism. While some incidents, like the massacre in Colorado Springs, continue to be narrated by focusing on the mental health of the individual perpetrators—hence avoiding any broader systemic critique of gun laws, political allegiances, and religious beliefs, et cetera—others, such as the recent attack in San Bernardino, immediately connect individuals to broader historic forces.

What about how we use the term "violence"? I have written before that it is used carelessly in the media. For instance, I have seen news reports that say a situation "turned violent" when in fact only property was being damaged or destroyed. That suggests that property can be a victim of violence. With regard to Ferguson, reports said that protests "turned violent," which suggests the situation was not violent already, ignoring the fact that there is no background state of peace or nonviolence when young black teens are being gunned down by police with impunity. Do you think we need a better conception of what actually constitutes violence? Do you agree that the word itself is used irresponsibly? How might we conceive of a better way to apply the term?

Violence remains a complex problem that defies neat description. The German philosopher Walter Benjamin saw the task of developing a critique of violence adequate to our times to be one of the most significant intellectual challenges we face. How can we critically engage the problem of violence and remain ethically sensitive to the subject while doing justice to its victims? Too often violence is studied in an objective and neutral way, forgetting that human lives are being violated and that its experience is horrific and devastating.

Violence does, however, remain poorly understood if we simply attend to mere bodily attacks. Not only is psychological abuse clearly a form of violence, often we forget how some of the most pernicious and lasting casualties of war are intellectual. There is also a compelling case to be made for arguing that extreme social neglect, unnecessary suffering

caused by preventable disease, and environmental degradation could also be written as forms of violence, given their
effects on lives. Key here is to recognize both the systematic
and all too human dimensions to violence, which requires us
to look more attentively to the multiple forms violence can
take, teasing out both its logical consistencies and novelties.

You do, however, raise an important point: once we
start to objectify violence—for instance, argue what its main
referent objects should be—it is easy to retreat back into
established moral and normative positions that neatly map
out justifiable versus unjustifiable forms of violence. The
justifiable being the violence we are willing to tolerate, the
unjustifiable the intolerable. With this in mind, it's much
better to ask how violence operates within a social order. By
this I mean to question regimes of power, less by their ideas
and more by the types of violence they tolerate, while asking
how such violence serves to authenticate and disqualify the
real meaning of lives.

So where does this leave us intellectually? Rather than
encouraging a debate about the true meaning of violence,
I'd like to deal with your final question by proposing the
urgent need to think against violence in the contemporary
moment.

As Simon Critchley intimated in a very powerful piece
in "The Stone" in 2011, breaking the cycle of violence and
revenge requires entirely new political and philosophical coordinates and resources to point us in alternative directions.

I'd like to add to this discussion by drawing attention to
Auguste Rodin's sculpture *The Thinker*, which is still arguably

one of the most famous human embodiments of philosophical and critical inquiry. The symbolic form given to Rodin's isolated and contemplative sculpture alone should raise a number of critical concerns for us. Not least the ways in which its ethnic, masculine, and all too athletic form, speaks to evident racial, gendered, and survivalist grammars.

But let's consider for a moment what the thinker is actually contemplating. Alone on his plinth, the thinker could in fact be thinking about anything. We just hope it is something serious. Such ambiguity was not, however, as Rodin intended. In the original 1880 sculpture, the thinker actually appears kneeling before *The Gates of Hell*. We might read this as significant for a whole number of reasons. First, it is the "scene of violence" which gives specific context to Rodin's thinker. Thought begins for the thinker in the presence of the raw realities of violence and suffering. The thinker in fact is being forced to suffer into truth.

Second, there is an interesting tension in terms of the thinker's relationship to violence. Sat before the gates, the thinker appears to be turning away from the intolerable scene behind. This we could argue is a tendency unfortunately all too common when thinking about violence today. Turning away into abstraction or some scientifically neutralizing position of "objectivity." Yet, according to one purposeful reading, the figure in this commission is actually Dante, who is contemplating the circles of hell as narrated in *The Divine Comedy*. This is significant. Rather than looking away, might it be that the figure is now actually staring directly into the abyss below? Hence raising the fundamental ethical question of what it means to be forced witness to violence?

And third, not in any way incidental, in the original commission the thinker is actually called "the poet." This I want to argue is deeply significant for rethinking the future of the political. *The Thinker* was initially conceived as a tortured body yet also as a freethinking human, determined to transcend his suffering through poetry. We continue to be taught that politics is a social science and that its true command is in the power of analytical reason. Such has been the hallmark of centuries of reasoned, rationalized, and calculated violence, which has made the intolerable appear arbitrary and normal. Countering this demands a rethinking of the political itself in more poetic terms, which is tasked with imagining better futures and styles for living among the world of peoples.

TWO

THEATER OF VIOLENCE

From Sophocles to soccer, or Donald Trump to Kendrick Lamar, we are all players on history's bloody stage.

Our *New York Times* series of wider dialogues on violence began with the following conversation with the renowned philosopher and writer Simon Critchley—a professor of philosophy at the New School for Social Research in New York City and the moderator of the *New York Times* forum "The Stone." Simon is a critical philosopher who is often associated with the anarchist tradition. Throughout his extensive corpus of work, he has raised important questions on the meaning of tragedy, along with the tensions between violence and our metaphysical longings for love and togetherness. In this conversation a range of issues are discussed, from the continued importance of tragedy and how we might make sense of the forty-fifth president of the United States to Shakespeare, soccer, art, and music.

Brad Evans interviews Simon Critchley

March 14, 2016

Simon Critchley is the author of many books, including *Bowie, Memory Theatre*, and *Notes on a Suicide*.

Brad Evans: I want to start the discussion by raising a seemingly basic yet elusive question: what actually is violence? In terms of media spectacles and popular culture, violence seems ubiquitous in liberal societies. Yet the very term "violence" continually escapes meaningful definition and critique. What do you understand by the term?

Simon Critchley: It is true, "violence" can be used in a very wide and somewhat vague manner. So let me try to restrict our discussion to physical violence of a rather direct form. Let's say that violence is behavior that uses physical force in order to cause damage, harm, or death to some living thing, whether human or not. It is pretty clear that we are not all going to be able to agree on a definition of violence, but let's see where this idea of it takes us.

First, violence cannot be reduced to an isolated act that could be justified with reference to some conception or principle of justice. Here I borrow a line of thought from the historian and cultural theorist Robert Young when he writes that violence "is a phenomenon that has a history." Violence is not so much a question of a single act that breaks a supposed continuum of nonviolence or peace. Rather, violence is best understood as a historical cycle of violence and counterviolence. In other words, violence is not one but two. It is a double act that traps human beings in a repetitive pattern from which it is very hard to escape. Violence, especially political violence, is usually a pattern of aggression and counter-aggression that has a history and stretches back deep into time.

This is how I would understand the patterns involving race and racialized violence that have taken on added urgency of late. Violence is not an abstract concept for those subjected to it but a lived reality that has a concrete history. To try to judge the racial violence that defines current life in the United States without an understanding of the history of violence that stretches back to colonization, the forced transport of Africans to the colonies of the Americas, and the implementation of plantation slavery is largely pointless. We have to understand the history of violence from which we emerge.

In that respect, as your colleague Richard Bernstein has argued, even massive historical events like the September 11 attacks don't necessarily provoke serious thinking on the problem of violence.

One way of looking at 9/11—let's call it the standard way—is that the United States was at peace with the world and then terror came from the sky and the twin towers tumbled. In that view, 9/11 was a single act that required a justified reaction, namely war in the Middle East, the infinite detention of suspected "terrorists" in places like Guantánamo Bay, and the construction of the vast institutional apparatus of Homeland Security.

But another way of looking at 9/11 is looking at what Osama bin Laden said about the matter. In a 2004 video called *The Towers of Lebanon*, where he first accepted responsibility for Al Qaeda's role in the 9/11 attacks, he justifies the attacks by claiming that they were a reaction to the persistent violation of Arab lands by the United States, especially the use of Saudi Arabia as a base during the first Gulf War. Bin Laden even adds that the idea of 9/11 came to him as a visual memory of watching TV footage of the Israeli bombardment of West Beirut's high-rise tower blocks in 1982. If the "Zionist-Crusaders," as he pejoratively puts it, could put missiles into towers, then so could Al Qaeda. Thus the idea for 9/11 was born.

The point is that if we are to understand violence concretely, then we have to grasp it historically as part of a cycle of action and reaction, violence and counterviolence, that always stretches back further than one thinks. If one doesn't do this, then one ends up like Donald Trump, emptily promising to flatten ISIS with bombs. It's in this light that we might also consider the Theater of Trump that has exploded with truly disturbing and racially coded violence in recent days.

If violence shouldn't be theorized in the abstract, as you rightly insist, we must pay attention to how it is enacted. In this, the importance of theater, which is a recurring theme throughout your work, is often overlooked. What do you think theater has to offer here?

We live in a world framed by violence, where justice seems to be endlessly divided between claim and counterclaim, right and left, freedom fighter and terrorist, believer and nonbeliever, and so on. Each side appears to believe unswervingly in the rightness of its position and the wrongness, or indeed "evil," of the opposition. Such belief legitimates violence and unleashes counterviolence in return. We seem to be trapped in deep historical cycles of violence where justice is usually simply understood as vengeance or revenge.

This is where theater can help, especially tragedy (but I think this is also true of the best movies and TV dramas).

It is useful to consider the Greeks. The history of Greek tragedy is the history of violence and war, from the war with the Persians in the early fifth century B.C. to the Peloponnesian Wars that run until that century's end; from the emergence of Athenian imperial hegemony to its dissolution and humiliation at the hands of Sparta. In 472 B.C., in the oldest extant play we possess, *The Persians*, Aeschylus deals with the aftermath of the Battle of Salamis in 480. It was therefore somewhat closer to the Athenians than 9/11 is to us. More than half of our surviving Greek tragedies were composed after the outbreak of the Peloponnesian Wars in 431. *Oedipus the King* was first performed in 429, two years after the beginning of the Peloponnesian Wars, during a time of plague that is estimated to have killed one-quarter of the Athenian population. The plague that established the entire environment of Sophocles's play is not some idle musing. It was very real indeed. It killed Pericles, the leader of Athens, that very same year. The frame of tragedy is war and its devastating effects on human life.

Greek tragedy, particularly with its obsessive focus on the aftermath of the Trojan War, is largely about combat veterans. But it was also performed by combat veterans. Actors were not flimsy thespians or the Athenian version of Hollywood stars but soldiers who had seen combat, like Aeschylus himself. They knew firsthand what violence was. Tragedy was played before an audience that had either participated directly in war or were indirectly implicated in war. All were traumatized by it, and everyone felt its effects. War was the life of the city and its pride, as Pericles argued. But war was also the city's fall and undoing.

How might we respond in a similar way to the contemporary situation of violence and war? It might seem that the easiest and noblest thing to do is to speak of peace. Yet, as Raymond Williams says in his still hugely relevant 1966 book, *Modern Tragedy*: "To say peace when there is no peace is to say nothing." The danger of easy pacifism is that it is inert and self-regarding. It is always too pleased with itself. But the alternative is not a justification of war. It is rather the attempt to understand the deep history and tragic complexity of political situations.

The great virtue of ancient tragedy is that it allowed the Greeks to see their role in a history of violence and war that was to some extent of their own making. It also allowed them to imagine a suspension of that cycle of violence. And this suspension, the kind of thing that happens in the trial at the end of Aeschylus's *Oresteia*, was not based on a fanciful idealism but on a realistic and concrete grasp of a historical situation, which was something the Greeks did by focusing history through the lens of myth.

The slim sliver of hope I have is that the same could

be true of us. To see the bloody events of the contemporary world in a tragic light exposes us to a disorder that is not just someone else's disorder. It is our disorder, and theater at its best asks us to take the time to reflect on this and to imagine what a world where violence is suspended might look like.

With that in mind, I'd like now to turn to Shakespeare. In Stay, Illusion! The Hamlet Doctrine *you show how Shakespearean figures are relevant for understanding the ways in which deeply tragic questions concerning life, death, and love are embodied today. What is it about Shakespeare that still captures the violence of the times?*

From the beginning to the end, Shakespeare's drama is a meditation on political violence. Whether one thinks of the wild excesses of *Titus Andronicus*, the vast majestic sweep of the history plays, or the great tragedies, Shakespeare had a tight and commanding grip on the nature of political power and its relation to violence and the claims and counterclaims of justice. What is most powerful about Shakespeare is the way in which his historically coded reflections on the politics of his time are combined with intense and immense psychological intimacy. Shakespeare, like no one before or since, binds together the political and the psychological.

To take the play that I know best, *Hamlet*, it is not just that this play is a drama of violence in a surveillance state where power is constituted through acts of murder (the Castle of Elsinore and the state of Denmark is clearly some kind of allegory for the late Elizabethan court and police state), but also that we feel an awful proximity to the effects of violence on the mind of the young Danish prince and the way in which it drives his feigned madness into something more real and frightening, as when he confronts his mother with terrifying psychic violence (act 3, scene 4).

What answer does *Hamlet* give that helps us understand our current political situation? Simply put, the play counsels us that time is out of joint. What people often forget is that Hamlet's father, before he was himself murdered, killed Fortinbras's father. And therefore it is fitting that *Hamlet* ends not just with the prince's death but also with the military occupation of Denmark by the forces of young Fortinbras, who is Hamlet's twin, insofar as they are both the sons of murdered fathers, one by the other.

So the point of Shakespeare is not to give us simple answers or reassuring humanistic moral responses to violence but to get us to confront the violence of our own histories. "Hamlet" gives us many warnings, but perhaps the most salient is the following: if we imagine that justice is based on vengeance against others, then we are truly undone.

How can we connect insights such as this to the historic and evidently prescient contemporary relationship between violence and sport? Are sporting arenas perhaps the real theaters of our times? Are they inevitably bound up with the problem of violence in both its glorified and its vilified forms?

Ah, now you're talking. Sport is obviously the continuation of war by other means. And sports stadiums are undoubtedly the closest thing to ancient theaters that we have, especially in terms of scale (nearly 15,000 people sat in the Theater of Dionysus in Athens). It's fascinating to me that when Bertolt Brecht was trying to imagine the ideal audience for the kind of epic theater he was developing in the 1920s, he pictured a sports crowd. That is, a crowd that is relaxed and not anxious, sitting under lights rather than in the dark, and that has knowledge of what is happening and a passion for it, rather than people either looking perplexed or quietly taking a nap, as usually happens in New York theaters. I think there is a lot to Brecht's idea.

Sport is obviously violent, and it is violence that we want to see. We want to see people putting their bodies on the line for their team and leaving their bodies on the field. This is why the whole debate about concussions in the NFL is so hypocritical, to my mind. Sport is a place where bodies break. If you don't agree with it, then don't watch it.

But sports is not just some gladiatorial spectacle of violence. It is violence honed into skill and masterful expertise, what psychoanalysts would call "sublimation." It is violence refined and elevated. And sporting drama is only made possible through an elaborate set of rules, which have to be observed and with which all parties agree.

But what is in the background of the rule-governed physical violence of sport is something more complex, something closer to what the ancients called fate. This is particularly the case with the sport that I take it you and I hold dearest, what our American pals call soccer. For the real fan, what is at stake in a soccer match is a sense of profound attachment to place, whether town, city, or nation, a sense of identity that is almost tribal and that is often organized around social class, ethnicity, dialect, or language. But what is driving the whole activity is something closer to destiny. This is usually experienced when one's team loses, as one has the sinking feeling that England must when playing Germany and the game has to end with penalty shots.

But the key phenomenon of sport in relation to violence is that although sport can and does spill over into actual violence (whether through hooliganism or ethnic or racist violence), this usually doesn't happen. As a fan, one follows the physical, violent intensity of the game with a mixture of intense passion and expert knowledge of what is happening, and then the game ends and one goes home, often a little disappointed. I think sport, especially soccer, is a wonderful example of how violence can be both made spectacular and harnessed for nonviolent ends. At its best, one accepts defeat, respects the opponent, and moves on eagerly to the next game.

The subtlety of the potential for nonviolence you express here seems crucial. In particular, how might we develop the necessary intellectual tools adequate to these deeply violent and politically fraught times?

My response is very simple: art. I think that art at its most resonant and powerful can give us an account of the history of violence from which we emerge and can also offer us the possibility of a suspension of that violence. Art can provide an image for our age.

For me, this happens most powerfully in popular music. For me, as for many others, one of the most coherent and powerful responses to the racialized violence of the past year or so was Kendrick Lamar's *To Pimp a Butterfly*. With dazzling linguistic inventiveness, steeped in intense inward knowledge of traditions of jazz, soul, and funk, Lamar does not provide easy solutions or empty moral platitudes but confronts us aesthetically with the deep history of racialized violence. You hear this very clearly on a track like "Alright." It is what Public Enemy, Curtis Mayfield, and Marvin Gaye did so powerfully in previous generations.

Some days I am inclined to agree with Nietzsche when he said that without music life would be error. Music like Lamar's doesn't give us the answers, but it allows us to ask the right questions, and it does this with a historical and political sensibility suffused with intelligence, wit, and verve. Great music can give us a picture of the violence of our time more powerfully than any news report. It can also offer, for the time that we listen, a momentary respite from the seemingly unending cycles of violence and imagine some other way of being, something less violent, less vengeful, and less stupid.

THREE

THE PERILS OF BEING A BLACK PHILOSOPHER

America needs a movement that transcends the civil rights movement.

Violence takes many different forms, from physical attacks upon bodies to the assault upon one's dignity and sense of self. In this emotionally charged conversation, philosopher George Yancy discusses his painful experiences of racism in response to his previous forms of public engagement. What it means to be a black public intellectual is not only to bring power into question; it is to be further exposed to the violence that has long been used to mark black thinkers as incapable of thinking philosophically, as Yancy explains. In this regard, what Yancy deals with in this discussion are questions far more searching than philosophical mediation. His response is testimony on, and indictment of, today's state of racial politics and violence in the United States and beyond.

Brad Evans interviews George Yancy

April 18, 2016

George Yancy is a professor of philosophy at Emory University and author, editor, and co-editor of many books, including *Backlash* and *Black Bodies, White Gazes.*

Brad Evans: In response to a series of troubling verbal attacks you received after your essay "Dear White America" appeared in "The Stone" in December 2015, the American Philosophical Association put out a strongly worded statement criticizing the bullying and harassment of academics in the public realm. But beyond this, shouldn't we address the broader human realities of such hateful speech and in particular how this sort of discursive violence directly impacts the body of the person attacked?

George Yancy: Your point about discursive violence is an important one. Immediately after the publication of "Dear White America," I began to receive vile and vitriolic white racist comments sent to my university email address and verbal messages sent to my answering machine. I even received snail mail that was filled with hatred. Imagine the time put into actually sitting down and writing a letter filled with so much hate and then sending it snail mail, especially in our world of the Internet.

The alarming reality is that the response to "Dear White America" revealed just how much racism continues to exist in our so-called postracial America. The comments were not about pointing out fallacies in my position but were designed to violate, to leave me psychologically broken and physically distraught.

Words do things, especially words like "nigger" or

being called an animal that should go back to Africa or being told that I should be "beheaded ISIS style." One white supremacist message sent to me ended with "Be Prepared." Another began with "Dear Nigger Professor."

The brutality and repetitiveness of this discursive violence has a way of inflicting injury. Given the history of the term "nigger," it strikes with the long, hate-filled context of violence out of which that term grew. This points to the non-spectacular expression of violence. The lynching of black people was designed to be a spectacle, to draw white mobs. In this case, the black body was publicly violated. It was a public and communal form of bloodlust. There are many other forms of violence that are far more subtle, non-spectacular, yet painful and dehumanizing. So when I was called a "nigger," I was subject to that. I felt violated, injured; a part of me felt broken.

Only now have I really begun to recognize how discourse designed to hurt can actually leave its mark. I recall after reading so many of these messages I began to feel sick, literally. So words can debilitate, violate, injure; they can hit with the force of a stick or a stone and leave marks on the body. In this case, I began to feel the posture of my body folding inward, as it were, under the attacks. Frantz Fanon talks about this as not being able to move lithely in the world.

How does this relate to the intellectual history of racial persecution, oppression, and subordination, especially the denial of the right of black people, and specifically black intellectuals, to speak with their own voice in a public setting?

I shared some of the malicious discourse used against me with some very prominent white public intellectuals. We began to exchange experiences. The exchange was helpful to me; it helped me to understand what is at stake when engaging in courageous speech. What was immediately clear, though, was the absence of specifically racist vitriol directed at these white public intellectuals, which in no way downplays their pain. Yet we must bring attention to the difference, to the perils of being a *black* intellectual. Not only was I being attacked for my courageous speech; I was being attacked as a *black man*. Yet I was also being attacked as a *black* philosopher.

There were some very nasty remarks that were designed to question my status as a philosopher because I'm black. The implication of those messages was that to be black *and* a philosopher was a contradiction, because "niggers" can't be philosophers. So I agree; the discourse was far more pernicious. But to understand this is to come to terms with the history of white violence in this country used to control and silence black people.

To see my experience as a single episode or an anomaly is to deny the logic of the long history of white racist violence. bell hooks recalls that as a child she thought of whiteness as a site of terror. In a country in which white people would brutalize and kill a black person on a whim, that is far from irrational.

For centuries, black people lived in fear of white terror. That fear partly captures the contradiction of being black and an American. Black people were not the American "we" but the terrorized other. The symbols of white sheets and cross burnings must be recalled. Think here of black World War II veterans who returned home from the war and were severely beaten and lynched by whites, even as they wore their uniforms. They fought against Hitler only to return home, to the land of "democracy," to be attacked by what might be called white terrorists.

Or think here of the slave trade, the institution of American slavery, black codes, convict leasing, the lynching of black men and women and the flaying of black flesh, the castration of black men, being burned alive. Violence, within these contexts, is a specific racialized form of inculcating black people with fear and controlling their social mobility. There is nothing episodic about it; this form of white violence is historically grounded and systematic.

The coldhearted use of white violence was very effective. Not only were there actual beatings, there was the fear of possibly being beaten. So the black imagination, though never defeated, was weakened. The lynching of a black person wasn't just a form of theater (where the root meaning suggests a kind of "beholding") but also a way of communicating fear and terror through mass displays of violence. For someone white, the spectacle was a sport, a kind of national pastime activity, but, for a black person, one could always imagine that one was next and thereby stand in fear of what could happen at any moment.

Cornel West talks about the "death shudder" as a kind of existential moment of realization that one is finite. I think that we are all open to experience that dreadful sense of our existence coming to an end. However, when black life is forever in a "state of exception," it is an additional weight. Black people not only experience the death shudder but also a specific kind of shudder that involves an emotional intensity that speaks to the disposability of black life.

For example, the other day, a white police officer walked into a store where I was buying some food, and I remember feeling this powerful sense of wanting to flee, of feeling as if the rules and laws that are designed to govern our (white) society didn't apply to me. I could move "too quickly," placing my hand into my pocket to pay for my food, and my life would end just like that. The white police officer would explain how he felt "threatened" and had "reasonable" suspicion. And I would be dead.

These connections between the continuum of racial violence and the terrors of the everyday are crucial to understanding the normalization of humiliation and the outright denial of the most basic qualities that make people feel part of a society and "human," as such. This demands a more serious intellectual engagement with the "marking out" of the black body as incapable of philosophical thought and deliberation. Does this make a return to thinkers such as Aimé Césaire and Frantz Fanon all the more relevant in the contemporary period?

Yes. And racial violence takes many forms and raises larger issues. For example, Judith Butler's concern about questions of grievability is important. Racial violence is linked to forms of racial vulnerability, disposability, and our tendency as a nation to grieve the deaths of certain racialized persons and not others. The disproportionate number of poor black people affected by Hurricane Katrina, the sentencing disparities when it comes to locking up black people for nonviolent offenses, and the shooting in the back of Walter Scott by the white police officer Michael Slager are all examples of forms of racialized disposability. They speak to how black humanity is deemed of little or no human value.

The process of marking the black body as incapable of philosophical thought is longstanding. It is one of those major myths that grew out of Europe, even as Europe championed "humanism." The poet Aimé Césaire, through immanent critique, knew that European humanism was a farce. Of course, Jean-Paul Sartre knew this as well. And Fanon knew what it was like to embody reason and have it denied to him. In "Black Skin, White Masks," he argued that when he was present, reason was not, and when reason was present he was no longer. So one might argue that reason and black embodiment, from this perspective, are mutually exclusive. Yet, at the end of that text, Fanon says, "My final prayer: O my body, make me always a man who questions!"

Fanon appeals to something that is beyond abstract political rights discourse. He appeals to his own body, something concrete and immediate. Fanon asks of his body not to allow him to be seduced by forms of being-in-the-world that normalize violence and dehumanization. Doubt can be linked to critique. In a society that hides beneath the seductions of normalization, critique is undesirable and deemed

dangerous. Yet in our contemporary moment, the fulfillment of Fanon's prayer is desperately needed.

These examples are manifestations of a racialized, selective misanthropy. This is why I have such a negative visceral reaction to Donald Trump's promises to build a wall
along the Mexican border. That discourse is one of labeling
certain bodies as "unwanted," "deviant," "sub-persons." And
to say that Mexico is sending "rapists" to the United States
is a form of deep insult, of marking certain bodies as violent
and pathological. Trump is, sadly, able to play on the racist
biases and fears in many white people. It is a divisive tactic
that exploits both latent and manifest bigoted assumptions
in many white Americans. It is not by accident that David
Duke, a former grand wizard of the KKK, supports him.

*As you point out, a conceptualization of political rights must also
include the right for the marginalized to critique power. Does
philosophical inquiry have to do with the ways we might recon-
ceptualize the meaning of rights, especially considering that the
denial of persons' humanity often occurs within normative legal
frameworks?*

Absolutely. After all, slavery, which was a vicious, death-
dealing, and violent institution, was legal. I think that
rights-based discourse is necessary, but there is this sense in
which rights can be given and, by implication, taken away.
Within this context, I think that America needs a movement
that transcends the civil rights movement. Applicative justice might be necessary but not sufficient. Imagine a sce-

nario where justice is being applied across the board, and the rights of people are being upheld. In a country like ours, saturated by racism, that scenario might still involve blacks being hated, seen as "inferior," as "sub-persons." In such a world, white people can continue to insulate themselves from the "others."

We are desperately in need of a movement that shakes us at the very core of how we think about ourselves as individuals, masters of our own destiny. While this isn't philosophically fashionable, I want to know what it means to love with courage. What would it mean to make love an integral feature of moral reasoning, the kind of love that risks profound ways of being mutually vulnerable, of placing no limits on who we call our neighbors? This means radically changing how we currently relate to one another. I recall when we killed Osama bin Laden in 2011 that there were Americans who were cheering. As unpatriotic as some will say I'm being, we must keep in mind that bin Laden was someone's son, father, and husband.

This speaks to the limits of our moral imagination as a nation. Can you imagine President Obama saying at a press conference that he is sorry that we killed bin Laden, that we loved him as a human being despite his violence? Can you imagine what would happen if Israelis and Palestinians were to cease their "peace" talks and radically deploy a discourse of love? Imagine the many whites who read "Dear White America" saying to me: "We return the love to you that you've shared with us!" I think that we are an impoverished nation when it comes to loving our "enemies." God bless America is an empty, politicized gesture if we are not also saying God bless our "enemies."

There is an ethical aspect to "Dear White America"—particularly the honest reflections put forward regarding your own prejudices and fallibilities when it comes to relations of power. While a critique of violence demands attention to historical forces of domination and exploitation, it also asks how each of us shamefully compromise with power, often against our better judgments.

Yes. This raises the issue of complicity. As I discussed in the essay, there are ways in which I have been shaped to believe that looking at women with a dominating gaze or desiring women only for sexual pleasure is "normal." Yet it is this process of "normalization" that produces a kind of "walking dead" mentality where many of my social practices (sexual desire being one, fixed gender role expectations being another) support the oppression of women. The process of normalization is often so effective that there isn't much resistance coming from one's "better judgment," especially as one's better judgment has already been defined by the terms of normalization.

In this case, one's "better judgment" has already been compromised, has already become an extension of the power of normalization. Your use of the term "shameful" is important. Shame implies a powerful sense of disgrace. It is not limited to the assignment of blame, which is more like guilt. Shame suggests the sense of disrupting one's ethical "certainty" or business as usual. After all, one can be guilty without ever feeling shame. So violence, for me, has to be attended to at those levels where we are going about our business as if we are not doing violence to other individuals.

The fact that we don't hear cries of pain doesn't let us off the hook. Ethical discourse and practice must be imbued with an effort to remain honest, especially about one's own ethical shortcomings and the pain and suffering that we cause others.

A critique of violence must include an understanding that one doesn't escape the many ways in which one perpetuates violence—violence against those who we may never see face to face, violence against those who are closest to us, violence against the earth, and perhaps even violence against one's own sense of self-integrity.

Violence is all around us. Yet we prefer to remain asleep—the walking dead. For me, personally, the more I become aware of the magnitude of violence in our world, what many of us would rather deny or not see, the more I enter into that space of the "dark night of the soul," a place where dread and hopelessness reside. The objective, though, is to continue, to remain awake, to keep fighting for a better world even as one endures the dark night of the soul.

FOUR

THE REFUGEE CRISIS IS HUMANITY'S CRISIS

Refugees have been stripped of their humanity and denied their "inalienable" rights.

"The world is now full," Zygmunt Bauman once wrote. "There is nowhere left to map, nowhere to run." The late sociologist and critical theorist dedicated his life and writings to the problem of the refugee but not simply out of academic curiosity. Having lived through some of the worst episodes in political history, he came to embody the intellectual refugee, endlessly in search of a safe place he might call "home." But what does the figure of the refugee really show us today? And does it reveal more about our prejudices than we care to consider? This conversation took place against the backdrop of the Syrian refugee crises, which for Bauman revealed more broadly a crisis of the political and philosophical imagination and the limits of our tolerability.

Brad Evans interviews Zygmunt Bauman

May 2, 2016

Zygmunt Bauman was emeritus professor of sociology at the University of Leeds, UK, until his death in 2017. His many books included *Retrotopia* and *Strangers at Our Door*, both published by Polity Press.

Brad Evans: For over a decade you have focused on the desperate plight of refugees. Your work draws particular attention to the many indignities and insecurities the refugee faces on a daily basis. You have also stressed how the problem is not entirely new and must be understood in a broader historical context. With this in mind, do you think the current refugee crises engulfing Europe represent yet another chapter in the history of flight from persecution, or is there something different taking place here?

Zygmunt Bauman: It does seem like "yet another chapter," though as with all political problems, which all have histories, something is added to the contents of its predecessors. In the modern era, massive migration itself is not a novelty, nor is it a sporadic event. It is in fact a constant, steady effect of the modern mode of life, with its perpetual preoccupation with order-building and economic progress. Those two qualities in particular act as factories endlessly capable of producing "redundant people," those who are either locally unemployable or politically intolerable and are therefore forced to seek shelter or more promising life opportunities away from their homes.

It's true that the prevalent direction of migration has changed following the spread of the modern way of life from Europe, its place of origin, to the rest of the globe. As long as Europe remained the only "modern" continent of the planet, its redundant populations kept being unloaded onto the still "premodern" lands—recycled into colonist settlers, soldiers, or members of colonial administration. Indeed, up to sixty million Europeans are believed to have left Europe for the two Americas, Africa, Australia during the heyday of colonial imperialism.

Starting from the middle of the twentieth century, however, the trajectory of migration took a U-turn. During this time, the logic of migration changed as it was dissociated from the conquest of the lands. The migrants of the postcolonial era have been and still are exchanging inherited ways of eking out an existence, now destroyed by the triumphant modernization promoted by their former colonizers, for the chance of building a nest in the gaps of those colonizers' domestic economies.

On top of that, however, there is a rising volume of people forced out from their homes, particularly in the Middle East and in Africa, by the dozens of civil wars, ethnic and religious conflicts, and sheer banditry in the territories the colonizers left behind in nominally sovereign, artificially concocted "states" with little prospects of stability but enormous arsenals of weaponry supplied by their former colonial masters.

Hannah Arendt once used the term "worldlessness" to define those conditions where a person doesn't belong to a world in which they matter as human beings. This seems to be equally resonant in describing the plight of contemporary refugees. Might the problem here be our framing of the debate in terms of "security"—that of either the refugees or their destinations?

Part of the issue is the way in which the political world is framed and understood. Refugees are worldless in a world that is spliced into sovereign territorial states and that demands identifying the possession of human rights with state citizenship. This situation is further compounded by the fact that there are no countries left ready to accept and offer shelter and a chance of a decent life and human dignity to the stateless refugees.

In such a world, those people who are forced to flee intolerable conditions are not considered to be "bearers of rights," even those rights supposedly considered inalienable to humanity. Forced to depend for their survival on the people on whose doors they knock, refugees are in a way thrown outside the realm of "humanity," as far as it is meant to confer the rights they aren't afforded. And there are millions upon millions of such people inhabiting our shared planet.

As you rightly point out, refugees end up all too often cast in the role of a threat to the human rights of established native populations, instead of being defined and treated as a vulnerable part of humanity in search of the restoration of those same rights of which they have been violently robbed.

There is currently a pronounced tendency—among the settled populations as well as the politicians they elect to state offices—to transfer the "issue of refugees" from the area of universal human rights into that of internal security.

Being tough on foreigners in the name of safety from potential terrorists is evidently generating more political currency than appealing for benevolence and compassion for people in distress. And to outsource the whole problem into the care of security services is eminently more convenient for governments overloaded with social care duties, which they are apparently neither able nor willing to perform to the satisfaction of their electors.

Central to your analysis has been to argue how many of the vulnerabilities people now face need to be explained in more planetary terms. Increasingly, individual nation-states seem incapable of responding to the multiplicity of threats defining our interconnected age. Does the figure of the refugee reveal more fully the globalized nature of power and violence today?

Seeing the problem in "more planetary terms" is indispensable to fully understanding not only the phenomenon of massive migration but also the genuine and widespread migration panic that the phenomenon has triggered in most of Europe. The influx of a great number of refugees, and their sudden high visibility, draws to the surface fears that we are trying hard to stifle and hide: those fears that are gestated by the premonition of our own fragilities in society and by the continuously reaffirmed suspicion that our fate is in the hands of forces far beyond our comprehension—let alone our control.

In part, they bring the mysterious and obscure but hopefully distant horrors of "global forces" right into our visible and tangible neighborhood. As recently as a few weeks ago, those newcomers may have felt just as safe at home as we do right now. But now they look at us, deprived of their homes, possessions, security, often their "inalienable" human rights, and of their entitlement to have the respect and acceptance that provide a guarantee of self-esteem.

Following the age-old habit, the messengers are blamed for the contents of their message. No wonder the successive tides of fresh immigrants are resented, to quote Brecht, as "harbingers of bad news." They are embodiments of the collapse of order—a state of affairs in which the relations between causes and effects are stable and so graspable and predictable—allowing those inside a situation to know how to proceed. Because they reveal these insecurities to us, refugees are easily demonized. By stopping them on the other side of our properly fortified borders, it is implied that we'll manage to stop those global forces that brought them to our doors.

Those who flee from war-torn situations ignite vociferous debates regarding their correct labeling: the "migrant" or the "refugee"? But both terms can be reductive. Might we need a new vocabulary here to emphasize more the human agency of those who are trying to escape such conditions? After all, as the poet Warsan Shire observed, "no one puts their children in a boat unless the water is safer than the land."

In most cases the choice open to a refugee is between a place where one's presence is not tolerated and another where one's arrival is unwanted and disallowed. Similarly, the choice open to the so-called economic migrants is one between famine or a prospectless existence and a chance, however tenuous, of tolerable conditions for oneself and one's family. This is not any more of a "choice," in any meaningful sense, than that faced by the refugee fleeing overt physical violence. Each one of us would be horrified by the necessity to make such choices. We do need a language and critical vocabulary for a worldly condition that forces millions of its inhabitants to do so.

Insofar as the label "economic migrant" stigmatizes these victims, its use should be condemned. Such discursive acrobatics leave the causes of these crises unexamined and those responsible untouched by guilt. In a culture that ennobles the pursuit of self-betterment and happiness by raising it to the rank of life's purpose and meaning, it is nothing less than utter hypocrisy to condemn those who try to follow this precept but are prevented from doing so by lack of means or proper papers.

When dealing with the racial and cultural politics of the refugee, you have used the metaphor "setting fears afloat" to emphasize how the refugee has become the signifier upon which many of our contemporary fears and anxieties are projected. Mindful of what you address above in respect to the politics of (in)security, is there not a danger that the heightened focus on the refugee adds to the scapegoating by presenting the problem as defining of our times (hence truly polarizing the debate and driving it to the extremes)?

As Hegel warned nearly two centuries ago, the owl of Minerva, that goddess of wisdom, spreads its wings at dusk. By this I mean that we tend to learn only what defines "our times" in retrospect, once they are over. And rarely even in hindsight do we learn this definitely. Eric Hobsbawm, perhaps the greatest historian of the modern era, gathered courage to attach the name of the "Age of Extremes" to the twentieth century only in 1994. And even then he felt the need to apologize for such attachments:

> Nobody can write the history of the twentieth century like that of any other era, if only because nobody can write about his or her lifetime as one can (and must) write about a period known only from outside, at second or third-hand, from sources of the period or the works of later historians. . . . This is one reason why under my professional hat as a historian I avoided working on the era since 1914 for most of my career.

Let's heed the advice/warning by the great historian and resist the temptation to overemphasize what Thomas Hylland Eriksen has called, with particular reference to the power of the media, the "tyranny of the moment." The refugees might have indeed more entitlements than most other categories to hold the status of "the defining scapegoats" of "our times"—but for how long? In my latest book I write that our insecurities keep "floating," as none of the anchors we cast proves to be solid enough to hold them in place with any degree of permanence. So it may go with the refugee, who embodies in the clearest way the liquidity of fear in the contemporary moment. Right now, at least, that liquidity creates a sort of affinity between the strangers at our doors and the mysterious, seemingly omnipotent global forces that pushed them there. Both stay staunchly beyond our reach and control, ignoring our deepest wishes and our most ingenious "solutions."

It is arguable that one of the "intellectual casualties" of the war on terror has been the humanitarian ideal that the world might be transformed for the better. Do we perhaps need a new humanism for the twenty-first century?

In his *Cosmopolitan Vision*, Ulrich Beck captured the predicament brilliantly: we have been already cast (without having been asked) into a cosmopolitan condition of universal, humanity-wide interdependence. But we are still missing, and have not yet started in earnest to compose and acquire, an accompanying cosmopolitan awareness. This creates a kind of cultural lag, as William Fielding Ogburn would call it, the evidence of which is the treatment of the refugee. They may well remain the collateral victims of this lack of understanding until such time that we try in earnest to attend to that lag's institutional, state-based foundations.

As Benjamin Barber crisply put it in his manifesto, *If Mayors Ruled the World*, "today, after a long history of regional success, the nation-state is failing us on the global scale. It was the perfect political recipe for the liberty and

independence of autonomous peoples and nations. It is utterly unsuited for interdependence." He sees that nation-
states are singularly unfit to tackle the challenges arising
from our planet-wide interdependence, in that they are "too
inclined by their nature to rivalry and mutual exclusion" and
appear "quintessentially indisposed to cooperation and incapable of establishing global common goods."

I trace much of the problem to the growing separation between power and politics, a rift that results in powers
free from political constraints and a politics that is suffering
a constant and growing deficit of power. Powers, particularly those most heavily influencing the human condition
and humanity's prospects, are today global, roaming ever
more freely in (to use the Spanish sociologist Manuel Cas-
tells's words) the "space of flows" while ignoring at will the
borders, laws, and internally defined interests of political
entities—whereas the extant instruments of political action remain, as they were a century or two ago, fixed and
confined to the "space of places," that of states. Alternative
"historical agents" are much in demand, and one may sur-
mise that until they are found and put in place, debating the
models of a "good" or at least a "better" society will seem to
be an idle pastime—and except in the extreme margins of
the political spectrum won't arouse much emotion.

All the same, I don't believe there is a shortcut solution to the current refugee problem. Humanity is in crisis,
and there is no exit from that crisis other than the solidarity
of humans. The first obstacle on the road to the exit from
mutual alienation is the refusal of dialogue: that silence

that accompanies self-alienation, aloofness, inattention, disregard, and indifference. Instead of the duo of love and hate, the dialectical process of border-drawing needs to be thought therefore in terms of the triad of love, hate, and indifference or neglect that the refugee, in particular, continues to face.

FIVE

OUR CRIME AGAINST THE PLANET AND OURSELVES

We are both offenders and victims. But some are more guilty than others.

While mainstream discourse continues to debate whether or not catastrophic climate change is caused by humans, discussions about what sort of disasters we're facing—and how they might yet be prevented—are stymied. Throughout her career, Australian philosopher Adrian Parr has addressed the problems of environmental degradation as being inseparable from the vise grip that capitalism has on our lives and political imaginations. Against a neoliberal landscape that might recognize the dangers of climate change but deploys a language of perpetrator-free disaster, Parr insists that we understand environmental degradation as not only a form of mass violence but also a crime against humanity, which demands no less than a questioning of what it means to be a human. Here we discuss why it matters to talk about the environment in terms of structural violence, and what justice could even look like for a crime in which we are all—to differing degrees—both perpetrators and victims.

Natasha Lennard interviews Adrian Parr

May 18, 2016

Adrian Parr is a professor of environmental politics and cultural criticism at the University of Cincinnati and the director of the Taft Research Center. Her books include *The Wrath of Capital* and *Birth of a New Earth: The Radical Politics of Environmentalism.*

Natasha Lennard: In your work, you raise the idea of framing climate degradation as a form of violence and potentially as a crime against humanity. What does it mean to speak of the human destruction of the climate in terms of criminal justice? Is there a distinct guilty party that can be held responsible for this crime?

Adrian Parr: There are three components to the claim that environmental degradation is a crime against humanity. First, it is an appeal to a universal, common humanity that stretches across space and time and that is oblivious to geographic and historical differences. Second, the crime in question is an existential one that is committed against the very experience of being human, the human élan. Third, it is a crime that calls the established legal order into question, because everyone, yet no one specifically, can be held responsible.

What is the nature of this crime? The human species is the agent of a terrible injustice being perpetrated against other species, future generations, ecosystems, and our fellow human beings. Examples include contaminated waterways, mass species extinction, massive fossil fuel consumption and greenhouse gas emissions, and unsustainable rates of deforestation, to name just a few. This is leading to extreme and more frequent weather events, expanding deserts, loss of biodiversity, collapsing ecosystems, water depletion and contamination, and the rise of global sea levels.

However, humans are not all equally guilty of this crime. Some, such as those advancing the interests of the fossil-fuel industry, or those whose high-income lifestyles carry a heavy environmental footprint, are implicated more than those living in poverty. Present and past generations are collectively more at fault than future generations.

At the same time, the human species is an agent of justice, having crafted laws designed to hold criminals accountable. Troubled when we witness violence, discrimination, and unnecessary cruelty, we also individually serve as vehicles of justice.

Yes, so if we consider our relations with our environment to be criminally violent in nature, we find ourselves in a tension as both potential perpetrators and victims but also as the vehicles whose obligation it is to deliver justice. Why do you think it's important or useful to frame climate degradation this way?

A crime against humanity is an action that causes severe and unnecessary human suffering, and environmental destruction unquestionably degrades the quality of human life.

The degradation of the environment is a record of past and present human activities. Ours is a landscape that bears the burden of human atrocities waged against other humans through war. The battered and burnt-out environments of Syria, Iraq, and Afghanistan are a few recent examples of this. The more than four million refugees fleeing the conflict in Syria reported by the United Nations High Commissioner for Refugees is the horrifying consequence of years of conflict decimating not only that country's social, cultural, economic, and political systems but its environmental resources as well. Then there is the continual annihilation of numerous habitats which both humanity and other species depend upon for their survival. All of this provides evidence of an environmental crime being committed against humanity.

If this situation continues unabated it will cause extreme harm to future generations and eventually a gratuitous loss of human life. Let me ask: should we confer greater existential importance upon present generations of human beings than future ones? Environmental degradation, and in particular climate change, denies future generations their agency through no fault of their own, leaving them with a world that could very well reduce what life remains to that of mere survival.

This is a crime against what makes us uniquely human—the creative agency that comes from a combination of reasoning, imagination, and emotion. We may all have different capacities and opportunities through which to realize our agency, but we share the same ability to collectively and individually realize our innovative potential.

Because human activities cause this environmental

damage, our species is culpable for a crime we are committing against ourselves. But in our defense, humanity is largely trapped by the political form of liberal state power, which facilitates the smooth functioning of global capitalism—the source of the problem.

On that point, you suggest that climate change cannot be properly challenged with the tools or "innovations" of the neoliberal, capitalist system that caused it. Can you expand on this?

Absolutely. In my view, it is futile to try to solve the harms being inflicted upon the environment using the same mechanisms that produced the problem in the first place. Environmental degradation is the concrete form of late capitalism. The failure to recognize and respond to this situation is in bad faith.

For instance, the idea that we can "green" a capitalist economy without radically rethinking the basic premises at the heart of neoliberal economic theory is truly an example of misplaced politics. The system is premised upon a model of endless growth, competition, private property, and consumer citizenship, all of which combine to produce a terribly exploitative, oppressive, and violent structure that has come to infuse all aspects of everyday life.

Yet you have worked with UNESCO in the past—an example of an organization that I think it's fair to say is more interested in mainstream climate "solutions" than in radical political change. How do you approach this contrast?

It is important to strategically work across a variety of political platforms in order to be effective. I am completely realistic about the limitations of my role as a UNESCO water chair, meaning I acknowledge the fact that I am not producing radical change in this context. That said, I maintain a strong and honest position, one that resists being mediated by the institutional power relations that define a large international organization. As a UNESCO water chair I am both external and internal to the organization. This allows me to maintain a position of partial autonomy.

The people whom I have been in dialogue with at UNESCO are deeply committed to creating policies and practices that address social and environmental injustices. We may not always agree on how to do this, but it is crucial that different voices, experiences, and situations are part of the discussion, even when the outcome falls short of radical change.

It is better to be at the table and contributing to the discussion than not at all. Every now and then, what one brings to the table animates the discussion enough to create small but meaningful changes.

During the 1990s, it was common in policy circles to link the causes of conflict and violence to conditions of poverty and underdevelopment. A number of critics challenged this, as it seemed to place the blame for insecurity and vulnerability onto the shoulders of the global poor. Is there a danger that the same is happening today as environmental concerns are increasingly brought into discussions concerning the likelihood of violence and war?

This question raises an important issue concerning displacement: the way in which structural and historical violence is obfuscated by pointing the finger of blame somewhere else. In much the same way that poverty has been identified as the cause of unrest, today environmental degradation is increasingly viewed as causing or having the potential to trigger social conflict, providing justification for the privatization of common pool resources or defensive strategies to secure and gain a monopoly over valuable natural resources.

Whether the conflict in Darfur is blamed on desertification, or water scarcity as underpinning the ongoing conflict between Palestinians and Israelis, the problem of the equitable distribution of scarce natural resources and the deeper power relations concerning who reaps the benefits of these, and at whose expense, remains dormant.

I am not suggesting that environmental degradation is unconnected to social and political unrest—it definitely is. However, to form a neat causal connection between the two disguises the myriad ways in which violence in the contemporary world operates.

For instance, the threat of environmental degradation is used as a weapon of war. Here I am thinking of ISIS taking control of Mosul Dam in August of 2014, or of Syria, where water supplies were cut off from residents in Aleppo in both government- and opposition-controlled areas of the city.

Environmental degradation is also used to justify the privatization of resources we share in common, under the guise of sustainable management, such as the privatization of water in Bolivia in the late 1990s, which increased the

price of water, exacerbated poverty in the country, and fueled mass unrest. In this case, entire groups of people, future
generations, and other species are denied or given limited
access to common pool resources. I don't see much difference between this and the previous example of ISIS seizing
Mosul Dam. In varying degrees, all are instances of what
the social theorist David Harvey might call "'accumulation
by dispossession."

*If we maintain that climate degradation is indeed a form of crim-
inal violence, and that neoliberal solutions cannot serve justice,
what might a practice toward justice look like?*

There are two dominant political strategies that currently
prevail in response to this problem. Either we try to medi-
ate capitalism (this would be the "greening" of the economy argument) or we work from the outside to resist it
(namely, the position of the radical activist). However, we're
now seeing a system of government that responds to environmental degradation by protecting the interests of the
corporate sector ahead of civil society. The government is
now a corporate actor that works with the private sector
to privatize our shared resources. Meanwhile, the radical
activist who frees minks from a fur farm, for example, can
now be prosecuted under federal terrorism laws. In this
way, tactics of working within the system to change it and
the alternative approach of radical resistance each, in their
own way, end up being absorbed into capitalist society and
facilitating its smooth functioning.

I am more interested in connecting conflicting political models, with the aim of creating new political solidarities. I don't mean solidarity simply based on an issue—for instance when climate-change activists link arms with indigenous-rights activists or the anti-fracking movement. While this is important to do, I think the whole notion of solidarity needs to be deepened and expanded to include solidarities across different political practices, strategically switching between oppositional intervention from the outside and working from the inside to find a more effective path forward.

This would be a bastard solidarity that combines the immanent politics of Spinoza and all its offshoots, which emerge by affirming the current situation differently to produce change, with the dialectics descended from Hegel and Marx, which begin by negating the current state of affairs so that contradiction leads to change. In my view, the change in question is only ever a provisional synthesis, not a stable, finished solution. As such, the struggle is necessarily continual and manifold, occurring in multiple ways and across numerous platforms. What unites them is a struggle premised upon love. A love of life, diversity, and openness. A love that works to defy hatred, oppression, and intolerance, and the violence this perpetuates.

An emancipatory politics needs to be quick on its feet and recognize how capital accumulation functions and in turn build its political practices and thinking as a strategic response to this. No one political program is immune to appropriation by capital. Working within the system to change it is always going to involve risks of co-option, just as much as a politics that positions itself outside of the capitalist system would. Recognizing this and developing a critical realism regarding this situation that can switch deftly and quickly between the two positions is the basis for crafting a path forward.

Environmental degradation is calling us to the witness stand of history. It demands we testify against ourselves and mount a case in our defense. Ultimately, we are all agents of history. To reduce ourselves to a role of mere observation is to deny us of our humanity.

SIX

THE VIOLENCE OF FORGETTING

When ignorance and power join forces, history itself can be erased.

How do we develop the necessary educational practices to challenge the problem of violence in our times? How might we differentiate between competing pedagogies of violence and hope? And what lessons might be learned so that we can build collective futures? The political and cultural theorist Henry A. Giroux has been at the forefront of these debates with his impassioned call to take the power of education seriously. Education is always a political form of intervention, Giroux maintains. This discussion begins from the very real presence of violence in the United States as witnessed in repeated mass killings and what this means for cultural memory and civic engagement. Confronting the raw realities of suffering, Giroux then directly addresses the politics of ignorance and the intellectual conditions that give rise to systems of oppression. Finally, he identifies the challenges and difficulties faced by the modern university when teaching students about violence.

Brad Evans interviews Henry A. Giroux

June 20, 2016

Henry A. Giroux is a professor in the Department of English and Cultural Studies at McMaster University in Hamilton, Ontario. A leading public intellectual and critical pedagogue, his latest books include *America at War with Itself*, *American Nightmare: Facing the Challenge of Fascism*, and *The Terror of the Unforeseen.*

Brad Evans: Throughout your work you have dealt with the dangers of ignorance and what you have called the violence of "organized forgetting." Can you explain what you mean by this and why we need to be attentive to intellectual forms of violence?

Henry Giroux: Unfortunately, we live at a moment in which ignorance appears to be one of the defining features of American political and cultural life. Ignorance has become a form of weaponized refusal to acknowledge the violence of the past and revels in a culture of media spectacles in which public concerns are translated into private obsessions, consumerism, and fatuous entertainment. As James Baldwin rightly warned, "Ignorance, allied with power, is the most ferocious enemy justice can have."

The warning signs from history are all too clear. Failure to learn from the past has disastrous political consequences. Such ignorance is not simply about the absence of information. It has its own political and pedagogical categories whose formative cultures threaten both critical agency and democracy itself.

What I have called the violence of organized forgetting signals how contemporary politics are those in which emotion triumphs over reason, and spectacle over truth, thereby erasing history by producing an endless flow of fragmented and disingenuous knowledge. At a time in which figures like Donald Trump are able to gain a platform by promoting values of "greatness" that serve to cleanse the memory of social and political progress achieved in the name of equality and basic human decency, history and thought itself are under attack.

Once ignorance is weaponized, violence seems to be a tragic inevitability. The mass shooting in Orlando is yet another example of an emerging global political and cultural climate of violence fed by hate and mass hysteria. Such violence legitimates not only a kind of inflammatory rhetoric and ideological fundamentalism that views violence as the only solution to addressing social issues, it also provokes further irrational acts of violence against others. Spurned on by a complete disrespect for those who affirm different ways of living, this massacre points to a growing climate of hate and bigotry that is unapologetic in its political nihilism.

It would be easy to dismiss such an act as another senseless example of radical Islamic terrorism. That is too easy. Another set of questions needs to be asked. What are the deeper political, educational, and social conditions that allow a climate of hate, racism, and bigotry to become the dominant discourse of a society or worldview? What role do politicians with their racist and aggressive discourses play in the emerging landscapes of violence? How can we use education, among other resources, to prevent politics from being transformed into a pathology? And how might we counter these tragic and terrifying conditions without retreating into security or military mindsets?

You insist that education is crucial to any viable critique of oppression and violence. Why?

I begin with the assumption that education is fundamental to democracy. No democratic society can survive without a formative culture, which includes but is not limited to schools capable of producing citizens who are critical, self-reflective, knowledgeable, and willing to make moral judgments and act in a socially inclusive and responsible way. This is contrary to forms of education that reduce learning to an instrumental logic that too often and too easily can be perverted to violent ends.

So we need to remember that education can be both a basis for critical thought and a site for repression that destroys thinking and leads to violence. Michel Foucault wrote that knowledge and truth not only "belong to the register of order and peace" but can also be found on the "side of violence, disorder, and war." What matters is the type of education a person is encouraged to pursue.

It's not just schools that are a site of this struggle. "Education" in this regard not only includes public and higher education but also a range of cultural apparatuses and media that produce, distribute and legitimate specific forms of knowledge, ideas, values, and social relations. Just think of the ways in which politics and violence now inform each other and dominate media culture. First-person shooter video games top the video-game market while Hollywood films ratchet up representations of extreme violence and reinforce a culture of fear, aggression, and militarization. Similar spectacles now drive powerful media conglomerates like 21st Century Fox, which includes both news and entertainment subsidiaries.

As public values wither along with the public spheres that produce them, repressive modes of education gain popularity, and it becomes easier to incarcerate people than to educate them, to model schools after prisons, to reduce the obligations of citizenship to mere consumption, and to remove any notion of social responsibility from society's moral registers and ethical commitments.

Considering Hannah Arendt's warning that the forces of domination and exploitation require "thoughtlessness" on behalf of the oppressors, how is the capacity to think freely and in an informed way key to providing a counter to violent practices?

Young people can learn to challenge violence, like those in the antiwar movement of the early 1970s or today in the Black Lives Matter movement.

Education does more than create critically minded, socially responsible citizens. It enables young people and others to challenge authority by connecting individual troubles to wider systemic concerns. This notion of education is especially important given that racialized violence, violence against women, and the ongoing assaults on public goods cannot be solved on an individual basis.

Violence maims not only the body but also the mind and spirit. As Pierre Bourdieu has argued, it lies "on the side of belief and persuasion." If we are to counter violence by offering young people ways to think differently about their world and the choices before them, they must be empowered to recognize themselves in any analysis of violence and in doing so to acknowledge that it speaks to their lives meaningfully.

There is no genuine democracy without an informed public. While there are no guarantees that a critical education will prompt individuals to contest various forms of oppression and violence, it is clear that in the absence of a formative democratic culture, critical thinking will increasingly be trumped by anti-intellectualism, and walls and war will become the only means to resolve global challenges.

Creating such a culture of education, however, will not be easy in a society that links the purpose of education with being competitive in a global economy.

Mindful of this, there is now a common policy in place throughout the education system to create "safe spaces" so students feel comfortable in their environments. This is often done in the name of protecting those who may have their voices denied. But given your claim about the need to confront injustice, does this represent an ethically responsible approach to difficult subject matters?

There is a growing culture of conformity and quietism on university campuses, made evident in the current call for safe spaces and trigger warnings. This is not just conservative reactionism but is often carried out by liberals who believe they are acting with the best intentions. Violence comes in many forms and can be particularly disturbing when confronted in an educational setting if handled dismissively or in ways that blame victims.

Yet troubling knowledge cannot be condemned on the basis of making students uncomfortable, especially if the desire for safety serves merely to limit access to difficult knowledge and the resources needed to analyze it. Critical education should be viewed as the art of the possible rather than a space organized around timidity, caution, and fear.

Creating safe spaces runs counter to the notion that learning should be unsettling, that students should challenge common-sense assumptions and be willing to confront disturbing realities despite discomfort. The political scientist Wendy Brown rightly argues that the "domain of free public speech is not one of emotional safety or reassurance" and is "not what the public sphere and political speech promise." A university education should, Brown writes, "call you to think, question, doubt" and "incite you to question everything you assume, think you know, or care about."

This is particularly acute when dealing with pedagogies of violence and oppression. While there is a need to be ethically sensitive to the subject matter, our civic responsibility requires, at times, confronting truly intolerable conditions. The desire for emotionally safe spaces can be invoked to protect one's sense of privilege—especially in the privileged sites of university education. This is further compounded by the frequent attempts by students to deny some speakers a platform because their views are controversial. While the intentions may be understandable, this is a dangerous road to go down.

Confronting the intolerable should be challenging and upsetting. Who could read the testimonies of Primo Levi and not feel intellectually and emotionally exhausted? Or Martin Luther King Jr.'s words, not to mention those of Malcolm X? It is the conditions that produce violence that should upset us ethically and prompt us to act responsibly, rather than to capitulate to a privatized emotional response that substitutes a therapeutic language for a political and worldly one.

There is more at work here than the infantilizing notion that students should be protected rather than challenged in the classroom; there is also the danger of creating a chilling effect on the part of faculty who want to address controversial topics such as war, poverty, spectacles of violence, racism, sexism, and inequality. If American society wants to invest in its young people, it has an obligation to provide them with an education in which they are challenged, can learn to take risks, think outside the boundaries of established ideologies, and expand the far reaches of their creativity and critical judgment. This demands a pedagogy that is complicated, taxing, and disruptive.

You place the university at the center of a democratic and civil society. But considering that the university is not a politically neutral setting separate from power relations, you are concerned with what you term "gated intellectuals" who become seduced by the pursuit of power. Please explain this concept.

Public universities across the globe are under attack not because they are failing but because they are considered discretionary—unlike K-12 education, for which funding is largely compulsory. The withdrawal of financial support has initiated a number of unsavory responses: Universities have felt compelled to turn toward corporate management models. They have effectively hobbled academic freedom by employing more precarious part-time instead of full-time faculty, and they increasingly treat students as consumers to be seduced by various campus gimmicks while burying the majority in debt.

My critique of what I have called "gated intellectuals" responds to these troubling trends by pointing to an increasingly isolated and privileged full-time faculty who believe that higher education still occupies the rarefied, otherworldly space of disinterested intellectualism of Cardinal Newman's nineteenth century and who defend their own indifference to social issues through appeals to professionalism or by condemning as politicized those academics who grapple with larger social issues. Some academics have gone so far as to suggest that criticizing the university is tantamount to destroying it. There is a type of intellectual violence at work here that ignores and often disparages the civic function of education while forgetting Hannah Arendt's incisive admonition that "education is the point at which we decide whether we love the world enough to assume responsibility for it."

Supported by powerful conservative foundations and awash in grants from the defense and intelligence agencies, such gated intellectuals appear to have forgotten that in a democracy it is crucial to defend the university as a crucial democratic public sphere. This is not to suggest that they are silent. On the contrary, they provide the intellectual armory for war, the analytical supports for gun ownership, and lend legitimacy to a host of other policies that lead to everyday forms of structural violence and poverty. Not only have they succumbed to official power, they collude with it.

I feel your recent work provides a somber updating of Arendt's notion of "dark times," hallmarked by political and intellectual catastrophe. How might we harness the power of education to reimagine the future in more inclusive and less violent terms?

The current siege on higher education, whether through defunding education, eliminating tenure, tying research to military needs, or imposing business models of efficiency and accountability, poses a dire threat not only to faculty and students who carry the mantle of university self-governance but also to democracy itself.

The solutions are complex and cannot be addressed in isolation from a range of other issues in the larger society such as the defunding of public goods, the growing gap between the rich and the poor, poverty, and the reach of the prison-industrial complex into the lives of those marginalized by class and race.

We have to fight back against a campaign, as Gene R. Nichol puts it, "to end higher education's democratizing influence on the nation." To fight this, faculty, young people, and others outside of higher education must collectively engage with larger social movements for the defense of public goods. We must address that, as the welfare state is defunded and dismantled, the state turns away from enacting social provisions and becomes more concerned about security than social responsibility. Fear replaces compassion, and a survival-of-the-fittest ethic replaces any sense of shared concern for others.

Lost in the discourse of individual responsibility and self-help are issues like power, class, and racism. Intellectuals need to create the public spaces in which identities, desires, and values can be encouraged to act in ways conducive to the formation of citizens willing to fight for individual and social rights, along with those ideals that give genuine meaning to a representative democracy.

Any discussion of the fate of higher education must address how it is shaped by the current state of inequality in American society and how it perpetuates it. Not only is such inequality evident in soaring tuition costs, inevitably resulting in the growing exclusion of working- and middle-class students from higher education, but also in the transformation of over two-thirds of faculty positions into a labor force of overworked and powerless adjunct faculty members. Faculty need to take back the university and reclaim modes of governance in which they have the power to teach and act with dignity, while denouncing and dismantling the increasing corporatization of the university and the seizing of power by administrators and their staff, who now outnumber faculty on most campuses.

In return, academics need to fight for the right of students to be given an education not dominated by corporate values. Higher education is a right, not an entitlement. It should be free, as it is in many other countries, and, as Robin D. G. Kelley points out, this should be true particularly for minority students. This is all the more crucial as young people have been left out of the discourse of democracy. Rather than invest in prisons and weapons of death, Americans need a society that invests in public and higher education.

There is more at stake here than making visible the vast inequities in educational and economic opportunities. Seeing education as a political form of intervention, offering a path toward racial and economic justice, is crucial in reimagining a new politics of hope. Universities should be subversive in a healthy society. They should push against the grain and give voice to the voiceless, the powerless, and the whispers of truth that haunt the apostles of unchecked power and wealth. Pedagogy should be disruptive and unsettling, while pushing hard against established orthodoxies. Such demands are far from radical and leave more to be done, but they point to a new beginning in the struggle over the role of higher education in the United States.

SEVEN

WHEN LAW IS NOT JUSTICE

Rule of law may be good for business, but in many parts of the world it's not enough to ensure basic rights.

Who actually gets to speak on behalf of the globally oppressed? The importance of language and the capacity to speak for oneself has been a central concern for the postcolonial theorist and activist, Gayatri Chakravorty Spivak. Such concerns expose the operations of power at the level of discourse and how they become integral to how we come to understand the normalization of oppression and the denial of rights "within" normative, progressive, and legal frameworks. Recognizing the limits of legalistic and developmental approaches to human rights, this conversation covers a range of issues from the violence of poverty, the problem of law, and the legacy of Frantz Fanon to the ways the imperialism of canonical thinkers such as Immanuel Kant might be affirmatively sabotaged. This provides a new opening into the meaning of revolution and how it might be detached from the violent dialectics of history.

Brad Evans interviews Gayatri Chakrvorty Spivak

July 13, 2016

Gayatri Chakravorty Spivak is a university professor in the humanities at Columbia University, New York. Her books include *Nationalism and the Imagination* and *An Aesthetic Education in the Era of Globalization*.

Brad Evans: Throughout your work, you have written about the conditions faced by the globally disadvantaged, notably in places such as India, China, and Africa. How might we use philosophy to better understand the various types of violence that erupt as a result of the plight of the marginalized in the world today?

Gayatri Chakravorty Spivak: While violence is not beyond naming and diagnosis, it does raise many challenging questions all the same. I am a pacifist. I truly believe in the power of nonviolence. But we cannot categorically deny a people the right to resist violence, even, under certain conditions, with violence. Sometimes situations become so intolerable that moral certainties are no longer meaningful. There is a difference here between condoning such a response and trying to understand why the recourse to violence becomes inevitable.

When human beings are valued as less than human, violence begins to emerge as the only response. When one group designates another as lesser, they are saying the "inferior" group cannot think in a "reasonable" way. It is important to remember that this is an intellectual violation and in fact that the oppressed group's right to manual labor is not something they are necessarily denied. In fact, the oppressed group is often pushed to take on much of society's necessary physical labor. Hence, it is not that people are denied agency; it is rather that an unreasonable or brutish type of agency is imposed on them. And the power inherent in this physical agency eventually comes to intimidate the oppressors. The oppressed, for their part, have been left with only one possible identity, which is one of violence. That becomes their politics, and it appropriates their intellect.

This brings us directly to the issue of "reasonable" versus "unreasonable" violence. When dealing with violence deemed unreasonable, the dominating groups demonize violent responses, saying that "those other people are just like that," not just that they are worth less but also that they are essentially evil, essentially criminal, or essentially have a religion that is prone to killing.

Yet, on the other side, state-legitimized violence, considered "reasonable" by many, is altogether more frightening. Such violence argues that if a person wears a certain kind of clothing or belongs to a particular background, he or she is legally killable. Such violence is more alarming because it is continuously justified by those in power.

At least some violent resistance in the twentieth century was tied to struggles for national liberation, whether anticolonial or (more common in Europe) antifascist. Is there some new insight needed to recognize forces of domination and exploitation that are separated from nation-states yet are often explained as some return to localism and ethnicity?

This is a complicated question demanding serious philosophical thought. I have just come back from the World Economic Forum, and their understanding of power and resistance is very different from that of a group such as the ethnic Muslim Rohingya who live on the western coast of Myanmar, though both are already deeply embedded in global systems of power and influence, even if from opposing sides. The Rohingya have been the victims of a slow genocide as described by Maung Zarni, Amartya Sen, and others. This disrupts an Orientalist reading of Buddhism as forever the peace-loving religion. Today we see Buddhists from Thailand, Sri Lanka, and Myanmar engage in statesanctioned violence against minorities.

The fact is that when the pro-democracy spokesperson Aung San Suu Kyi was under house arrest there, she could bravely work against oppressive behavior on the part of the military government. But once she was released and wanted to secure and retain power, she became largely silent on the plight of these people and has sided with the majority party, which has continued to wage violence against non-Buddhist minorities. One school of thought says that in order to bring democracy in the future, she has to align herself with the majority party now. I want to give Ms. Aung San Suu Kyi the benefit of the doubt. But when the majority party is genocidal, there is a need to address that. Aligning with them cannot possibly bring democracy.

However, rather than retreating back into focused identity politics, resistance in this context means connecting the plight of the Rohingya to global struggles, the context of which is needed in order to address any particular situation. Older, national, identity-based struggles like those you mention are less persuasive in a globalized world. All of this is especially relevant as Myanmar sets up its first stock exchange and prepares to enter the global capitalist system.

In globalization as such, when the nation-states are working in the interest of global capital, democracy is reduced to body counting, which often works against educated judgments. The state is trapped in the demands of finance capital. Resistance must know about financial regulation in order to demand it. This is bloodless resistance, and it has to be learned. We must produce knowledge of these seemingly abstract globalized systems so that we can challenge the social violence of unregulated capitalism.

What are the implications when the promotion of human rights is left to what you have called "self-appointed entrepreneurs" and philanthropists, from individuals such as Bill Gates to organizations like the World Bank, who have a very particular conception of rights and the "rule of law"?

It is just that there be law, but law is not justice.

The passing of a law and the proof of its existence is not enough to assure effective resistance to oppression. Some of the gravest violations of rights have occurred within legal frameworks. And if that law governs a society never trained in what Michel Foucault would call "the practice of freedom," it is there to be enforced by force alone, and the ones thus forced will find better and better loopholes around it.

That is why the "intuition" of democracy is so vital when dealing with the poorest of the poor, groups who have come to believe their wretchedness is normal. And when it comes time to starve, they just tighten their nonexistent belts and have to suffer, fatefully accepting this in silence. It's more than children playing with rocks in the streets. It takes over every aspect of the people's existence. Yet these people still work, in the blazing heat, for little or next to nothing for wealthy landowners. This is a different kind of poverty.

Against this, we have this glamorization of urban poverty by the wealthier philanthropist and aid agencies. There is always a fascination with the picture-perfect idea of poverty; children playing in open sewers and the rest of it. Of course, such lives are proof of grave social injustice. But top-down philanthropy, with no interest in an education that strengthens the soul, is counterproductive, an assurance that there will be no future resistance, only instant celebrity for the philanthropist.

I say "self-appointed" entrepreneurs because there is often little or no regulation placed upon workers in the nongovernmental sector. At best, they are ad hoc workers picking up the slack for a neoliberal state whose managerial ethos cannot be strong on redistribution, and where structural constitutional resistance by citizens cannot be effective in the face of an unconstituted "rule of law" operating, again, to protect the efficiency of global capital growth. The human rights lobby moves in to shame the state and in ad hoc ways restores rights. But there is then no democratic follow-up, and these organizations rarely stick around long enough to see that.

Another problem with these organizations is the way they emphasize capitalism's social productivity without mentioning capital's consistent need to sustain itself at the expense of curtailing the rights of some sectors of the population. This is all about the removal of access to structures of reparation: the disappearance of the welfare state or its not coming into being at all.

If we turn to "development," we often see that what is sustained in sustainable development is cost-effectiveness and profit-maximization, with the minimum action necessary in terms of environmental responsibility. We could call such a thing "sustainable underdevelopment."

Today everything is about urbanization, urban studies, metropolitan concerns, network societies, and so on. Nobody in policy circles talks about the capitalization of land and how this links directly to the dispossession of people's rights. This is another line of inquiry any consideration of violence must take into account.

While you have shown appreciation for a number of thinkers known for their revolutionary interventions, such as Frantz Fanon, you have also critiqued the limits of their work when it comes to issues of gender and the liberation of women. Why?

I stand by my criticism of Fanon, but he is not alone here. In fact he is like most other men who talk about revolutionary struggle. Feminist struggle can't be learned from them. Yet, in *A Dying Colonialism*, Fanon is really trying from within to understand the position of women by asking questions about patriarchal structures of domination.

After the revolution, in postcolonial Algeria and elsewhere, those women who were part of the struggle had to separate themselves from revolutionary liberation organizations that were running the state in order to continue fighting for their rights under separate initiatives. Gender is bigger and older than state formations, and its fight is older than the fight for national liberation or the fight between capitalism and socialism. So we have to let questions of gender interrupt these revolutionary ideas, otherwise revolution simply reworks marked gender divisions in societies.

You are clearly committed to the power of education based on aesthetic practices, yet you want to challenge the canonical Western aesthetic ideas from which they are derived, using your concepts of "imaginative activism" and "affirmative sabotage." How can this work?

Imaginative activism takes the trouble to imagine a text—understood as a textile, woven web rather than narrowly as a printed page—as having its own demands and prerogatives. This is why the literary is so important. The simplest teaching of literature was to grasp the vision of the writer. This was disrupted in the 1960s by the preposterous concern "Is this book of relevance to me?" which represented a tremendous assault on the literary, a tremendous group narcissism. For literature to be meaningful it should not necessarily be of obvious relevance. That is the aesthetic challenge, to imagine that which is not immediately apparent. This can fight what is implicit in voting bloc democracy. Relevant to me, rather than flexible enough to work for others who are not like me at all. The inbuilt challenge of democracy— needing an educated, not just informed, electorate.

I used the term "affirmative sabotage" to gloss on the usual meaning of sabotage: the deliberate ruining of the master's machine from the inside. Affirmative sabotage doesn't just ruin; the idea is of entering the discourse that you are criticizing fully, so that you can turn it around from inside. The only real and effective way you can sabotage something this way is when you are working intimately within it.

This is particularly the case with the imperial intellectual tools, which have been developed not just upon the shoulders but also upon the backs of people for centuries. Let's take as a final example what Immanuel Kant says when developing his *Critique of Aesthetic Judgment*. Not only does Kant insist that we need to imagine another person, he also insists for the need to internalize it to such an extent that it becomes second nature to think and feel with the other person.

Leaving aside the fact that Kant doesn't talk about slavery whatsoever in his book, he even states that women and domestic servants are incapable of the civic imagination that would make them capable of cosmopolitan thinking. But, if you really think about it, it's women and domestic servants who were actually trained to think and feel like their masters. They constantly had to put themselves in the master's shoes, to enter into their thoughts and desires so much that it became second nature for them to serve.

So this is how one sabotages. You accept the unbelievable and unrelenting brilliance of Kant's work, while confronting the imperial qualities he reproduces and showing the contradictions in this work. It is, in effect, to jolt philosophy with a reality check. It is to ask, for example, if this second-naturing of women, servants, and others can be done without coercion, constraint, and brainwashing. And, when the ruling race or class claims the right to do this, is there a problem of power being ignored in all their claimed benevolence? What would educated resistance look like in this case? It would misfire, because society is not ready for it. For that reason, one must continue to work—to quote Marx—for the possibility of a poetry of the future.

EIGHT

WHAT PROTEST LOOKS LIKE

These are times for visionary organizing, not outraged reposting.

As an activist and academic, Nicholas Mirzoeff demands that we look at violence with persistence and organization. Working at the intersection of politics and visual culture, he addresses what it means to make violence visible and what concepts of violence are offered by the media. Mirzoeff illustrates how Western, capitalist hegemony has used visualization to secure itself as legitimate and how oppressed subjects have fought against this visuality. There are more images published on a daily basis today than there were published in the entire nineteenth century. The importance of visual culture in organizing our world can't be underestimated, but neither can the way in which existing power structures determine the shape of that culture and who can see and be seen within it. Here we look at culture, protest, and how a visual politics can be used to refuse state accounts of violence.

Natasha Lennard interviews Nicholas Mirzoeff

August 3, 2016

Nicholas Mirzoeff is a professor of media, culture, and communication at New York University. He is the author of many books, including *How to See the World* and *The Right to Look.*

Natasha Lennard: It is common in reports on protests to see or hear the phrase "turned violent"—"events turned violent," "protesters turned violent," et cetera. This usually means some sort of property damage, physical altercations between protesters and cops and the use by police of force. What does the suggestion of a violent "turn" imply? To me, it seems to suggest that the situation being protested—say, police brutality and racism—was not already "violent."

Nicholas Mirzoeff: Where there is violence, there is a message. Because so many forms of human action can be defined as violent, it is always a key political moment when a particular group or person is identified in this way. Defining violence as a personal choice, as if it were a consumer purchase, hides systemic or structural violence, such as poverty or racism. It presents the state as the only legitimate user of violence, in an implied social contract in which citizens renounce violence in exchange for protection. To be violent, in defiance of the state's monopoly on violence, is therefore to be a kind of traitor.

This theory of the state underlies media and state

reporting of political protest, in which violence is always invoked to disqualify the grievances of protesters. In the 1960s, the Rev. Dr. Martin Luther King Jr. was able to use media coverage of disproportionate violence against nonresisting demonstrators in Birmingham or Selma to convey his message as a form of martyrdom. He wrote: "We'll wear you down by our capacity to suffer . . . we will so appeal to your heart and conscience that we will win you in the process."

Today if police dogs attack demonstrators it is no longer national news. Ironically, the example of King himself, so often vilified as a traitor and a Communist in his lifetime, is used to berate today's protesters with the demand for nonviolence, meaning compliance with police instructions. King never intended nonviolence to mean compliance with the state. But when the term "violence" is used, it now signifies a moral and political failing by the "people," those not authorized to use force. Whenever Palestinians protest against the occupation of their land, the response in some quarters is always to call it violent, no matter what has happened. So I find myself avoiding the term altogether in relation to protests.

In terms of the images that have led to much recent protest: why do you think we seem to rely on images of broken black and brown bodies in order to recognize the oppression they face? We don't seem to need video of the deaths of, say, white school shooting victims to evoke similar public anger.

When Mamie Till-Mobley insisted that the body of her son Emmett Till be displayed in an open casket in 1954 after

his murder in Mississippi by white supremacists, she dramatically broke with convention and insisted people look at
what they would rather not see. It was Ferguson residents,
outraged by the callous treatment of eighteen-year-old Michael Brown's body—in full view of many children—who
tweeted the picture of his corpse to social media. A social
movement was started through the combination of popular
refusal to accept the police account of what happened with
the spread of the photographs both of Michael Brown and
of the subsequent protests. From the legend of Antigone to
Ferguson and the ongoing Israeli refusal to release Palestinian bodies for burial, there is a strong sense that justice—
aside from any law—requires that those meeting untimely
death receive proper burial. With the consent of the families
and communities concerned, images can help do that work.

What activists then did in the U.S. was to create a per-
formative form of protest that insisted we not look away but
consider over and over again what had happened. "Hands
Up, Don't Shoot" calls our attention to the instant before
the definitive violence, a moment where a reasonable person (to use legal phrasing) could and should have decided
against shooting, for example, twelve-year-old Tamir Rice.
By performing this collectively, it also became a challenge to
the police, saying in effect, "you don't dare to shoot, there
are too many of us."

The mass "die-in," an action appropriated from earlier movements in which protesters mime death as a group,
further emphasizes that all are potential targets. Performed
death, a visual act, makes each person appear vulnerable but

simultaneously creates a sense of freedom as you rest your body with others in spaces where you never normally are at rest. Both these forms of protest create what I call a "persistent looking," a repeated return to the place of loss so that it is possible to move past the first shock of violence to an understanding of the systemic violence that brought it about.

By comparison, the pictures of the body of Aylan Kurdi, the three-year-old drowned Syrian toddler who washed up on a Turkish beach, broke through the shield that we all create in what the German philosopher Walter Benjamin called "the optical unconscious." An outpouring of grief in the West made it seem as if we were seeing refugees die for the first time, although such drownings have been common for decades. The picture of a Turkish policeman carrying his body resonated because of its association (whether conscious or not) with the Christian image known as the *pietà*, in which the Virgin Mary carries the body of the dead Christ. We looked at Aylan's body and realized that he had indeed died for our sins.

A few months later, however, Britain voted to leave the European Union, largely because of intense resentment of all immigrants, including refugees. Here then is the dilemma. Certain images have the capacity to break through the defenses of our optical unconscious, but, precisely because that unconscious is a way of dealing with the intense violence of modern life, it seals over quickly. When these moments occur, change results only if people organize around the general principle that such images convey.

Black Lives Matter has done this. But in the case of

Aylan Kurdi, while efforts were made for individual refugees, no general case for immigration and asylum was effectively promoted after his death. Still less did Western media outlets turn to the Kurdish community for understanding.

But as far as the outrage that images provoke, sometimes it can be fleeting, and people move on to the next tragedy quickly. Do you think this speaks to the limitations of witnessing from afar and through a screen?

Your question speaks to the difference between click-tivism and activism. To click the "angry" icon on Facebook or retweet in outrage can be useful. But it is clearly not enough. There are differences to be noticed within online activism. For example, finding people with whom you might be able to associate and become an activist via a hashtag, like #BLACKLIVESMATTER, leads to the possibility of new communities being created and new ways of acting. This relies on a co-presence between online association and physical assembly. Sometimes this co-presence is simultaneous, as when people watch events on livestream. Other times the digital connection sets the stage for a physical assembly, whether that might be a meeting, a march, a protest, and so on.

Within these activist communities online, people often speak of being connected by love. This love is not romantic love between individuals but the collective bond that Dr. King called "the beloved community." For his colleague and friend Grace Lee Boggs, the result was what she called "visionary organizing." Such organizing thinks about how to make a life, not make a living. These exchanges are horizontal, requiring a good deal of time and energy to sustain. But they can make change.

The negative alternative is simply following. Millions of people now follow @realdonaldtrump, and the primary emotion of his supporters is indeed outrage, channeled via the iconic figure of Trump, who even refers to himself in the third person. In the medieval period, an icon was not distinct from the form it depicted, it was equivalent to that person or thing. An icon today, a figure like Trump's persona, is without content of any kind, taking on the shape and form that the person who believes in it wishes it to be. Whereas the religious icon was given meaning by faith, today's avatar expresses anger.

These are times for visionary organizing, not outraged reposting.

We find ourselves in the moment of the protest vote or the protest candidate—the Sanders and Trump campaigns, populist parties from the right and left gaining ground throughout Europe, and, of course, Brexit. What are your thoughts on the way the idea of a "protest" option gets invoked in these sorts of political circumstances?

Here I want to distinguish between two figures: the protester and the reactionary (meant literally, not pejoratively). Both respond to events in what political theory sometimes calls the "public square," the place where the political gets debated and decided that is now coextensive with both media and social media spaces. The philosopher Hannah Arendt further defined this space as what she called "the space of appearance." Who can and cannot appear in this space and on what terms is both the properly political question and the key to understanding the importance of the visible in globalized societies. What matters is not that there are many new forms of visual materials, interesting though that is to some of us. It is the question of appearance that is literally and metaphorically vital, because when a person deemed black, Palestinian, or any number of other designations appears in public, they may be killed.

However, it is becoming apparent that present-day politics cannot easily be configured around the demand for what Judith Butler has called "the right to appear." Protest is a form of appearance that makes a wrong visible and seeks to have it set right. Often that demand is aimed at authority, whether the government or some other body. In 2003, an estimated fifteen million people worldwide protested the predetermined decision to go to war in Iraq.

President George W. Bush dismissed them as a "focus group." As the Chilcot report has made clear, war was already the policy. This was not just a bad decision. It was exemplary of how appearance in the public sphere has lately lost its ability to have political impact.

There have been two notable responses to the breakdown of the space of appearance. Former protesters and the disillusioned have either set out to create a new politics of appearance or they have reacted by looking for groups to blame.

From the Zapatistas to the global Occupy project and today's Nuit Debout movement in France, the politics of appearance is no longer about submitting a petition to power but instead organizing so that people can appear to each other. That means suspending the regulation of the space of appearance by norms, above all the norms of racial hierarchy, and then refusing to move on out of that space. I believe that is why Black Lives Matter has acted to disrupt all the major presidential campaigns in 2016. It is seeking to form a new manner of being "political," a new way to see and be seen in the world.

But the other possibility, the blaming of other groups, is a reaction to a sense of powerlessness. As we have seen in the past, these reactions are not correlated to factual evidence or even specific local experience. The Brexit vote was above all motivated by a hostility to immigration. But those voting on these grounds often live in places with low immigration, just as anti-Semitism in the past did not result from proximity to Jewish people.

"Take back control" in Britain and "Make America great again" are then calls for a re-regulation of the space of appearance to exclude certain groups.

When Trump speaks of a wall, his followers understand this to mean both a physical structure (which may or may not actually be constructed) and, more importantly, a conceptual exclusion from participation.

There is no "common ground" between the politics of appearance and those of exclusion. In the United States, as the Black Lives Matter co-founder Alicia Garza has noted, "when black people get free, everybody gets free." Which means that unless black people get free, nobody gets free. Until and unless there is a politics of recognition that might form a new space of appearance that is not structured on exclusion, there will be no liberation.

But the resurgent politics of exclusion sometimes overwhelms our sense of that necessity. We seek expedient solutions and look to established leaders. Brexit showed that the defense of what W.E.B. Du Bois called the psychological "wage" of whiteness, its relative privileges, was more important to the majority population than actual economics. If Hillary Clinton fails to realize that it is no longer "the economy, stupid," a second reactionary victory might occur.

Talk of tolerance and diversity has failed. The urgent task at hand, especially for people who are not themselves black, is to construct an antiracist politics that is a common good. As Dr. King long ago realized, such politics can only work in tandem with antipoverty and antiwar strategies. In the end, it comes down to this: When we see another person, do we see them as another human being, not just equal to us in law but also someone that we can listen to, learn from and fall in love with? Or not?

NINE

WHO IS "EVIL" AND WHO IS THE VICTIM?

There are victims, and there are perpetrators, but it can be dangerous to think only in these terms.

Modern politics is full of theological resonances and traces. This is most apparent in the frequency that the term "evil" is used to describe atrocities and acts of extreme violence. Why do we still use such terms in the contemporary period? Does it not bind our politics to forms of moral absolutism and righteousness? Addressing these issues, the Italian philosopher Simona Forti talks about the recurring problem of evil within Western political and philosophical traditions, the importance of Dostoyevsky in setting out absolutist paradigms, and the need to rethink the perpetrator/victim relationship.

Brad Evans interviews Simona Forti

September 16, 2016

Simona Forti is a professor of political philosophy at the University of Eastern Piedmont in Italy. Her most recent book is *New Demons: Rethinking Power and Evil Today.*

Brad Evans: Since the September 11 attacks, right up to today's battles with the Islamic State, politicians have had no hesitation using the concept of evil to achieve their aims. George W. Bush's "axis of evil" or Barack Obama's assertion in his Nobel Peace Prize speech that "evil does exist in the world" are obvious examples. But as the philosopher Richard J. Bernstein points out in his book Radical Evil: A Philosophical Investigation, *intellectuals have been reluctant to deal with the concept. Do you believe that is true? And if so, why?*

Simona Forti: Evil has been a powerful mobilizer for centuries, going back long before September 11—from the Crusades, aimed at purifying Christianity of the evil of nonbelievers, to Ronald Reagan's portrayal of the Soviet Union as the "empire of evil." Speaking in such ways proves very expedient as it can be a powerful political strategy to revive the theological and metaphysical dichotomy between good and evil, with the latter obviously presented as the essential trait of the enemy we must defeat.

Bernstein is right in noting the recurring "evil talks" following September 11. At the dawn of the twenty-first century, these simplistic formulations were coming under attack in the intellectual world. But the egregiousness of the September 11 attacks lent itself very easily to a vision of good-evil dualism and a radical account of evil based on that vision.

Today we can see that both fundamentalist militant ideologies and the Western rhetoric of antiterrorism deploy a similar good-evil scheme as an instrument to divide the world along a simplistic dichotomy.

Take, for instance, the recent example of the Islamic State. If we were to write of its violence as being merely irrational or even barbaric, our condemnation wouldn't resonate as strongly in the popular imagination. Presenting the violence in terms of "evil" not only ensures that the fight against it is imperative, it also places us unreservedly on the right side of moral history.

What if someone were to argue that the concept of evil itself is philosophically and politically compromised, as it necessarily leads to such absolutist moral proclamations that leave no room for discussion or deliberation?

Calling attention to such absolutism is exactly what I aim to do. If we heed discussions about political evil, in the classics of political philosophy and elsewhere, we notice that behind the most diverse arguments stands a similar pattern. From the critics of the French Revolution to today's public speeches against radical Islamism, the question of evil and the power it unleashes is nearly always subsumed under the sign of nihilism. Evil, in short, becomes shorthand for the unleashing of death.

It was the literary genius of Fyodor Dostoyevsky who gave this nexus between evil and power its most iconic configuration, embodied in the main characters of his novel *Demons*. In Dostoyevsky's writings, there is a particular logic to evil born of the desire to take the place of God and his infinite freedom. Since finite creatures are unable to create the world from nothing, they try to become godlike by reducing being to nothing, by destroying. This is how evil enters the world for Dostoyevsky and for the many who, knowingly or not, follow in his tracks. It signals a condition where evil is said to enter the world as a diabolical disease of power, a power that, because it exceeds all given limits, can only be the pure energy of oppression and domination. This is the basis for thinking about absolute violence.

Of course, Dostoyevsky's conception of evil is much more complex, but I believe we can talk—beginning with *Demons*—about a "Dostoyevsky paradigm" as a theoretical framework within which many philosophers inscribed the evil they saw in the history of the twentieth century. It is as if the book offered transhistorical models of an exemplary scene of evil. We see this embodied in Nikolai Stavrogin, the most malicious character in this work, who directs its plot of nihilistic destruction.

Sucked into a destructive maelstrom of unlimited freedom, he seems to finally give a true representation of the "radical evil" glimpsed and named by Kant. He sexually violates a young girl, Matryosha, without apparent reason or desire. His perversion reaches its apex when he stands by impassively as the poor Matryosha hangs herself. For Dostoyevsky, this means Stavrogin goes past the point of no return as evil has as its object and target the absolute innocence of the victim. This expresses what I believe is Dostoevsky's idea of evil in its absolute, pure form.

The problem, however, is that the Dostoyevsky paradigm captures only this final scene. What is more relevant for the question of evil today is to critically question everything that happens before this utterly asymmetrical relationship between the perpetrators of violence and their absolute victims develops.

How then might we rethink the relationship between evil and the victim to allow for a more nuanced understanding of historical and contemporary forms of violence?

Without doubt, the way in which Michel Foucault rethinks relations of power opens a way here. He allows us to deconstruct the easy partitioning of the political field into just two distinct main characters, one with all the power (and, for this reason, guilty) and the other an absolute victim (thus, totally innocent.)

Evil doesn't always require absolute negativity, as it does in the Dostoyevsky paradigm. It can in fact be made by mediocre actions and actors and thrive through the gradual accumulation of unnecessary suffering over time. By "mediocre," I am referring to the unremarkable or the seemingly mundane.

Inspired here by the powerful and unsettling work of Primo Levi, I would say that before we reach a stage of domination polarized between victims and perpetrators, there is a "gray area" of strategies of power, domination, co-option, and resistance. This calls on us to address many challenging ethical and moral complexities that defy absolutist positions.

For example, Foucault's now widely cited reflections of biopolitics (the politics of life), and its ever possible slippage into thanatopolitics (a politics of death), reveal that the evil of domination comes not only from a will to destruction and death, as the classics imply, but also from a will to maximize life.

To understand this, consider that killing often takes place so that certain ways of life can thrive, not just out of some nihilistic urge. It was, in this sense, quite enlightening for me to read some key Nazi texts—texts of so-called "philosophical anthropology"—and to note how, despite how comforting it is to think of the perpetrators of genocide as absolute nihilists, such actors often think of themselves as maximizing some conception of life. They see themselves as the "true humanists" who fight against a "culture of death" (the Jewish one, in this case) in the name of "the value of life."

All of this further puts into question the Dostoyevsky paradigm. Now the characters are more than two (malevolent demons on one side and absolute victims on the other) precisely because the plot of political evil does not center only on death and the will to power but also on the unquestioned priority of "life" and the dangerous ways it can be pursued and conceived. Out of the shadow emerge mediocre demons and their desire for normality and positivity.

Your mention of "mediocrity" and evil inevitably recalls the work of Hannah Arendt. How does all this relate to her now infamous dictum on the banality of evil?

My debt to Hannah Arendt here is obvious. She was the first to grasp the complexity of a system of evil, to understand that it does not live only of evil intentions. With "Eichmann in Jerusalem" she no longer speaks of radical evil but of the banality of evil, that matter-of-fact way that the officer Eichmann and other Nazis pursued the day-to-day operations of genocide. Thanks to this theoretical shift, Arendt makes available for us a constellation of concepts, even though she did not have the time to arrange into a fully developed philosophical reflection. My goal is to pick up where she left off, while addressing the limitations of her important and empirically grounded work. Talk of "banality," in my opinion, runs the risk of turning merely into a linguistic provocation. If we talk about normality instead, a whole new field of insights comes to the fore, including that of compliance with a norm.

Our present times, in the West, are ruled by a paradoxical kind of normativity, where on the one hand there is a stated commitment to universal claims regarding rights, as if this discourse is now uncontroversial for liberal societies, yet on the other hand the painful reality for many is the experience of unnecessary suffering and hardship.

For example, consider the unnecessary violence represented by the frequent drownings of people fleeing to Europe. The treatment by European leaders and officials of this situation as in a way normal, in the absence of serious political commitments to resolve it, could be usefully spoken about in terms of normative or mediocre evil in the world today.

Looking at the other side of the relationship, it seems that an essential political strategy for many groups today is to present themselves as the undeniable victim of violence and suffering in order to stake out their own moral claims. How do we make sense of this?

For a long time in European history, being identified as a victim of a war or a genocide carried with it the shame of not having been able to defend oneself. This is one of the reasons, for example, in the first few years following World War II, that the Jewish victims of Auschwitz could not fully tell their story.

In the last few decades the situation has completely changed. Not only does the status of victim elicit respect, it has also become the object of some kind of competition. Who is the true victim? Who is most victimized? Who can boast about being an absolute victim, free from any compromise with power and from any responsibility?

The identity of victim can produce political benefits. But most of all, it allows us to think of ourselves as morally superior and innocent and therefore holding the right to inflict violence ourselves, but now a violence that is morally legitimate and hence a nonviolent violence. It is an identity then that dulls our perception of abusing our own power, of having become perpetrators.

Let us be clear: victims exist, as perpetrators exist. There are different degrees of responsibility and abuse, because all actors are not equally guilty. Yet, as Primo Levi teaches us, being a victim in itself does not automatically confer a certificate of innocence. Before and after we were victims, we have been and are responsible: for actions and inactions, for wrongs and indifference, for negations and shrugs.

Where does this all leave us in terms of Nietzsche's famous critique of all forms of dogmatism and the violence it can cause, thinking instead "beyond good and evil"?

I do not stand opposed to Nietzsche. In fact, in many ways I would place myself within a philosophical context that embraces at least some readings of his work. And that is the challenge: to take his "untimely," contested concepts and to try to rethink them within a new ethical and political framework.

The problem I aim to solve is that despite his appeal to think beyond good and evil, Nietzsche himself cannot quite step out of that distinction. He can change its terms, overturn them, but he does not escape from the dynamic of ethical judgment, which distinguishes between actions that are good on account of the ways they affirm the "human," as opposed to actions that are patently dangerous and negate those qualities that enable a dignified life.

Instead, I believe that the distinction between good and evil, just and unjust—the very act of distinguishing—is constitutive of the human animal's search for meaning. And if people think deeply, they cannot but ask themselves questions, questions not only about the existence of things but also about the meaning of actions and the relations that exist between humans living in a shared world

If we believe in the critical function of philosophy, we cannot, and, more important, should not, stop talking about political evil, precisely because of the expressive and provocative force of the term and the concept. It is the most powerful way to signify the complex entanglement of subjectivity, facts, ideas, intentional and unintentional actions, indifference, and passivity that come together in a fatal weave of atrocity and destruction.

TEN

ART IN A TIME OF ATROCITY

It can heal and restore memory when witnesses have been erased.

Societies are saturated by images of violence. As a result, we are continually forced to witness brutal events and the aesthetics of their representation. This comes at a time when the arts and humanities are facing considerable pressures as they try to respond to the challenges of the world and what it means to be human. Moving beyond the all too reductive claim that art is merely a cultural pastime, artist and critical thinker Bracha L. Ettinger confronts the problem of violence by making an impassioned case for the importance of art as a form of political and ethical intervention. Art provides openings for developing new ethical sensibilities and compassionate feelings toward others. Doing so, explains Ettinger, offers possibilities for connecting to trauma and suffering, allowing us to rethink legacies of violence in our times.

Brad Evans interviews Bracha L. Ettinger

December 16, 2016

Bracha L. Ettinger is a visual artist, philosopher, and psychoanalyst. Her publications include *Art as Compassion* and *And My Heart Wound-Space*, published on the occasion of the fourteenth Istanbul Biennial.

Brad Evans: You have consistently brought together in your works the often-disparate fields of art, psychoanalysis, and critical theory. How can this approach address violence?

Bracha L. Ettinger: I begin with art. We are connected through art even if we are, as individuals, retreating from one another and from the world. Each of my paintings starts from the traces of images of human figures—mothers, women, and children—abandoned, naked, and facing their death. The figure's wound is her own, but as we witness it, we realize traces of her wound are in me and in you.

Painting for me is an occasion to transform the obscure traces of a violent and traumatic past. Residues and traces of violence continue to circulate throughout our societies. Art works toward an ethical space where we are allowed to encounter traces of the pain of others through forms that inspire in our heart's mind feeling and knowledge. It adds an ethical quality to the act of witnessing.

Painting leads to thought and then leaves it behind. The space of painting is a passageway. By trusting the painting as true, you become a witness to the effects of events that you didn't experience directly, you become aware of the effects of the violence done to others, now and in history—a witness to an event in which you didn't participate, and a proximity to those you have never met. The coming together of art, psychoanalysis, and critical theory allows me to approach images of devastation, praying I can cure in viewers a blindness to violence and persecution that continues to lead to the dehumanization of others and of ourselves.

Theodor Adorno and others have questioned the relevance of art in response to realities of extreme violence. How do you respond to this so-called unrepresentability of human atrocity?

Painting pains me. And it will pain you. We join in sorrow so that silenced violence will find its echo in our spirit, not by imagination but by artistic vision. After an earth-shattering catastrophe, must I not allow the traces of the horrifying to interfere with my artwork? Why should this be any different to psychoanalytical and critical interventions?

The question "What is art?" is certainly not a question of aesthetics, styles and technique alone. Art proceeds by trusting in the human capacity to contain and convey its rage and its pain, and to transform residuals of violence into ethical relations via new forms of mediation that give birth to their own beauty and define them. It is to trust that we will be able to bear in compassion the unbearable, the horrible, and the inhuman in the human. Critique is not lost in this artistic entrustment. Rather, critique becomes participatory in it.

The purpose of art is not to represent reality or to aestheticize it. Art invents images and spaces. Art works like a maternal healing when it solicits against all the odds the human capacity to wonder, to feel awe, to feel compassion, to care, to trust and to carry the weight of the world. What you see doesn't reflect reality or your own self; the image is not a mirror. When violence kills trust, art is the space where a trust in the other, and by extension of one's being in the world, can reemerge.

Like psychoanalysis, painting in this regard is a form of healing when it discerns the space of what I have called the "subreality"—a net of strings of aesthetic and human connections—and makes of this space its subject. It creates connections of "co-emergence": "I feel in you," "you think in me," "I know in you," and so on, in which subjective existence is articulated through one another. Art alone can achieve such an encounter. Its figures appear when both light and darkness are in light.

Your art deals with some of the most difficult and challenging aspects of the Holocaust. Why have you been particularly compelled to focus on the symbolic violence against women?

I draw upon a recurrent image of the woman with shaven head. My mother's sister Etka was deported to Auschwitz at the age of eighteen with her sisters Hella and Sara. How could she adequately symbolize the private meaning of the violence she endured? Having returned from Auschwitz, she used to repeat: "I have no memories except this one: my head had been shaved, and when I passed in front of the windows of the barracks I couldn't recognize myself. I didn't know, out of all these women, which one was me. That's my only memory." One day, a second memory emerged, an image: the hair clip another girl from our family, shaven-headed too, refused to be separated from.

She lost her intimacy, what marked her out as unique. Alain Resnais's masterful *Hiroshima Mon Amour* aside, very few artists have tried to deal with the burdens of a similar symbolic act of shaming. My aim is not to construct or de-construct memory. Aesthetics today is the ethical challenge. When the witnesses disappear and only witnesses to those first-generation witnesses can speak, art's role is to create a humanizing space. While art evokes memory, it invents a memory *for* the future. Crucially, the subject that emerges in the painting doesn't simply correspond with the subject of a violated identity that will turn into an object of gaze. Nonviolent encounters with transformed traces of violence are humanizing. Take Goya, for example, or Resnais, Marguerite Duras, or Paul Celan.

How would you respond to those who would argue that art has no place in any serious political critique, as it is limited when it comes to resisting oppressive systems and transforming violent and catastrophic conditions?

Painting works slowly. It allows us to enter the space of the trauma of others and of our own with neither fight nor flight and to dwell in its resonance. Painting is about bringing into visibility that which is not ordinarily visible, including the forms that violence takes. Painting produces a suspension in time. It not only makes us confront the atrocities of the past but also provokes how we see and feel about the present moment.

Art as a primary ethical form of compassion might be one of the only realms left from which we can open channels towards the humane. When I touch the canvas to reopen a wound whose "memory" is not necessarily mine I instantly resist the counter-desire to ignore it. Beauty is not pre-given by an image but is the result of the process of working the abstract space.

Art in this regard, like love, appears as a form of fragile communication in which complete strangers can understand one another by resonance, both inside and outside one's close "community." One then realizes that humans are part of fragile and shared systems.

If a transformation in the traces of violence is possible through painting, a slow and indirect working through of a special kind of Eros, a nonsexual love, emanating from a sense of the vulnerable other accessed by our fragility, occurs. Painting activates a deep capacity to join in love and in suffering, in sorrow and joy, in compassion.

Can you elaborate more on your conception of beauty, as it directly challenges some well-established criticisms of the aesthetics of violence, which are precisely concerned with how it can be dangerous by rendering it pleasing for public consumption?

What I refer to as beauty, the source of which is the experience of trauma and pain as well as, without contradiction, of joy, signals an encounter with the horrible that we are trying to avoid, to paraphrase Rilke, as well as with the other's desire for another life to a wretched existence and longing for light. Art that denies violence abandons its victims as if they are irrelevant to human life. In the painting, the subject matter is not simply a representation. It should work like a passageway, through which a blurred idea—as it is breathing its new form through color, line, and light—elicits an affective response in the viewer that paves the sense of personal responsibility.

However, most cultural representations of violence do indeed produce objects ready for consumption. Painters, poets, and filmmakers who address the catastrophes of the last century and still reach beauty and the sublime in the sense I am speaking of are very rare.

Think of Paul Celan's poetry, for me a source of inspiration. It forms the frontier of death in life, where life glimpses at death as if from death's side, to paraphrase Jacques Lacan. But beyond this, I would like both the figurative and the abstract form to evoke their own humanized *passage* from nonlife to life. There is no real beauty without compassion; art humanizes the shock and transforms trauma as you realize the *impossibility to not share* your psychic, mental, and physical space.

What do you understand to be the political importance of the arts in the twenty-first century? And what ethical burden does this place on the artist as we seek to break out from the logic of violence and look toward more nonviolent futures?

Art today is the site of a trust that comes *after the death of trust*. Our generation has inherited and lives through a colossal requiem, from the harrowing memories of the twentieth century and before, to the continued violence we witness today. Our time is pregnant with the impression of loss and suffering. So the question of art, like that of the human subject it is intended to be experienced by, is always also the question of this loss and of the bringing of compassion back into life, for the future, starting from both image and an abstract horizon.

Art has the power to relink and invent new subjects and forms in and by light and space. Enlarging the capacity to elaborate, carry, and transform traces of violence, whether private or historical, is a responsibility. This is one of art's most important functions. "To bear" and "to carry" comes from the same root in Hebrew, in German, and in French. But in Hebrew it also means "subject." To make the world more bearable means to infiltrate the function of what I call "carriance" into the structure of subjectivity. It is to carry the burden of the suffering of others in the hope of a better time to come. Celan wrote, "The world is gone. I must carry you."

The move from simply experiencing art to social and political acts of caring or witnessing is not automatic. But individuals encountering art create a potential for more caring collective action. Art enters the domain of community and of the political without opposing aloneness. But to dwell pensively with traces of violence is to tolerate anxiety, welcome the contingent and the unknown, and open yourself up as an individual to a possibility of collective love.

Art entails a potential resistance to structures based on violence. To the vulnerability of the other, known or unknown, we become more responsible There are no promises; a painting might not do its work. Yet it does give us a chance. Breaking with the violent past demands paying intimate attention to its often-erased figures. To not sacrifice yourself while not sacrificing the other—this is the challenge. And today we must take care of the other, the refugee. It doesn't matter why and where; the refugee is your sister. She could be your mother; she can one day be you.

ELEVEN

IS HUMANISM REALLY HUMANE?

The idea of the "human" has brought us human rights, but it's not enough to ensure justice.

Structural violence is consistently predicated on dehumanization—systems of oppressive hierarchy in which certain groups and individuals can be deemed less than human and are violently mistreated as such. It would seem that the obvious path of struggle against such violence would be to demand that all people be treated equally. For Cary Wolfe, however, such an approach risks perpetuating its own violent taxonomy, while maintaining a status quo in which to be deemed nonhuman carries the constant threat of brutal treatment. Enter posthumanism. Wolfe's conception of posthumanism seeks to challenge an entrenched liberal ideology that gives primacy to "the human" or a notion of human knowledge. What would it mean to challenge the human/animal hierarchy? Do we risk throwing the baby out with the bathwater by challenging humanism and the frameworks of human and animal rights that have emerged from it?

Natasha Lennard interviews Cary Wolfe

January 9, 2017

Cary Wolfe is a professor of English and the director of the 3CT Center for Critical and Cultural Theory at Rice University. Noted for his work on posthumanism, his books include *Animal Rites* and *Before the Law.*

Natasha Lennard: "Posthumanism" could mean a variety of things. What is it for you, and how does it challenge the standard, liberal humanism we're familiar with?

Cary Wolfe: Well, let's start by acknowledging that the subject of "humanism" itself is a vast one, and there are many different varieties of it—liberal humanism, the humanism associated with the Renaissance, "secular humanism," and so on and so forth. "Posthumanism" doesn't mean "anti-humanism" in any of these senses, nor does it simply mean something that comes historically "after" humanism, as if in 1968 or 1972 or whenever, the scales suddenly fell from our eyes and we realized the error of our ways.

There is in fact a genealogy of posthumanist thought that stretches back well before the twenty-first or even twentieth century. You find hints of it in anything that fundamentally decenters the human in relation to the world in which we find ourselves, whether we're talking about other forms of life, the environment, technology or something else. Perhaps more importantly, you find it in the realization that when you don't allow the concept of the "human" to do your heavy philosophical lifting, you are forced to come up with much more robust and complex accounts of whatever it is you're talking about. And that includes, first and foremost, a more considered concept of the "human" itself.

The sketches of the "human," "the animal," or "nature" that we get from the humanist tradition are pretty obviously cartoons if we consider the multifaceted, multidisciplinary ways in which we could address these questions. Humanism provides an important cultural inheritance and legacy, no doubt, but hardly the kind of vocabulary that can describe the complex ways that human beings are intertwined with and shaped by the nonhuman world in which they live, and that brings together what the humanist philosophical tradition considered ontologically separate and discrete domains like "human" and "animal," or "biological" and "mechanical."

Darwinian thought was a huge step in this direction. So was Marx's historical materialism or the Freud of *Civilization and Its Discontents*. For me, one of the big breakthroughs was the emergence at mid-twentieth century of the wildly interdisciplinary type of thought known as systems theory, where fundamental processes such as the feedback loop allow you to describe how cruise control in a car works but also how thermoregulation in warm-blooded animals happens—without ever invoking (or really even being interested in) the old humanist taxonomies that would have separated such questions.

It's given us a language with which we can now describe much more intricately and robustly how human beings—not just their minds but their bodies, their microbiomes, their modes of communication, and so on—are enmeshed in and interact with the nonhuman world.

Gregory Bateson's work on human and animal communication is a wonderful example. He once wrote that when a guy says to a woman "I love you," she would do well to pay more attention to his body language, the dilation of his pupils, the tone and timbre of his voice, whether his palms are wet or dry, and so on, than to the denotative content of his words. That's because communication is a multilayered phenomenon that requires attention to both its "human" and "nonhuman," or evolutionarily inherited, involuntary elements. Bateson said that's why we don't trust actors, and I tell my students that's what makes email such an incendiary form of communication: all those dampening and texturing dimensions of the communication go away, and so the communication becomes all the more thin and brittle, and to try and get some of it back we start inserting emoticons, and so on. In all this, the properly "human" is only part of the story; it's nested in a larger, and in many ways nonhuman, set of contexts and forces.

Your work emphasizes that humanism—the hierarchical distinguishing between human and nonhuman animals based on a certain notion of "knowledge" or "intelligence"—is inherently oppressive and violent. Many would agree but see a solution within humanism itself—for example, in talk of human rights and the inclusion of animal rights and environmental protections. Many people may be skeptical of the inherent oppressiveness of humanism, given the historic victories won by appeals to a human rights discourse and in appeals to "humanity." Indeed, in this political moment, in response to Donald J. Trump's ascendance and the attendant upsurge in racist nationalism in the United States and Europe, there seems to be a renewed urgency in defending hard-won human rights and liberties. How would you respond?

I agree entirely that these should be vigorously defended, now more than ever, but for me these are not mutually exclusive projects, because of the different terrains and contexts in which these projects are carried out. On the one hand, rights discourse is Exhibit A for the problems with philosophical humanism. Many of us, including me, would agree that many of the ethical aspirations of humanism are quite admirable and we should continue to pursue them. For example, most of us would probably agree that treating animals cruelly, and justifying that treatment on the basis of their designation as "animal" rather than human, is a bad thing to do.

But the problem with how rights discourse addresses this problem—in animal rights philosophy, for example— is that animals end up having some kind of moral standing insofar as they are diminished versions of us: that is to say, insofar as they are possessed of various characteristics such as the capacity to experience suffering—and not just brute physical suffering but emotional duress as well—that we human beings possess more fully. And so we end up reinstating a normative form of the moral-subject-as-human that we wanted to move beyond in the first place.

So on the other hand, what one wants to do is to find

a way of valuing nonhuman life not because it is some diminished or second-class form of the human but because the diversity and abundance of life is to be valued for what it is in its own right, in its difference and uniqueness. An elephant or a dolphin or a chimpanzee isn't worthy of respect because it embodies some normative form of the "human" plus or minus a handful of relevant moral characteristics. It's worthy of respect for reasons that call upon us to come up with another moral vocabulary, a vocabulary that starts by acknowledging that whatever it is we value ethically and morally in various forms of life, it has nothing to do with the biological designation of "human" or "animal."

Having said all that, there are many, many contexts in which rights discourse is the coin of the realm when you're engaged in these arguments—and that's not surprising, given that nearly all of our political and legal institutions are inherited from the brief historical period (ecologically speaking) in which humanism flourished and consolidated its domain. If you're talking to a state legislature about strengthening laws for animal abuse cases, let's say, instead of addressing a room full of people at a conference on deconstruction and philosophy about the various problematic assumptions built into rights discourse, then you better be able to use a different vocabulary and different rhetorical tools if you want to make good on your ethical commitments. That's true even though those commitments and how you think about them might well be informed by a deeper and more nuanced understanding of the problem than would be available to those legislators. In other words, it's only partly a philosophical question. It's also a strategic question, one of location, context, and audience, and it shouldn't surprise anyone that we can move more quickly in the realm of academic philosophical discourse on these questions than we can in the realm of legal and political institutions.

So much contemporary cultural emphasis and investment is focused on the importance of "self" realization, "finding" ourselves, and so on, despite the fact that this self isn't even necessarily something completely embodied anymore, considering the prevalence of social media and other technologies that have lately influenced our practical experience of identity. How does this relate to your critique of humanism?

I think the simplest, most mundane answer to the question of why the Enlightenment idea of the self has been so hard to budge is that everything in our culture encourages us to invest in it, for economic and legal reasons that are not far to seek. We're encouraged more and more to develop our "brand," as it were, whether by accruing more and more friends on Facebook or by perfecting the kind of balanced "portfolio" between academic, athletic, and nonprofit work that university admissions committees want to see. So your term "investment" is to be taken quite literally at this moment in late, neoliberal capitalism.

Having said all that, however, social media merely dramatizes something that has always been true of the "self"—that it is in fact a prosthetic entity, a distributed, dispersed "assemblage" constituted by many elements, some of them physical and material and biological, some of them not, the constitution of the self by language and how it rewires the brain being the most obvious example. That is, if you like, the "truth" of the self: that it exists nowhere as a totality.

As Gregory Bateson put it, the bioenergetic physical entity called "Socrates" ceased to exist a long time ago. But "Socrates" understood in a more complex way, as a network of texts, readers, cultural legacies, the institutions they depend on, and so on, is still alive and exerts a powerful influence on the world, every day, to this day. The false move—"false desire" would be more apt—is to think that "it," that "self," exists as a totality somewhere. There is no "self" in that sense, even though the tip-of-the-iceberg phenomenon called "consciousness" encourages us to think that there is, understandably enough.

How might a posthumanist approach to undoing interspecies hierarchies intervene with structures of violence among humans themselves? Trump's election reflects and emboldens white supremacy and misogyny to a frightening degree. Could a posthumanist intervention risk moving focus away from a direct and much-needed struggle against these things, or could it help?

Oh, I think it can help enormously, by drawing out more clearly the broader base that these struggles share in what I've called a posthumanist ethical pluralism. My position has always been that all of these racist and sexist hierarchies have always been tacitly grounded in the deepest—and often most invisible—hierarchy of all: the ontological divide between human and animal life, which in turn grounds a pernicious ethical hierarchy. As long as you take it for granted that it's OK to commit violence against animals simply because of their biological designation, then that same logic will be available to you to commit violence against any other being, of whatever species, human or not, that you can characterize as a "lower" or more "primitive" form of life. This is obvious in the history of slavery, imperialism, and violence against indigenous peoples. And that's exactly what racism and misogyny do: use a racial or sexual taxonomy to countenance a violence that doesn't count as violence because it's practiced on people who are assumed to be lower or lesser and who in that sense somehow "deserve it."

That's why the discourse of animalization is so powerful, because it uses a biological or racial taxonomy to institute an ethical divide between who is "killable but not murderable," those who are "properly" human and those who aren't. So the first imperative of posthumanism is to insist that when we are talking about who can and can't be treated in a particular way, the first thing we have to do is throw out the distinction between "human" and "animal"—and indeed throw out the desire to think that we can index our treatment of various beings, human or not, to some biological, taxonomic designation. Does this mean that all forms of life are somehow "the same"? No, it means exactly the opposite: that the question of "human" versus "animal" is a woefully inadequate philosophical tool to make sense of the amazing diversity of different forms of life on the planet, how they experience the world, and how they should be treated.

TWELVE

THE INTELLECTUAL LIFE OF VIOLENCE

Resisting violence means knowing many of your efforts will fail. But that doesn't mean there is no hope.

Violence is not just a physical problem, it often begins and continues within the life of the mind. As such, violence can have lasting impact on reasonable thought and the imagination. How are we to take seriously the concept of violence and develop a critique that is adequate to the times? Richard Bernstein explores this question through a range of issues that includes the continued importance of movement organizing in revealing everyday structural forms of violence, his personal friendship with Hannah Arendt and what she might make of the present condition and its forms of oppression and exclusions, and the need for continued vigilance against violence in all its forms, including what this means for resistance by recognizing the failures of the past, while also retaining hope.

Brad Evans interviews Richard Bernstein

January 26, 2017

Richard J. Bernstein is Vera List professor of philosophy at the New School for Social Research, New York. His books include *Why Read Hannah Arendt Now?*

Brad Evans: A considerable part of your work has attended in detail to the intellectual, rather than physical, dimensions to violence, including structures of violence like those the Black Lives Matter and anti–Dakota Access Pipeline movements are meant to address. Why?

Richard J. Bernstein: These groups are important because they are challenging the difficulties faced when attempting to critique structural violence, which is often hidden in plain sight.

Let me first address an issue that is implicit in your question. I think we need to be alert to the historical context in which we speak about violence, including structural violence. Too frequently we take physical harm and/or killing as the only paradigm of violence. But this can blind us to other forms of violence that involve humiliation and suffering.

But what is even more important is that there are forms of behavior that are not considered to be violent at one stage of history that need to be exposed as violent in another. Let me give a classic example. Many people read Frantz Fanon's *The Wretched of the Earth* as a glorification of revolutionary violence. I think this is a serious misreading. The primary point of the book is to expose the sheer brutality of the colonial violence that these struggles resisted. For long periods of history colonialism was viewed as a "legitimate" way to civilize native populations. To the extent that violence was even recognized by colonial empires, it was "justified" as an instrument of law and order.

Today as a result of works like Fanon's and other works of postcolonial studies, the full horror of colonial violence has been exposed. We can also tell an analogous story about how what were once considered acceptable ways of abusing women are now recognized as forms of violence. There is always political struggle required to make people aware of hidden and new forms of violence, and then in opposing that violence.

What is most important about the Black Lives Matter and the anti–Dakota Access Pipeline movements is precisely that they politicize issues that involve violence. In the United States, there has been a prevailing myth that the civil rights movement and the election of a black president show significant progress in addressing and solving "the problem of race." But the truth is that African Americans have been (and continue to be) subject to all sorts of manifest and hidden violence, while structural violence against Native American populations has long been characteristic of American policy.

One can never predict when new political movements will arise that will expose and challenge new forms of violence, but I reiterate: political struggle (even when it fails) is necessary to expose and challenge violence.

You knew Hannah Arendt, to whom we still undoubtedly owe a considerable intellectual debt, especially in terms of thinking about oppression and violence. How do you think she might see the world today?

Yes, I did meet Hannah Arendt in 1972, and we had many intellectual exchanges before her death three years later. I have been engaged with her thinking ever since. I have no doubt that if she were alive she would be horrified about what is happening in the United States and throughout the world today. It would confirm her worst fears about the disastrous and politically debasing social tendencies of the modern age.

When Arendt spoke of dark times, she was not exclusively referring to the horrors of totalitarianism. In her book *Men in Dark Times* she writes: "If it is the function of the public realm to throw light on the affairs of men by providing a space of appearances in which they can show in deed and word, for better and worse, who they are and what they can do, then darkness has come when this light is extinguished by 'credibility gaps' and 'invisible government,' by speech that does not disclose what is but sweeps it under the carpet, by exhortations, moral and otherwise, that under the pretext of upholding old truths, degrade all truth to meaningless triviality." She wrote this statement in 1968—but I think it is even more relevant today.

But there is another side of Arendt. She rejected all appeals to doom and historical necessity. She stresses the possibility of new political beginnings, what she calls "natality." She had a deep conviction that people can come together, create a public space in which they deliberate and act, and change the course of history.

This is why having a conceptual approach to violence is so important. Arendt draws a sharp distinction between power and violence as well as between liberty and necessity.

What does this mean? In her lexicon, power and violence are antithetical. Initially this seems paradoxical—and it is paradoxical if we think of power in a traditional way where what we mean is who has power over whom or who rules and who are the ruled.

Max Weber defined the state as the rule of men over men based on allegedly legitimate violence. If this is the way in which we think about power, then Arendt says that C. Wright Mills was dead right when he declares, "All politics is a struggle for power; the ultimate kind of power is violence."

Against this deeply entrenched understanding of power, Arendt opposes a concept of power that is closely linked to the way in which we think of empowerment. Power comes into being only if and when human beings join together for the purpose of deliberative action. This kind of power disappears when for whatever reason they abandon one another.

This type of power was exemplified in the early civil rights movement in the United States, and it was exemplified in those movements in Eastern Europe that helped bring about the fall of certain communist regimes without resorting to violence. Violence can always destroy power, but it can never create this type of power.

Arendt's distinction between power and violence is also closely related to her distinction between liberty and freedom. Liberty in her understanding is liberty from—whether it is liberty from the misery of poverty or liberty from tyranny. And liberty from tyrants and totalitarian rulers may require armed struggle. But this type of liberty is to be sharply distinguished from public freedom, which for Arendt means a worldly reality that comes into being when people actively participate in public affairs and act together in concert.

So what does all this have to do with the "real" world? Plenty! A painful illustration is the way in which the Bush administration "justified" the military intervention in Iraq in 2003. The American people were told that once Saddam Hussein was overthrown with violence, then democracy and freedom would flourish, not only in Iraq but also in the wider Middle East. This was and remains sheer nonsense.

Unfortunately, we have to learn over and over again that liberty from oppressors is never sufficient to bring about the public spaces in which public freedom flourishes. Achieving public freedom means cultivating practices where people are willing meet one another as peers, form and test opinions in public, and act in a responsible manner.

I'd like us to now turn to the work of Walter Benjamin, another thinker whose work has been important in considering violence. How might we use his work to develop our own critique of violence, adequate to our own times?

Walter Benjamin is a very complex thinker. His early essay "Critique of Violence" has been one of the most discussed essays on the topic. I believe that Benjamin's intervention is important because he poignantly raises the fundamental questions, not answers, that need to be confronted in dealing with violence. For example: What is the relation between law and violence, and when does the law further violence? What is the role of the police in violence, and how do states tend to resort to violence at times of perceived crisis?

Rather than posit easy answers to these and other queries, his questioning shows us challenging truths, including how difficult it is to draw a distinction between legitimate and illegitimate violence, or to break the systemic cycles of violence.

Hannah Arendt, who was a very close friend of Walter Benjamin, once said that the only way to teach people to think is to infect them with the perplexities that one is confronting. What I find so valuable about Benjamin is that he infects us (his readers) with the perplexities concerning violence that so deeply concerned him.

You have talked about the difficulties of breaking cycles of violence. What can we learn from the history of violence in order to develop more peaceful relations among people both in the United States and across the world?

I don't think that violence will ever completely disappear from the world. In the future we will become aware of new forms of violence that we can't anticipate now. But I am certainly not pessimistic. What we learn from the history of violence is that we need to be specific and concrete when we speak about violence. I don't believe in Progress with a capital "P," but I do believe in progress with a small "p."

Earlier I mentioned the work of Fanon and others who critiqued "traditional" forms of colonial violence and participated in social and political movements to oppose and overcome this colonial violence. Of course, there can always be regression, and some will argue that we now have new, more subtle varieties of colonial violence. I am not contesting this. But the breakup of the old colonial system was progress in overcoming a dehumanizing form of violence. In the United States, the lynching of blacks was once a common practice. It took decades to combat this form of violence. That is progress with a small "p" even though there are now new, invidious forms of violence against black populations.

And throughout the twentieth century, we have many instances of the power of nonviolent movements to overcoming state violence, from Gandhi in India to Solidarity in Poland. We discover similar progress in overcoming violence in the feminist, gay, and lesbian movements. There will always be those who say that such progress is insignificant because it doesn't eliminate violence but only displaces it with new forms of violence. This can lead to what my colleague (and "Stone" series moderator) Simon Critchley calls "passive nihilism." I do not accept the nihilist or cynical response.

So I believe that we must constantly be alert to new (and old) forms of invidious violence, oppose and resist them when we can with full knowledge that many of our efforts will fail. We should never underestimate the importance of overcoming the suffering, pain, and humiliation of those who are victims of violence. Let me conclude by citing

Christopher Lasch's characterization of hope. I think it is especially relevant to the issue of identifying, opposing, and resisting violence:

"Hope implies a deep-seated trust in life that appears absurd to those who lack it. . . . The worst is always what the hopeful are prepared for. Their trust in life would not be worth much if it had not survived disappointments in the past, while knowledge that the future holds further disappointments demonstrates the continuing need for hope. . . . Improvidence, a blind faith that things will somehow work out for the best, furnishes a poor substitute for the disposition to see things through even when they don't."

THIRTEEN

THE VIOLENCE OF LOVE

Our cultural idealization of love could use a revision.

It might seem facile to respond to recent political events—political upheaval, Trump's ascendence, mass shootings, police violence, cruel deportations, and buoyed racism—with a call to "love." But in violent times, it's worth considering: Can love (as we know it) act as a radical force rather than a distraction? Does our current idea of love need revision? Is there a new kind of love emerging in today's social justice movements, one that works against the narrow kind of love fostered by capitalism? Author and academic Moira Weigel discuss how a mystified conception of love, particularly romantic love, has served to damage and exploit women, upholding dangerous, essentialist ideas of gender and "nature." But if we take seriously the ways in which romantic and family relationships are labor relationships, the question becomes: can we free romantic love from its capitalist, patriarchal trappings into something transformative? What could this even look like?

Natasha Lennard interviews Moira Weigel

August 17, 2016

Moira Weigel is a writer and social commentator. Her latest book is *Labor of Love: The Invention of Dating.*

Natasha Lennard: From Romeo and Juliet, *to* Wuthering Heights *to Hollywood romance tales like* The Notebook, *the mainstream Western view of love has long been that—to borrow from the former Supreme Court justice Potter Stewart's thoughts on obscenity—we know it when we see it. True love. Real love. Love at first sight. We treat romantic love as some unchanging, metaphysical object waiting to be found and grasped, even though these "traditional" modes of courtship and coupling are actually relatively recent developments. A number of feminist thinkers see violence in this traditional conception of love, and for good reason. Firstly, why does love continue to be upheld as something timeless and transcendental?*

Moira Weigel: Although there is a long and rich tradition of philosophers' writing about love, in everyday life we often act and speak as if love itself cannot be analyzed. You bring up Justice Stewart's famous dictum on obscenity. I have often heard folks tell friends in the dating doldrums: when it's right you'll know. When I myself was dating I used to think (often woefully) of the Bob Dylan line: if something ain't right, it's wrong. These kinds of tautologies crop up all over conversations about sex and romance. They obscure the wide range of emotions and experiences that all go by the name of "love."

But what love is, and what it could be, are hardly self-evident. Sometimes we speak of love as if it is a form of instinct, emanating directly from our biology. Goethe borrowed a metaphor from chemistry to describe how, spontaneously, bonds of attraction and affection can form: "elective affinities." These kinds of metaphors are tempting because attraction and affection surely do involve biological and bodily processes that we may not clearly perceive or intellectually understand. Yet they are incomplete.

The kinds of tautological definitions of love that I alluded to above—"when it's right you'll know," "if something ain't right, it's wrong," etc.—all emphasize its spontaneity. To put it another way, they refuse to acknowledge that it could involve any element of effort or intention. I think that this separation between love and labor is misguided. What's more, it is conservative, to the extent that it suggests that we have no agency, no power to shape the world as we recreate it.

What do you think the risks are, what potential violences emerge, from the perspective of feminism and political change, when we treat romantic love as this sort of timeless object?

Historically, the mystification of romantic love has been particularly damaging to women. It is difficult to separate from the entire tangle of ideas about female nature that have served to justify the exploitation of our labor—for instance, that we are instinctively emotional and innately giving, whether to our lovers, our children, or our co-workers.

(Convenient, isn't it, that the very group of humans forced by their material conditions to smile and meet the emotional needs of others for centuries are so "naturally" adept at doing so?)

Marxist feminists have done a lot of important work elucidating the extent to which romantic and family relationships are labor relations. Even as stay-at-home wives or mothers, women contribute a great deal to the economy. By caring for family members who perform wage labor, they sustain and help reproduce the work force; giving birth to and raising children to be productive members of society increases gross domestic product in direct, measurable ways.

We are paid for none of it. The re-creation of the world reproduces a social good that people of all genders hold in common. Yet very few public conversations about women and family acknowledge that these activities do anything more than gratify a personal impulse. The fact that childbearing and child rearing are not paid or subsidized reinforces the idea that these activities are not valuable labors: they are love.

We may be seeing the first steps toward policy changes that could help set straight this centuries-old con with the new paid family leave laws in California and New York. It is critical that any such laws offer paid leave to parents and caregivers of all genders; otherwise, while they may alleviate the pressures on individual women, they may reinforce the prejudice that says that care work is women's work. We still have a long way to go.

The question of whether romantic love can be unmoored from its relationship to the violences of patriarchy and capitalism, or whether it should be discarded altogether, has fostered various responses from feminist thinkers. bell hooks, seeking to salvage and elevate love as a radical and healing practice, argues for a specific definition of love as a mutual, life-affirming choice and practice— a verb as well as a noun—that cannot coexist with abuse. Others, like Silvia Federici, see the concept of love as something necessarily, violently doomed.

I owe a huge debt to the work of Marxist feminists like Silvia Federici, Selma James, and Mariarosa dalla Costa, or Nancy Holmstrom and Nancy Fraser, who have elucidated the extent to which romantic and sexual relationships are labor relationships, and the ideology surrounding female nature and the role of women in the nuclear family have served to justify our exploitation. Our society calls the work of mothers priceless while treating it as worthless. Indeed, all the crowing about priceless love serves as a way of romanticizing exploitation. If money can't buy you love, love won't get you paid.

But at the end of the day, I find myself more persuaded by the vision of the philosopher and activist bell hooks. As you mentioned, she emphasizes that love is a verb, as well as a noun—an active form of care that we can extend to ourselves and others, in a world riven by abuse and violence. I believe that love, when we approach it as such a purposive activity, can reshape our realities.

Angela Y. Davis too has written very lucidly on how

love can be used to forge new counter-public spheres—
say, antiracist family units. Davis specifically describes how
white middle-class feminists, because they had experienced
the home as a site of oppression, tended to downplay its creative possibilities; she proposes that African American wom-
en, who constantly encountered violence and racism in the
outside world of work, saw the family as a liberating space to
create other possibilities.

It follows directly from recognizing love as a form of
labor implicated in social reproduction that it can be creative: we do not have to reproduce the world as it is now.
For me, the key questions are not about what love is but
about what love does. Or perhaps more precisely, what we
can do with it. What we do does not have to be reproducing white-supremacist, heterosexist, capitalist patriarchy. It
really doesn't.

*The cultural theorist Dominic Pettman has written: "It is worth
speculating whether love is the only discourse still available to us
that is capable of salvaging singularity in a late capitalist epoch, or
whether it is rather a case that 'love' has become (or perhaps always was) a decoy that lures us into a libidinal economy no less indifferent to individual suffering than the macroeconomy overseen
by the IMF and the World Bank." How would you respond to this?*

"Salvaging singularity"! I like that. Love is an emotion you
feel for someone you wouldn't trade up if you could. It seems
worth stressing that the singularity of love also involves a
form of collectivity—even if it's just a primitive communism

of two. We owe it to ourselves, and to one another, to honor that love and not let it be entirely enclosed or co-opted.

So I like what Pettman says here. We should be wary of how the language of love can discipline us to consume and work. Yet I do have reservations about the ways that some anti-capitalist thinkers like Alain Badiou, Jean Baudrillard, and Slavoj Zizek, have tried to treat love and erotic experience as the "other" of capitalism or its outside—a last refuge of authenticity in a corrupt world. I think there's often a kind of crypto-misogyny at work in that kind of romanticism.

There is such a long tradition in European philosophy that idealizes women—or, more precisely, the concept of "woman"—by defining us in opposition to the male world. This kind of rhetoric purports to elevate "us." Yet it dehumanizes us in the process. We become the shadow of what exists. I am thinking, for instance, of how Nietzsche uses the concept of "eternal feminine," inherited from earlier German Romantics, and how Jacques Derrida and other poststructuralists pick up on his famous proposition, "What if truth is a woman—what then?" And Sigmund Freud, and the psychoanalytic tradition that defines women in terms of "lack." Lack, that is, of a phallus.

The great irony is that, by romanticizing the feminine and the erotic, avowed anti-capitalists like Baudrillard, Bourdieu, and Zizek end up perpetuating one of the founding lies of modern capitalism. This may be its most important myth: that the work that women do in bearing and raising children is not work. It is simply part of nature.

And nature is what you can take for free, without having to feel bad about it.

Left thinkers who view the existing world order as corrupt, and fail to see that pregnancy, labor, and child rearing are labor, miss the key fact that social reproduction can be creative. They see the work of care and mothering as simply passive—part of biology or a self-renewing "standing reserve" that the natural world is. As a result, they fail to see that care can transform social conditions. This is why they remain stuck in the negative modality of critique: because they have no account of how we come into the world and grow, they can only imagine change coming from the outside, as an apocalypse. It's also why, however petulantly they insist otherwise, they hate women.

Disconnecting the idea of romantic love from the violences of capitalism is particularly challenging in a culture that eroticizes and romanticizes labor. We are supposed to love what we do and find our passions in work. This is the message upheld by female power players like Sheryl Sandberg and certainly seems central to the sort of feminism attributed to Hillary Clinton—whose marriage and "love life" have also been a site of intense focus. The language of love being applied to work is not an age-old phenomenon, of course, but it certainly seems to further entangle, rather than disentangle, love with oppressive systems. What are your thoughts on this and the relevance of this love-your-work phenomenon and the figures embodying it?

Hillary is an interesting case: She inspires such intense feelings in those who love and hate her. We can certainly agree that right-wing misogynists have vilified her for her entire career because she is female. But among liberals too feelings about Hillary often seem to be inspired by her identity rather than her political record.

For me, Hillary epitomizes a kind of representative feminism. Many of the policies that she has supported throughout her career have been terrible for women. As First Lady, she supported welfare reform that impoverished mothers and children, a crime omnibus bill that fueled the "New Jim Crow" of mass incarceration, corporate education reforms that vilified teachers' unions, [in] a predominantly female profession. As a New York senator and secretary of state, she has consistently promoted hawkish foreign policies that have led to the deaths of women and children abroad.

The George W. Bush administration was most shameless in mobilizing a combination of feminism and Islamophobia to legitimate the war on terror—I am thinking of Laura Bush and Condoleezza Rice, talking publicly about the need to "free" women in Afghanistan and Iraq. But Clinton has continued to use women and children rhetorically, to justify war. Still, for many women, because she is a woman, she inspires feelings of identification and love. From the left and the right, her lovers and haters do seem to engage in the same kind of tautological thinking that we talked about earlier. When it's right you'll know. Or when something's not right, it's wrong.

As for the rest of us, I definitely think we could lean out and take a long critical look at the entire ideology surrounding "do what you love." The mantra that sex sells has been around for long enough that most people know how to approach it skeptically. However, in the past few years, as work and play have become less and less distinguishable, we have seen an eroticization of labor as well as leisure.

I believe that this language conflating passion and profession is becoming an increasingly shameless pretext to exploit precarious workers. It makes us feel that if we do not want to work all the time for not enough pay we have personally failed. You should not have to talk about your "passion for food and beverage service" to get a job as a barista, nor your "passion for retail" to get a job folding sweaters. We should not feel so bound to love our work that we do not have time or resources for love—or life—itself.

FOURTEEN

THE DIRECTOR'S EYE

Movies can point out violence. But how effective can they can be?

The filmmaker and director Oliver Stone needs little introduction. Recipient of multiple academy awards, he has focused his attention directly on the conduct of war and its enduring legacies. Our exchange with him, which launched the ongoing "Histories of Violence" series in the *Los Angeles Review of Books*, returns to a number of Stone's acclaimed movies. In doing so, Stone questions the importance of culture in developing a public conversation on violence while appreciating some of the limits of the genre when trying to steer history in a more democracy-conscious direction. The director himself is cautiously pessimistic about the role cinema can play in terms of mobilizing effective political responses to violence and atrocity.

Brad Evans interviews Oliver Stone

January 23, 2017

Oliver Stone is a film and documentary director. His many acclaimed productions recently include *The Putin Interviews* and *Snowden*.

Brad Evans: Each of your films deals in different ways with the relationships between power, war, and oppression. What role do you think filmmakers have when confronting the problems of violence and injustice in the world today?

Oliver Stone: *Platoon* was made almost twenty years after that war, [Vietnam] and it was a small slice of an infantry unit in a war that was misunderstood by most Americans. It was truly an ugly slice, and people recognized that. Do you realize how much information actually got out about that war when it was in progress? Very little! We still have the same issues. As Chris Hedges points out, we still have the same issues; so few reporters really see the war. They get "embedded" by the U.S. military, and they spend their time getting "briefed" from the U.S. point of view, rarely see real action, and they miss the big picture.

I didn't see one press person in the field my entire time in combat units in Vietnam, which stretched over approximately thirteen of my fifteen months. They would go out to the elite units such as the marines, as they're always looking for publicity, or the First Cavalry Division, a novel concept at the time, but the grunt units are not glamorous. The same is true essentially of filmmakers, because they also get seduced by a fabricated reality put to them by the Pentagon.

The current Syrian conflict is the latest example of

this behavior. American TV is terribly good at removing the ugliest side of war. You get a much more direct picture on France 24 or Russian Television (RT). We in the United States cut out the body bags or coffins coming back from Iraq and Afghanistan because it's bad publicity for the war effort. As a result, Americans are sanitized to the concept of death in a Disney War. And that's why I believe we have the ability to have wars that continue for fifteen years without coming face to face with them. This is where film has a role—but a small one. After all, *Platoon* can come out twenty years afterwards; so can *Born on the Fourth of July* and *Heaven and Earth*, the three films I made. But few Americans to this day still realize that 3.8 million Vietnamese, according to McNamara, were killed. That's more than half of Jews killed in World War II, yet every schoolkid in America knows that!

I'd like to ask you about your personal relationship with and experience of violence. In particular, how your firsthand encounters with war and injustice shaped and continues to inform your own director's eye.

Occasionally, I did see and engage with the enemy. I spent quite a bit of time in the bush, and I saw a lot of fuck-ups. A lot of "friendly fire," that is a lot of getting killed by your own men, often in close combat when you don't know who is killing whom or where the explosions are coming from.

We tend in the U.S. military to overreact to incoming fire. We send out a ton of artillery and sometimes planes with bombs for what often is a simple ambush that can be handled without overreaction. Sort of like George Bush in 2001 who thinks the attack on the World Trade Center is the start of World War III and calls for a war on the world. Us against them. War on terror, et cetera. So we go into this overreaction. It's in our makeup.

I'd argue that it goes back to our childhood. Those who grew up after the war in the shadow of the bomb were born into a paranoid society that wasn't necessarily nurturing. We're set up in schools by an Anglo-Saxon mentality for a fierce competition, wherein to succeed you must assert yourself and win. Which often means the other person has to lose and lose badly. Otherwise you're weak. The films of John Wayne or, for that matter, so-called thoughtful films like *Shane* and *High Noon* show that even a good man has to carry a gun and be able to protect the weak—and in the end, of course, he has to use that gun. You can't have a gun in an American movie and see it not used.

I don't think our movies, with few exceptions, have veered from that equation. I've made several antiwar movies, but look at our country now. It's even more militaristic than before. When the kids saw *Platoon* they joined up; they didn't go and see *Born* so much because their hero, Tom Cruise (from *Top Gun*), was castrated halfway through the film. Suffering a paralyzed life is much harder for the young people to understand. I think young people want to see excitement, and most of them don't care about the moral consequences. It's in our national DNA.

From Salvador *to* Platoon *and* Born on the Fourth of July *there is a clear dimension to your work that addresses head-on the intimate nature of violence and the ongoing trauma of all too human suffering. What has been the most difficult scene you have filmed in this regard?*

In *Born on the Fourth of July*, we concentrated on a moment in which Tom Cruise is shot near-fatally in the lung area. He'd already been wounded in the heel and was continuing to fire on his knees, partly out of a sense of guilt from an earlier encounter when he believed he'd killed his own man in a combat situation. In this case, as he stays up, firing without purpose, we built the music and the montage to that one bullet that cracks into his spine and severs his spinal cord. Basically it's one bullet that does this—just one bullet that changes your life.

There is also a very powerful scene in *Heaven and Earth* where Tommy Lee Jones, a war veteran failing to make a living by selling arms back in the United States, has married a Vietnamese woman who has experienced every form of warfare up to this point. Now back in San Diego, frustrated with his life, he almost kills her. He points his shotgun at her head and all her past life passes before her. We have the faces and the shotgun, the shells, the ammunition box and its descriptions all passing before us with the music. In the end, he pauses long enough not to kill her. He puts the shotgun away and momentarily we see them reconcile with a loving scene where she forgives him ("different skin, same suffering"). But in the end he kills himself, as many veterans are doing. So we really dig into the power of violence and what one bullet can do. We show clearly that this happens in U.S. domestic life; that you don't have to go to Vietnam to see the power of the bullet. In fact, kids are being cut down left and right in our cities. We really are in a war situation, but we are not facing up to it. Movies can point out this violence. But how effective they can be, I have my doubts.

The abuse of power as we all know comes in many different forms. Turning to your latest film release Snowden, *what was it about this story line in particular that compelled you? And how do you see it in relation to your broader critique of the role of the United States?*

I think the 2013 revelations were not very clear to many people. It was so technical. But it doesn't really register, and we tried with the movie to get really into what they were doing by showing the NSA, the dialogue, the maps, the way they think, to try and show some of that world. The only way we could find out about it was to talk to Snowden. And he was the guy who in nine different visits gave us some remarkable insight into these new systems with tremendous power—and why surveillance isn't about terrorism, which can be dealt with through selected targeting, but really about a desire to dominate the world with social and economic control in all countries.

This is not just about Internet surveillance. It is about drone warfare and cyber warfare. This is about global satellite systems and the most intimate forms of knowledge from our personal details to the operations of all leading multinational corporations. And, of course, interfering in nation-states, including conducting digitalized coup d'états against countries whose politics we'd like to change. It's no longer necessary to club the other guy to death. When you can control the media and the minds of the populace, you can control the country's spirit and break it. This truly is Orwell's *1984*.

One of the dangers of dealing with the legacies of war is the tendency to beautify and make amenable for public consumption the suffering. How does the industry play into these demands to turn violence into mere spectacle?

Most of American war movies are propaganda; soldiers die in small numbers. But, of course, we dote on it. Most recently Michael Bay made a spectacular-looking movie called *13 Hours about Libya*. The Americans are shown killing hundreds of Libyans before you see a handful of them taken down. They get blown up so spectacularly and rolled over in cars; you'd think dozens are killed! But in the end, we see four, maybe five coffins, and their deaths are so scripted as to give you a sense of justification coming from how many Libyans they've killed—aka a heroic last stand á la Custer. The same is common in movies like *Lone Survivor*, which again offers a most ridiculous representation. Hundreds of Taliban were killed in an event in which probably none were killed or at most a few. And most or all of the American soldiers died dirty, without even firing a shot. It's really, in the end, much more about luck, poor pre-planning, and politics than combat skills.

I saw it again in *Black Hawk Down*, which was an Oscar-nominated best picture, released on the eve of our second Iraq War. Imagine the impact of that on our culture. Think about the probability that George Bush must have seen this picture—like Nixon saw *Patton*. And think about the "nobleness" of our mission to Somalia. In the movie they kill so many black people, as we did with the Libyans, and our soldiers are glorified. Every one of them who dies in this fucked-up mission. There's not one guy who's shitting in his pants when he goes to meet his maker. In fact, they're dying in a military fashion, which is going down in a helicopter and obeying perfectly the protocol. That's what the Pentagon does. "You want to get our state-of-the-art Black Hawk choppers and use them, that's fine, we'd just like to view the script." And they tell you how a man should die when his helicopter is going down in flames. It's all bullshit! It doesn't happen that way. And that's what goes on. This distortion in American cinema has been gigantic. I understand there is always propaganda in times of war, and we sentimentalize one side over the other, but I've never seen it this bad in terms of directors using highly technical skills to render so realistic something so unrealistic as their interpretations of the war. I find that disgusting. As good as the film was, its message is a detriment to humanity. On top of it, America's failures in Somalia and wherever we intervene are glossed over as simple technical glitches or failures of communications.

Americans have never really been attacked in a war.

We've never experienced the bombings and deaths the Europeans, Russians, and Asians have felt. And we never have this worship of the military like we now have. On football games, baseball games, I see it everywhere on commercials on TV, this recruiting of poor people to join the military. They make it look so good to join the military, and they don't ever question the purpose of the war or the morality of that war. We can just go to another country and invade, kill local people, and it's no sweat off our sense of guilt. None at all! What wrong with us? I mean Vietnam? We should have had a major reexamination of our country. Never happened! What kind of leadership do we have or lack of in this country?

So what can movies do? Nothing. *Salvador* was a powerful movie, but, my god, it didn't mean one iota, it didn't turn one eyeball. We were doing horrible things in Central America, supporting the Contras and the death squads. So here we are in a situation where we have no sense of reality. And you want to talk about violence? I mean how much violence has the U.S. visited on the rest of the world? It's just gigantic and disproportionate to the guilt we feel.

The director Michael Haneke once argued that the perfect scene in regards to violence is the one that forces the viewer to turn away. What would be your understanding or idea of the perfect scene?

"It forces a viewer to turn away," I don't know about that. The point of violence is to engage the audience and show the power of it and what it means. It need not be delicate, so as not to offend the viewer. Eisenstein certainly didn't look away. He showed the shock at the Potemkin Steps. The worst thing to do is to lie about it and make it look seductive. Life is much more complicated than good guy/bad guy. Often it's somebody in your own family who is acting violently or is a bully. All these issues are complex, but we should do violence as accurately as possible.

12 Years a Slave certainly drove home the point about violence. How many whippings were there in the movie? Do you really need that many to sell the point? I got it, and for me it was too much. I actually turned away from the screen bored, so maybe that's what Haneke meant. You need to be pushed. You knew from a few minutes into the film that slavery was this brutal thing; whereas when Tarantino did it in his slave picture it was way over the top and disgusted me in the wrong way. Remember at the end, the last half hour is just about getting even. It meant nothing to me because these were pointless killings done gratuitously, as when you beat an opponent but then you keep beating him to show how powerful you are. So violence is a relative scale, and as a filmmaker you have to decide when it's doing its job. But truly I'm not sure movies make a difference. Because there have been so many great movies with violence, done so effectively for over one hundred years now, yet it hasn't seemed to deter people from acting violently and stupidly.

Moving forward, there has been a marked increased in recent times with critical thinkers' engagement with cinema as a serious medium for social and political critique. How might we resource cinema better in order to develop a more effective resistance to the present?

It's so hard. You can make a small independent film, but few are going to see it. It has to be distributed, marketed; before you get a movie into any viable format to get people to see it, you've spent a lot of money. You know in some ways one of the most revolutionary movies was actually *Avatar*, which cost and made the most amount of money. It really was a statement about the American empire. But the director, scared of losing his American audience, kept denying it. I suppose you have to be very subtle about this and make sure the American audience does not feel threatened or guilty. But the imperialists on that planet are so clear, and every character is American. That one beats me. It seems that every congressman would've seen it and gotten the message. But none of them did, and here we are rooting for more wars in the Middle East than ever before. When do we wake up?

It's so difficult now because movies in theaters are dying. Mostly young people would rather see it on a device at home. The ideal is to marry the two but that's not happening right now. And movies have been superseded by television, which is a lot easier to access.

On the other hand I miss movies. I think there is a certain form to it that is beautiful, elegiac. I think if you can tell a story in two hours, it's much better to do so than in eight to ten hours like a TV series. There is a purity to movies that will disappear. I hope we never lose them, but it doesn't look good right now. In fact, so many movies from 1930s through the 1980s and the 1990s are lost to our culture because they're not available from the cloud. Only people with libraries have evidence that there's a tremendous culture, a tremendous amount of work done in those fifty years. Netflix, for example, would rather make an original series (and make more money) than to store old films. This is as bad, in its way, as the sack of Baghdad under Donald Rumsfeld. "Shit happens," he said. That's the American way.

So, in the meantime, it seems these kinds of pro-American, pro-System movies like *Zero Dark Thirty*, *Black Hawk Down*, and *American Sniper* will get made. It's the guys who attack the system who have a hard time getting the resources to make their films; it seems they'll be marginalized and even erased if the empire wins out.

FIFTEEN

CONFRONTING THE INTOLERABLE

Creating means standing up, rebelling, resisting—it means striking back.

What actually makes an image intolerable? Should art respond to violence by reproducing explicit images of suffering? How might we mobilize violent aesthetics to create new openings in political discussion? Recalling his personal journey as an artist growing up in postwar Vienna, Gottfried Helnwein insists upon the need for art to confront the intolerable so that we might reimage the world anew. Violence should be intolerable. And it should make us recoil. But the worst we can do, Helnwein insists, is to surrender to violence by domesticating its appearance and not addressing its visual realities head-on. Issues regarding violence against children, in particular, are engaged here, as doing so allows for mediations on innocence, humanity, and the sacred.

Brad Evans interviews Gottfried Helnwein

January 23, 2017

Gottfried Helnwein is an Austrian-born visual artist, photographer, sculptor, filmmaker, and director currently based in southern Ireland.

Brad Evans: What is it about violence that continues to capture your attention as an artist?

Gottfried Helnwein: For me, art is the most direct and efficient way to approach the difficult questions and complex realities of existence. The reason for my decision to become an artist was therefore not primarily about aesthetics, it was about confronting the elementary questions I struggled with. This began when learning about the Holocaust.

I was born in Vienna right after World War II, and I vividly remember how dark and depressed this place was. I can't remember ever hearing someone sing or laugh. I was caught in a world that stood still, without sounds, without colors, without movement—I had the feeling the grown-ups around me tried to be overlooked—not to be perceived. The only thing they seemed to fear was to be seen, to be discovered. A city played dead. From the very beginning I knew something was wrong, but I didn't know what, because nobody talked, nobody answered my questions.

There was complete silence. It was as if history simply didn't exist. What I didn't know at that time was that my parent's generation had just lost the second of two world wars and were responsible for the most devastating genocide in modern history.

Then came the war crime tribunals. Reading the newspapers I became suddenly aware of the concentration camps, the torture, the brutality, and the numbers of people killed.

Shock took hold of me. How can life go on after that? What also disturbed me was how many of the war criminals in Austria seemed to be acquitted of their crimes.

By learning about the violence, I effectively removed myself from that society. I didn't want to be part of that system. I didn't want anything to do with its traditions, its beliefs, or its ideals. I think many of my generation around the Western world shared this feeling. And so, by the 1960s, you have a generation of disenchanted, angry youths ready to revolt and fight against everything the previous generation stood for. My personal journey was to research as much as I could about the history of cruelty, violence, and the human obsession to inflict pain onto other human beings.

Once you're exposed to such things, they never leave you, especially as I became more and more aware of the violence done to children. That's when I decided to become an artist.

I realized art would allow me to communicate something that society didn't want to talk about. To show people something of the horror that perhaps couldn't be put into words. I guess I was searching for a different concept of justice in art. So I went to study at the Academy of Fine Arts in Austria, which to my surprise accepted me immediately on the basis of a single painting I did of one child killing another child.

I started to paint without any specific expectations. I was not even sure if anybody would bother to look at my paintings, but I didn't really care, I just needed to get my images on paper. To my surprise, I learned very quickly that my work provoked strong emotional responses in people. No one was ever indifferent. Some people got angry, others laughed hysterically or had tears in their eyes. I was amazed by these reactions, and I thought: "Wow, did my little watercolor just do this to a grown-up person?" It was at that moment that I realized the potential power of an image.

I don't know how it works or why, but again and again I experienced that instant metaphysical connection, I saw that my pictures could touch people and reach much deeper into their hearts and minds, or the subconscious if you will, than words ever could. It's a very intimate process, a dialogue, without the need for words.

It's exactly what Marcel Duchamp said: "The work of art is always based on the two poles of the onlooker and the maker, and the spark that comes from the bipolar action gives birth to something—like electricity."

I am fascinated by this idea concerning the metaphysical nature of art. Can you elaborate more on what you mean by this and how it links to the question of ethics?

In 2000, when I moved to downtown Los Angeles, I suddenly had doubts. I wasn't sure if painting was a complete anachronistic, outdated activity. I looked around and thought: who would bother to look at a simple old-fashioned painting on canvas in our digital age, where everybody is flooded with overwhelming special effects and virtual realities of a multitude of media and an omnipresent entertainment industry?

Soon after that I had my first museum solo show in San Francisco; after the curators overcame their doubts, whether my work was too controversial to be shown, I experienced the most emotional response to my work to date. When I visited the exhibition, people would come up to me, hug me, and thank me. Again, many of them with tears in their eyes. An elderly lady said to me: "You probably don't even know how important it is, that you are showing your work here and right now."

It shows that people need relevant art, and in those moments I feel that what I am doing is worthwhile. To have such a reaction means you have arrived. You're part of something that is much deeper than the work itself. It still amazes me how strangers approach me and completely open up to me, telling me the most intimate things, which perhaps they have never before told anybody else. And all that because they have seen one of my paintings. As I said, I don't know how that works, I can't explain it. It's not rational. But it shows that art can have a meaning beyond the aesthetic.

A girl who had written a dissertation about my work told me later that when, at the age of fourteen, she saw my work for the first time she reacted in total shock and trembled and cried, but then she realized that it was the painful memories of her childhood that had begun to surface, which had been bottled up for years. She had been abused as a child, and she said that my pictures helped her to confront and work her way through these traumatic experiences.

So in this case, the paintings had a therapeutic effect that helped her overcome her nightmares. And that's what I understand to be the metaphysical or the spiritual. It is precisely that which you cannot explain but is no less real. Or as David Bowie put it: "Religion is for people who fear hell. Spirituality is for people who have been there."

The centrality of the wounded child in your work is notably striking and provocative. I do, however, think there is something more at work here than mere shock art, which I feel simply provokes a reaction without any meaning or depth. How does the wounded child resonate for you in terms of its political and philosophical significance?

History shows us time and time again how the corrupt old world preys upon the defenseless, the children. In our loud and frantic adult world where children are usually marginalized or kitschified, I guess I wanted to force people to confront purity or innocence and the vulnerability that you can see in the face of a child and the pain of innocence betrayed.

With my work I wanted to take their side. I wanted to see the world through their eyes. When I made the image of the child the center of my work, what I was actually referring to is the existence of a human being. Everybody is a child at some point in their life. Not everybody reaches adulthood or gets old, but childhood is a phase nobody can avoid. It is this brief moment in time, when we are still much more connected to the boundless universe of fantasy, dreams, imagination, and visions than to the constricted material world. For a child, physical laws don't exist, and constant creation comes as naturally as breathing.

As Picasso once said, "Every child is an artist. The problem is how to remain an artist once he grows up."

Because, unfortunately it's the grown-ups that rule the world and make the laws, and all kids have to go through their demolition program called education. Once they come out on the other side, they are usually broken, and their magic is gone. And then they can be citizens, soldiers, clerks, psychiatrists, politicians, bankers, undercover agents, prostitutes, or other useful entities in this brave new world of consumerism.

"You know what the issue is with this world?" said Lewis Carroll. "Everyone wants some magical solution to their problem and everyone refuses to believe in magic." Dreaming and fantasizing are nowadays considered a chemical imbalance in the brain of the child. For reasons of national security there are no realms of imagination anymore in which to escape—children are held in the merciless headlight of the adults' level-headed, common-sense madhouse: a world of stock markets, war, rape, pollution, television-moronism, Prozac, prison camps, Miss Universe competitions, genetic engineering, child pornography, Ronald McDonalds, Kardashians, and torture.

In a child, the full potential of humane values and virtues, of innocence, trust, love, compassion, and creativity are intact. Children are sacred. But they are vulnerable, defenseless, and dependent on our fairness. And it seems that we tend to betray that trust.

Do you detect any differences in the ways audiences react to your work in different countries?

Originally I expected people to react differently, due to their cultural and ethnic background, but this is not the case. It seems that aesthetics can cut through the inherited social veneer and acquired reality. With visual art and music there are no language barriers, you directly hit the individual human being at his core. But the reactions of individuals differ. It seems to have more to do with their personal inner world than the country they are coming from.

I think that a work of art can be a screen for the subconscious. People seem to project their own mental images onto my paintings so that the artwork in fact becomes a co-creation. Depending on who is looking at the painting, it will always be something unique and different. For me, my work is an ongoing dialogue with my public, and I must say I have learned more from the spontaneous reaction and responses of the onlookers or "naïve observers," as Kandinsky called them, than from any art theory.

When I look at a work of art, I ask myself: Does it inspire me? Does it touch and move me? Do I learn something from it? Does it startle or amaze me—do I get excited, upset? And this is the test any artwork has to pass: can it create an emotional impact on a human being even when he has no education or any theoretical information about art? I've always had a problem with art that can only be understood by somebody with a degree in art history. I think the importance of theory in art is totally overrated. Real art is self-evident. Real art is intense, enchanting, exciting, and unsettling; it has a quality and magic that you cannot explain. Art is not logic, and if you want to experience it, your mind and rational thinking will be of little help. Art is something spiritual that you can only experience with your senses, your heart, your soul.

There are some stylistic influences from Caravaggio, Goya, and Francis Bacon in your work. I'd be interested in your thoughts on these influences. Why are these artists important in terms of the aesthetics of violence?

Actually I was lucky to have never been much influenced by anybody, because, as I said, from early on I rejected everything my parents' generation stood for, their traditions and their values. And I hated art history as it was taught in school. So it was a conscious decision to be a proudly ignorant street kid. The art I could relate to was comics and rock music, and when I decided to become an artist I approached painting like an autistic child. I didn't know much about techniques, and I didn't care about traditional methods and rules. It was fun to try things out and follow only my own curiosity.

It was much later as my resistance against traditional art was wearing off that I became interested in the work of artists of the past. I wanted to check it out and see if it would do anything to me. I was kind of neutral, without any preconceptions or expectations. I was just curious, but what I saw took my breath away, it turned my world upside down. I was shaken to my core when I encountered the works of Rembrandt, Caravaggio, Goya, and others. The aesthetic power was totally overwhelming. I didn't really understand or explain what exactly happened, but I was so deeply touched and moved, it was like a religious experience.

It's a strange feeling when you realize that, a long time ago, there was somebody who created something that touches you so deeply and that is so close to what I try to express in my own work.

Some forty years after Pasolini's Salò, *which remains one of the most devastating cinematic treatments of violence, you collaborated with Hans Kresnik to create a new version of* 120 Days of Sodom *for the Volksbühne in Berlin. What compelled you to return to this script?*

Pasolini is one of the great visionaries of the twentieth century. He's up there along with Orwell and Huxley. Pasolini's vision of a new type of totalitarianism whereby hyper-materialism destroys our culture can be seen now as brilliant foresight into what has happened to the world generally in the Internet age. When he said: "I consider consumerism a worse fascism than that the classical one," he referred to the dystopia of a super-capitalistic world where consumerism is the sole purpose of human existence.

Pasolini is one of the most radical but at the same time

one of the most poetic of thinkers, who really understands the stakes. It was almost logical therefore that society would have to kill him. He was too close in confrontation with the truth.

Mindful of this, we wanted to bring our version of Pasolini's film *120 Days* to stage for the very first time. I wanted to put the emphasis on all the things he was predicting: the consumerism, the wars and violence carried out in its name. As you know, this was a film that had been banned and widely condemned due to its graphic nature. It seemed to me that now was the time to do it due to its relevance to what we are experiencing now.

After a very successful first season, we were suddenly told it would no longer be showing. No explanation was offered. Later we found out that somebody from the government had intervened and terminated the show. I understand why it was forbidden. It was an assault on the system.

To conclude, how do you think critical thinkers and writers might connect better with artists and creative producers in order to develop a better critique of violence that is more adequate to our times?

Throughout the entire history, the only forces capable of resisting tyranny and suppression are artists, thinkers, and writers. These are the makers of what we call culture, which means the combination of aesthetics and spirituality. Dictators know that; they have a very good sense for the only serious threat to their power: free creation and free communication.

Most societies are ruled by mediocre people that have

no vision and no imagination. Most rulers are scared of creation and creative people. Artists are funny people: all they want is to touch and move, challenge and surprise. But dictators hate surprises more than anything else.

Nothing scares authoritarian regimes more than art and free creation. Why would Hitler burn mountains of books and paintings and ban all arts? Why would Stalin—the master over life and death of almost three hundred million people, a man who commanded the biggest army and secret service that ever existed—be afraid of the poems written by Anna Akhmatova? Why would Mao be so obsessed with destroying China's entire cultural heritage? Why would FBI director J. Edgar Hoover, while denying the existence of organized crime in the United States, put so much effort into harassing and investigating every artist of any significance from Hemingway to John Lennon?

Rulers throughout history have always hated those who stood out from the masses—the geniuses, the poets, artists, witches, and saints; and usually they burned them or put them in dungeons, concentration camps, or mental institutions, thinking of what a nice and peaceful slave camp this planet could be without them.

On this planet, creating means to stand up, to rebel, to resist; it means striking back. While I am pessimistic about the conditions we face in the short run, in the longer run I remain optimistic. We need to remember empires can fall overnight. What may seem to be invincible now evaporates tomorrow without a trace. Power in this regard is defined by its moment in time, whereas the creation is timeless.

SIXTEEN

VIOLENCE IS OUR PRESENT CONDITION

Can art reveal forms of violence that are hidden or invisible?

The visual artist Alfredo Jaar has transformed art in terms of how we recognize ourselves as witnesses to suffering. For Jaar, the most sublime work of art manages to create a perfect balance where those engaged with it experience information, humanity, and complexity in such ways that makes them want to search and explore beyond the work of art. This requires taking seriously manifestations of violence as they appear in everyday broadcasting, as well as those more subtle forms that may be hidden in plain sight. Jaar's message is clear: while violence is no doubt devastating and endemic to modern societies, art still has the capacity to move people and, in the process, inspire a new form of politics.

Brad Evans interviews Alfredo Jaar

February 16, 2017

Alfredo Jaar is a Chilean-born visual artist, architect, writer, curator, and filmmaker currently based in New York.

Brad Evans: Your work directly deals with power, war, and violence. As an artist, why did you feel it was important to address such issues in your work?

Alfredo Jaar: I have never studied art. I am an architect. For an architect context is everything. As you can see if you look around my studio, we do not produce anything here. I am not a studio artist. I am a project artist. And I am interested in responding to the conditions of the world that surrounds and immerses us—especially the world of images. I confront this world, trying to understand the context and to act within that context. My modus operandi has always been the same: before acting in the world, I need to understand the world.

I have been faced with contexts where violence has been the catalyst for a series of political events and tragedies, which have forced my work in a particular direction. I must face and deal with the obligation to confront that violence. And in that process of engagement, I have tried to design the complex representations of that violence and give justice to the deep intricacies of the subject. Because I am aware that my work does not have an answer to this problem, I find myself creating what I call exercises in representation. And because I have confronted quite a few situations of violence, one exercise has taken me to another exercise, and today I think that I have learned a few things along the way. At least I hope that my most recent works deal with the problem of violence in a more considered and sensitive way. And perhaps this can be seen in my recent practice; where the more recent representations have deeper complexity and resonance, I think they communicate better my intentions.

Was there a particular moment in your life in which you felt or realized this was the direction you wanted your work to take?

It is not that I specialize in violence. I just think violence is our present condition. And it is not only physical violence that concerns me here, it is also psychological and political forms of violence. Some forms of violence suffer from total invisibility. Let us consider the case of killing drones, for example. I have become almost obsessed with them. We are killing thousands of people, most of them innocent, and they are dying in complete invisibility. Sadly, nobody is demanding that we stop this carnage. The casualties are always people without names. Will we ever know their names?

That violence might be invisible to us, but it exists out-there, and we will see the consequences of it sooner or later. I was thinking about this on my way to the studio this morning, when they announced they were searching for the Chelsea bomber who is from Afghanistan. New Yorkers are shocked by this event at this moment. They are probably thinking: *"How barbaric this guy who comes here and tries to blow us up!"* How many thousands have we killed exactly in Afghanistan with our unmanned drone technology? It is a very well-known fact that we have killed hundreds of women and children. So why are we surprised that this Afghan man is trying to bomb us?

Everything is connected. The only difference between these different acts of violence is that the violence we carry out remains mostly hidden. So how do we deal with this? How do I deal with this as an artist?

Let us remember that the artist is free and that the world of art is probably the last remaining space of freedom. I would never demand that any artist must deal with these issues, especially the invisible forms of violence that I have mentioned. That is not my intention. I personally feel the obligation, the need and the responsibility to respond to that because I think it has consequences, and it says a lot about how we think about the world and our position within it, especially our relationship to other people. I am compelled to deal with the forms of violence our system exercises against less powerful peoples. It is something I have felt in a very spontaneous and natural way to confront because it was something I could not ignore. Our present condition, which as I said is violence, demands it.

I would like to now turn specifically to your piece The Eyes of Gutete Emerita. *A number of critical theorists and philosophers have been particularly taken by this piece. Especially the way in which it disrupts notions of voyeurism and what it means to witness the brutalities of violence. What do you strive for in your work when dealing with the problematic issue of witnessing violence as a spectacle?*

I have always said that I am a frustrated journalist. I feel that in a way my work tries to combine what I would hope journalism should accomplish with what I think art does best. That is why my objective has always been to inform and to touch people emotionally through visual media. Art at its best illuminates us, and it should also move us. I aspire to do all these things at the same time, but I have struggled to find the perfect balance. Many times I am accused of being too didactic, or it is said that my work appears purely informative because of the need I feel to include a certain amount of information, which I believe cannot be ignored, while sometimes I fall on the other extreme, in which the work becomes too aesthetic and beautiful in its form. Perhaps in that context the information is lost. I am always struggling with this balance between information and spectacle. Working in that space between ethics and aesthetics.

For me the most sublime work of art manages this perfect balance where the spectator is illuminated by the information and at the same time is moved by the beauty and also attracted by the complexity of the work in a way that makes the viewer want to go deeper and triggers within them the need to go and search further beyond the work of art. So that for me is the definition of a perfect work of art. Sadly, I do not think I have ever reached that perfection, though it is certainly the objective that I aspire to and approximate.

What does this mean when thinking about intolerable images? Should the artist force us to confront the intolerable in order to reflect more intently?

I think this is the conundrum we face. We must represent the intolerable in such a way that it can be visible. That is really the big question of our times. And I do not have an answer to that question. Again that is why I like the concept of exercises in representation. The entire Rwanda project, for example, was an exercise in dealing with the intolerable in one way or another. Now I feel that most of the works failed. But it is also true that working on that project for six years taught me something, so the later works were, I think, more successful in their attempt to navigate this intolerable situation.

I do not think there is any formula to this. Each tragedy or each intolerable image has its own specificity that we have to strive to understand and try to communicate to the audience in an ethically sensitive fashion. There is really no formula and no answer to this question. But we must still be compelled to continually ask it all the same.

Too often political and cultural theorists will take the so-called aesthetic turn to appropriate the arts for new modes of deconstruction and critique. How might we resource the arts better in terms of both a critique of violence and rethinking alternative political futures?

I think we are doomed because in the present moment we simply do not control the narrative. I think it is quite tragic and sad that the world of art and culture have such a bad representation in the popular world of media communication. It is absurd that intellectuals, who work with the means of representation, inventing every day different means of representing images of the world, do not control the narrative of even their own work. Most of the media is simply interested in the glamour of its spectacle, in the $100-million Picasso painting. And that is the issue we have to try to overcome. Artists do not have the image of a group of professionals that is seriously trying to deal with a major conundrum.

The major media networks, in terms of political or social commentary, by and large ignore artists. When they are interested in us it is only because we contribute to the society of the spectacle in one way or another, and so I dream of a new relationship between art and journalism. Some artists and thinkers and philosophers are deeply committed to these issues. Only then might we perhaps create a new information world where we contextualize our shared problems and read them properly. But I do not know if the present state of media information controlled by a few global conglomerates that are more interested in entertainment is ready for this kind of resistance. But you and I keep doing this because we are hoping that suddenly people will at least understand the potential for a real revolution in communication. And perhaps we would create a better society by understanding these issues and acting upon them together.

I am taken by the title of a previous interview you gave where you suggest the artist is a thinker. Does society need to take more seriously the idea of the artist as a public pedagogue whose visions are integral to how we might reimagine the world for the better?

This raises an important question, namely [about] education. We need to begin with education here. How we deal with images ethically is of profound importance. But we do need to rethink how we educate in this age where violence and its spectacle are defining of the moment. Our image of art needs to change as much as the need to challenge the spectacle shaping our society must change. Art is so much more than a $100-million Picasso.

There is also a need to rethink how we educate about art in both its historical and contemporary contexts. I am often invited to give graduate seminars, and I begin by telling the students to stop producing stuff. Our societies demand that we simply produce and produce things without seriously thinking about what it contributes. This is as true for art as it is for any other form of production. There is a need to be mindful that we do not reproduce the spectacle. It is to take seriously the ethics of art as a form of social output.

I think your project is tremendously important, though we all need to collectively question our impact on societies when the narrative is so dominated by a corporate conglomerate, which controls and mediates the image. I dream of an alliance between journalists, artists, and critical thinkers like [you] that will allow us to take the educative value of art and its broader impact much more seriously. I remain pessimistic but retain the slightest of hopes.

SEVENTEEN

SONGS IN THE KEY OF REVOLUTION

How can we take our understanding of revolutionary poetic interventions a stage further?

Can music inspire revolutionary change? What is the difference between music as propaganda and its more radically politicized compositions? What can music reveal about power? Drawing upon his personal life and the political climate while growing up in the brutal landscapes of apartheid South Africa, composer and musician Neo Muyanga addresses the revolutionary potential of music, how its scores are revealing of many of the subtle and hidden transcripts of cultural resistance, and why music stands the test of time when thinking about political interventions. According to Muyanga, song is not simply key to understanding the joys of existence. It is key to revolutionary change.

Brad Evans interviews Neo Muyanga

March 27, 2017

Neo Muyanga is a South African composer, musician, and cultural activist born in Soweto.

Brad Evans: The historical links between politics, violence and music are well established. From early documented uses of musical accompaniments in the conduct of war, both to heighten the passions and signal the onslaught, to the psychological desire to utilize the power of sound (broadly understood) as a weapon of warfare, history is littered with examples of how the artistic can be appropriated for violent means. What remains neglected, however, is the way in which the lyrical has a more emancipatory dimension. Can you tell me more about your interest in this often forgotten history of revolutionary struggle?

Neo Muyanga: I can't pinpoint exactly when I became interested in revolutionary songs. This is largely because I was immersed in their presence long before I understood their significance. I grew up in Soweto during the last two decades of apartheid—a system of imposed racial segregation and the securing of white privilege that came to a legal end at the conclusion of the first democratic elections in South Africa in 1994. The songs I heard growing up were revolutionary chants and hymns that spoke directly against this system; they were, happily, also songs that spoke of the valor and the dignity of the downtrodden in my own community. I don't even remember how we learned them—the songs just seemed to accompany every aspect of our lives, be it going to school, playing sport, attending worship on a Sunday (if church was your thing), or when attending celebratory township gatherings or funerals over the weekends.

We used to sing the songs whenever we went out to protest against "the System" in the streets of Soweto, and they provided us with the stamina and the fervor needed. It didn't matter if one was a good singer or not, what counted was being one among a mass, chanting in unison. The songs are particularly easy to learn, which makes them very effective for spontaneous outbursts of political solidarity too.

How might we meaningfully differentiate here between forms of music that, produced in a certain way, have a clear and distinct relationship with regimes of power and those arrangements that put themselves on the side of protest?

I'd like to come at this by adding another question. What is it we actually do when we sing during a protest? Singing seems a distinctly counterintuitive expression of, say, anger or militancy, which are some of the key elements one expects it takes to animate a protest during a tense confrontation on some anonymous street corner of the globe. In her book *Anthem*, Shana Redmond tells us, "Beyond its many pleasures, music allows us to do and imagine things that may otherwise be unimaginable or seem impossible."

There are countless famous songs included in the global repertoire of resistance that, on the surface, often seem so simple and straightforward as to offer very little in the way of revolutionary threat.

Take, for instance, "*Senzeni na?*" (What have we done?) This is a song which has been frequently sung during protests at least since the beginning of formal apartheid in South Africa (1948). Or "We Shall Overcome," a so-called Negro spiritual sung by countless marchers during the American civil rights movement of the 1960s. Or more [recently], the song "Ezzay," written by Mohamed Mounir, asking "how come?," which was chanted widely and wildly in the megapolis of Cairo and elsewhere as Egyptians brought down the reign of Hosni Mubarak in 2011.

On the surface, all three of these songs are laments of one kind or another. They appear to operate on a level akin to what the perennial iconoclast Fela Kuti sought to describe the vectors inside his own music when he said during an interview, "Despite my sadness I create joyful rhythms . . . through happy music I tell you about the sadness of others."

Is there not a danger here that we see these songs as part of the comforting blanket of culture, which, as you say, allows for a little escape despite the horrors of the everyday?

During a presentation I recently delivered entitled "Revolting Mass: A Survey of South African Songs of Protest," I suggested pointedly that such songs could in fact be deployed—in the parlance of South African pseudo-technocrat-speak—to great effect against a marauding enemy by virtue of the songs' inherent ability to simultaneously suggest and access multiple registers and rationalities within those standing in opposing camps during a heated political stalemate.

Being a committed improvising musician, I chose to begin the presentation with this riff on the words associating the title: Revolting = disgusting = overturning = overthrowing mass = church liturgy = weight = the masses = the great, lumpen mob!

One of the political points I sought to make in presenting this barrage of jumbled words was the following: these songs of protest are not, in actual fact, music. That is to say, we certainly do not regard them in the way we would describe, say, a hymn or a pop song performed in its usual context. You won't hear these protest songs played on your favorite radio station in the same way—certainly not in South Africa—since no one listens to this material; everyone (potentially) does this material when the circumstances call for it to be enacted.

To illustrate this idea, I shared a brief clip from film director Rehad Desai's 2014 Emmy-winning documentary *Miners Shot Down*, which tracked the progress of a miner's strike near Johannesburg in 2012 that culminated, tragically, in the shooting of more than seventy protesters and the ultimate killing of thirty-four strikers.

There is a chilling moment during the documentary, about eighteen minutes in, when the police threaten to use force to confiscate the miner's traditional weapons (sticks, spears—their symbols of ethnic pride). That is when the striking miners who, in a show of respect, were kneeling down until that moment, begin to clang their wares and break out in song. While singing, they rise up to their haunches and begin moving forward, past the line of policemen.

Incredibly, the song they chose to sing, at this very tense moment during the negotiations, was a song about "testicles going hard." This was a move which may well have been meant as an insult to the very policemen they faced squarely, [after] which policemen promptly began to cock and aim their shotguns.

The miners managed to walk away, on this occasion, without any shots being fired. That tragedy was to occur just two days later. After watching the scene in the film just described, it is my contention that the reason why violence didn't occur on [the] occasion in Marikana was because the song the miners sang put up for them a kind of invisible screen, a protective shield that either confused or marginally diffused the situation just enough so negotiations could be carried forward another day. The revolutionary power of song in this moment was all too apparent.

Do you think there is something unique to the colonial context here, where the use of song is not only part of a broader fabric of day-to-day revolutionary struggle but also integral to the politics of memory and the proud assertion of identities across generations?

I tend to focus on the South African repertoire of the past four decades or so, as these are the songs of my own uprising; the songs with which I am most familiar. Songs like "*Senzeni na?*," "*Nkosi sikelel' iafrika,*" and others like them exemplify what Abdullah Ibrahim was referring to when he asserted, "The revolution in South Africa is the only revolution anywhere in the world that was done in four-part harmony."

In this instance, four-part vocal harmony relates to the kind of musically hybrid aesthetics uniquely espoused by South Africa's nineteenth- and twentieth-century modernists: the Marcus Garvey/Du Bois-reading, missionary-schooled Africanists and founders of South Africa's liberation movements, the ANC, and later the PAC and others. Many of these leaders were church folks: women and men for whom political manifestation had to do with exhibiting a dignity, discipline, a racial pride. Laments like "*Senzeni na*?," therefore, express what I would argue is a redoubtable and righteous indignation towards the rampant inhumanity operative in the kind of oppression they experienced due simply to the biological fact of their race. So, yes, there is undoubtedly a colonial context to these harmonies—or to paraphrase Stevie Wonder, they are songs in the key of revolution.

And in this regard, as your question intimates, we must take our understanding of these revolutionary poetic interventions a stage further. Songs such as "*Senzeni na*?" held in them not only a shared pathos among those who saw themselves as victims but also signaled that constituency's fervent aspirations towards a political delivery from the extant systems of racial oppression—colonialism and apartheid. To the extent that such simple and straightforward songs were able to serve so effectively as ammunition against an oppressor during those periods in history exposes not only the horrifically technocratic lengths to which articulators of those same oppressive systems had to go to impose the will of the state but also the everyday banalities of evil (as Hannah

Arendt and Frantz Fanon understood all too well) it took to keep such humiliating, unjust maltreatment operable on a grand social scale.

The songs you have highlighted so far relate to an often "brack-eted" conception of anticolonial struggle. Yet as authors such as David Theo Goldberg and Achille Mbembe, among others, show, the very idea of the "post-colony" is a fiction often deployed by those in positions of power. How might we connect all this history to the contemporary political moment?

Today protest music appears through the voices of the marginalized and oppressed in many countries around the world. Songs in revolt are now part of a common repertoire for those who confront highly combative political contexts, much exemplified in movements such as Fees Must Fall and Rhodes Must Fall both in South Africa and Britain, Black Lives Matter in the United States, the Zapatistas in Mexico, and Movimento dos Trabalhadores Rurais Sem Terra in Brazil. These groupings are attracting more and more attention from scores of young people of color and the global media, arguably, both in response to untenable levels of continuing systemic racism, intolerance, and neglect and the way they bring color to those who seek to suffocate existence.

In South Africa, for example, many well-rehearsed *revolting songs* are often recycled and remixed, posing an added irony: whereas chants like, "*siyaya epitoli*" (meaning: we are going, or rather *marching*, to Pretoria) were sung fervently in October 2015 by some of the youth marching on the government buildings to call for no fees increase, that particular *revolting song* was pelted like a rock at the glass house now run by those erstwhile radicals of the 1970s, 1980s and 1990s who sang the very same ditty to threaten apartheid, then ensconced in those selfsame hallowed halls of the union buildings. A kind of poignant switch had therefore been flipped, transposing a new band of revolutionaries at the door—in this case, the *kids*—out where the *parents* once revolted.

I will hazard a guess here and claim the poetic justice of the occasion will have struck a South African president much lauded as well as reviled for gleefully singing "Umushini Wam" at various high points during his rise up to high office. It was the same president who soon sanctioned a no-increase to all university fees for 2016, thus temporarily securing a reprieve. Yet it is also true that while revolting songs can shield, they can also cut like the sharp edge of truth against forgetting, against the arrogance and delusion of power. This political poignancy in South Africa today leaves a lingering confusion about which side of the generational pianoforte deserves the right to deploy these revolting songs on occasions such as the one mentioned above.

This raises a whole number of challenging questions. Are the "authentic" instrumentalists, for instance, those who were pointed to by Abdullah Ibrahim earlier? Namely, the ones who sang the songs against apartheid, or are the "real authentic" instrumentalists the ones who are now stuck without any defenses against a globalism-captured state, like the miners in Marikana and their children? If so, do we need to write new revolting songs then, to shield the new revolting marginals?

My sense is the power of revolutionary songs is witnessed in their ability to stand the test of time. Such songs, we should remember, were not written against particular oppressors alone but also against a pervasive and highly articulated system of racial, gender-based, and classist oppression. It is for this reason that the older songs are just as relevant (and as revolting) today as they have ever been. After all, systems of stratification by race, gender, and class remain at play. Perhaps the songs can, however, be restrung and tuned to agitate at a higher frequency, making those who enter the hallowed halls of power as the new captains remember what is at stake. And in doing so, what may change is the mode agitating assumes now, as it performs itself in a posture no longer revolutionary in inflection, as was the case at the turn of the twentieth century, but targeting new forms of oppression and domination in the key of something different.

EIGHTEEN

LITERARY VIOLENCE

The task of democracy is both exhaustive and inexhaustible.

Violence has been a favorite theme of literature throughout the ages. Literature itself, explains acclaimed British author Tom McCarthy, begins with a fascination with primal acts of violence and the annihilation of others. But what can literature offer to us today when confronting violence in the world? Can we still learn from the classics in our attempts to develop a meaningful critique of violence? And why does tragedy in particular still capture the literary imagination? Moving beyond the crude reductiveness of "fact" versus "fictional" narratives in respect to the importance of the literary canon, McCarthy offers a culturally rich survey of the history of literature, his continued fascination with Kafka, Patty Hearst, and the recurring question of death as it appears beyond the limits of scientific enquiry.

Brad Evans interviews Tom McCarthy

May 8, 2017

Tom McCarthy's books include *Satin Island*, *C*, and an essay collection, *Typewriters, Bombs, Jellyfish*, which is discussed below.

Brad Evans: I recently had the pleasure of reading your eclectic mix of published essays, Typewriters, Bombs, Jellyfish. *Fully in keeping with your broader literary corpus, what strikes from the outset is a distinct fascination with violence in both implicit and explicit forms in your work. Why does the problem of violence continue to capture your attention as an author?*

Tom McCarthy: It seems to me that it has always been at the core of the literary experience in some form or other. This goes all the way back to the Greeks, for whom space is usually grounded in primal acts of violence. The city or polis of Oedipus Rex, the urban and political order of Thebes, is built on the murder of Laius, who himself abducted and raped Chrysippus. The political order of Athens—the cornerstone of modern democracy—is built in the Oresteia on the murder of Clytemnestra, who herself murdered Agamemnon, whose own father butchered Thyestes's children. It goes back and back. Faulkner has this brilliant image in *Absalom, Absalom!*, a novel that unearths a family history of slavery and war and incest, where Quentin muses that an event is not a unique occurrence but more like a set of ripples on a pool that itself is connected by an umbilical water-cord to another pool in which a stone was dropped—but you don't see the stone dropping in the first pool, you only see the ripples in the second. It's less an event than an event-

field—an expansive zone whose patterns are both set by and bear witness to an ur-trauma.

Freud sees all mental and biological life like this: we're just jellyfish, replaying the original shock of photosynthesis as we propel ourselves deathwards. What's really interesting about this particular image is that Freud couches it within a larger consideration of those magic writing-pad toys that kids still play with—the ones where the upper, waxy-paper surface can be erased and written over again and again, but the lower, gelatinous one retains all the traces. This is his decisive model for consciousness: a writing machine scored with the wounds of time.

The collection of essays is littered with literary references, from Joyce to Pynchon to Kafka. What is it about these authors that collectively still resonate in terms of understanding both the timelessness of tragedy and the contingency of the modern condition?

I wouldn't say tragedy is timeless. It has its temporality—a complex one. On the one hand, it's backwards-facing, like Walter Benjamin's angel of history (who, where humans see "progress," instead discerns a trail of debris, wreckage upon wreckage piled up behind him); on the other hand, it moves forwards towards some inexorable conclusion. I would question the notion of an exclusively "modern" condition too. What interests me about the best takes on the modern is their primitivism. So Joyce sees in twentieth-century telecoms "loftly marconimasts from Clifden" beaming "open tireless secrets . . . to Nova Scotia's listing sisterwands," and "television kills telephony in brothers' broil"—in other words, he sees these technologies playing out ancient Egyptian incest stories and biblical tales of fratricide. Similarly, Pynchon finds something totally regressive in state-of-the-art rocketry: his V2 is a repository of all these Brothers Grimm fables and Holy Grail myths and so on. It's this overlay of times and temporalities that interests me.

Your writing style is widely acclaimed for its attention to intricate details. This collection is no exception as it attends to the various ways human are immersed in various organizing systems, from the ecological to the technological, which continue to do great violence upon humans' and nonhuman bodies. What is to be gained by insisting as an author upon such detailed ecological and technological framings?

These things you identify here—systems and framings—are everything. Subjects that traditionalists might think of as the "true content" of literature—such as truth or justice or feelings or subjectivity itself—are only possible within these systems and inseparable from them. To understand one we must understand the other—and this understanding must by necessity (since it's of structures and infrastructures) be structural. That's what I love about Kafka: he completely undoes humanist "psychology" by making psychic space indivisible from the whole architecture of communication and containment that forms—to adapt your own term—its ecosystem. Josef K.'s anguish and anxiety are spun into existence around the corridors and waiting rooms and courtyards, the files and backup files and general feedback loops of juridical bureaucracy. It's similar in Lynch's films: to get a grip on them you have to map their relays and the layout of their spaces—which room opens to which other cell or chamber, which phone (or intercom or CCTV or cryptic utterance) is connected (via which operator) to which sender or receiver. . . . Like Freddie says in *Inland Empire:* "There's a vast network, an ocean of possibilities."

I'd like to turn to your philosophical influences. Alongside the literary acknowledgments, the essays are also notably populated with the voices of Bataille, Deleuze and Guattari, and Derrida. I am particularly interested in the latter and the idea that we are already walking amongst the ruins of the future. What are your thoughts on this, especially when thinking about the violence of cityscapes?

Ballard says that we have annexed the future into the present. That's a kind of collapse, a ruination—materially, in Ballard's own novels; it translates into endless visions of ruined cityscapes. Every great city, at least when it writes itself, seems to anticipate its own destruction: so in *The Waste Land*, London becomes Jerusalem, Athens, Alexandria, Vienna, all burning with towers falling and so on. In Robbe-Grillet's *Topology of a Phantom City*, he doesn't even give the city a name: it's just "the city," already an archaeological ruin even before it's built, replaying in its theaters and frescoes various scenes that dance around the central episode of its own sacking. I like how when Gerhard Richter paints Paris, the deliberate blurs and smudges make it look like it's being nuked, like Marker's apocalyptic photo-montage in *La Jetée*. And then Richter's Paris painting is already (since it's depicted from the skies above the city) framed by the picture he made a few years earlier of bomber planes; visually, painting and bombing become one and the same thing. I'm also very struck by Eldridge Cleaver's call for revolutionaries to reimagine urban space as a war zone: streets criss-crossed by armored vehicles, the sound of tommy guns and snipers' rifles, barbed wire closing off whole sections of the city, "and everywhere the smell of cordite." It's political, of course—but it's aesthetic too.

I was particularly taken by the scene you depict concerning Patty Hearst, especially the final meditation on "America" as captured in a hotel room "watching the apocalypse on television." This description seems tragically apt for the contemporary moment—albeit with the added drama of new mobile technologies, which offer new ways to capture the gaze. Is this how you still recognize America in the contemporary moment?

Patty Hearst is a figure who fascinates me. I think there should be statues to her all over America; hers is one of the great American stories. Revolution, self-reinvention, celebrity, catastrophe, all played out in real time on the broadcast networks. Not only is she Citizen Kane's granddaughter, but also her comrades went and hid inside a cinema screening that very movie when they were on the run from the authorities. There's an involution, an accretion, an overload of cultural histories there that's teetering on the edge of collapse. The fact that she's a woman is significant. I've been rereading lots of Kathy Acker recently—a writer who's also fascinated with the figure of the urban guerrilla whose operations straddle the fields of the recognizably "militaristic" (raids with guns and bombs) and the symbolic—what DeLillo calls "raids on consciousness." And reading Acker sent me back to the work of the philosopher Julia Kristeva, who she leans on heavily. Again, Kristeva is a figure whose heyday was the 1980s—but it's uncanny rereading her now, because her work is all about the relationship between technological or linguistic systems and bodies and power, and questions of inclusion and exclusion. Feminism—in particular French feminism of several decades ago—seems to anticipate so much of what's at stake under the Trump regime and to map it out really well.

There is a wonderful moment in the book when you consider the question of realism. Predating much of this contemporary fixation with so-called "fake news," there is an evident frustration in your voice to the marked separation between the fictional and the real, as if the likes of Nietzsche and Foucault never actually walked this earth! Sharing these concerns, what political role do you think fiction has to play in a moment where the fabrications of power are being countered by remarkable positivist purity for unconditional truths?

I try to undo the distinction that's usually made between "fiction" and "reality," as though "fiction" were synonymous with fakery. I don't think that's the right layout to work with; I think there's something else going on. In *Typewriters, Bombs, Jellyfish*, I try to argue that "fiction" is best understood in terms of a gap or interim, a delay or *décalage*—what Hamlet calls an out-of-jointness. Another way of thinking about this would be (and this perhaps goes back to Faulkner's ripple image) as a kind of asynchronic overlay. And vitally, what this overlay gives rise to, in its collisions and its recesses, is a possibility—and an ethics—of *witnessing*. Tell him we were here, says Vladimir to the boy-angel amid all the replays and repetition loops and waiting periods of *Godot*: don't turn up here tomorrow and deny you ever saw me. Then, watching Estragon sleeping, he asks himself, "Was I sleeping, while the others suffered?" And he muses that someone is also watching over him (Vladimir) and thinking: "He is sleeping, he knows nothing, let him sleep on." Now, of course, someone is watching him—it's a play! But beyond that, I think Beckett is invoking the notion of literature as a shared or consensual hallucination in which the act of witnessing, of affirming the existence of "the others," becomes possible. This is not a journalistic or "scientific" act; it's ultimately an imaginative one, an act of the imagination.

To conclude, I'd like to deal with the literary question of death. As you have written, every period proclaims and indeed celebrates the death of the novel. You have also suggested that Joyce in particular exhausted all literary possibilities. I want to press you on this idea of exhaustion, which Deleuze argued was central to the emergence of new forms of subjectivity. How might we think about this in terms of "inventing" (a phrase you dwell upon in the book) better styles for living?

While writing the more recent of these essays, over the last few years, I became obsessed with Mallarmé. He sees literature very much in terms of exhaustion and rites of burial and interment. So his non-character Igitur experiences all of cultural history as a tomb, or crypt, into which he has to descend in an attempt to bring about his own extinction—but, of course, he doesn't bring this about, he brings about the work. Similarly, in the wild, typographically exploded poem "A Throw of the Dice," the Master, "corpse at his arm," is going down for the third time as the ship of poetry disintegrates on the rock of oblivion and chance—and, of course, it's from this very abyss or void that literary modernity is born. Mallarmé spent the last decades of his life trying to bring into existence a giant, expanded, multimedia *Gesamtkunstwerk* that he called "The Book," which would somehow contain absolutely everything ever. But he never realized this: it remained in a state of imminence or potentiality—and half of twentieth-century literature and visual art and music, from Joyce to Duchamp to Cage, responds to that potentiality, that call—but without realizing or completing it either. The "Book" is always and inherently to come. That's where Derrida gets his idea of democracy from: it's always and inherently to-come, too. It needs to be invented—a task that's both exhaustive and inexhaustible. Ballard says a similar thing, about reality *tout court*: it's not there yet; the writer needs to invent it.

NINETEEN

LANDSCAPES OF VIOLENCE

Can art can inspire people to be open to new challenges and obligations as worldly citizens?

Art, when done properly, allows for a fundamental questioning of politics and its segregation of life into naturalized hierarchies of inclusion and exclusion. It is directly concerned with questions of oppression and injustice, creating a new dialogue through alternative mediums of public engagement. Such claims about the importance of art and the moving image are central to the pioneering work of the artist and filmmaker John Akomfrah, whose unique documentary style provides a visual history of our violent present. Talking directly about the often occluded intersections between violence, race, and aesthetics, and the influence of the British thinker Stuart Hall and Russian film director Andrei Tarkovsky on his work, the artist looks to mobilize art in the struggle over memory, while using aesthetics as a critical weapon to break out from the cultural amnesia washing over global politics today.

Brad Evans interviews John Akomfrah

June 5, 2017

John Akomfrah is a British artist, writer, curator, and film-maker whose recent projects include *Vertigo Sea* and *The Stuart Hall Project.*

Brad Evans: What role do you think artists and filmmakers have when confronting the problems of violence and injustice in the world today?

John Akomfrah: Most of my work has been concerned with this question, but I would say more through an ongoing "worrying" over the relationship between the aesthetic and the political, a worrying about form and about signature.

And one of the main reasons why that worrying and attempting to get the formal balance right between them matters is because it allows for and "licenses" interventions in those spaces "outside" of my work; it emboldens me to trespass, if you like, into those "spaces" conventionally designated as off-limits for the art practice. Done properly, this coming together, this emphasis on form, makes things happen, things often unintended, and creates a frisson, a charge between the art and its "outside." And this fusion, this alignment, has a major role to play for me when it comes to talking about questions of violence.

What is also really important for me to say—through the work and by implication to others—is this: I understand what's going on in the "spaces of the political" and engage with their significance. But the work is not in some crudely mimetic relation to that political, not just mirroring it in the work. What I think I am offering are a set of propositions. Some of that is about the landscapes of violence. But those propositions are not "mere" recognitions or acknowledgements of that "political." I am in dialogue with that "outside" about its narcissisms, its untruths, its epistemic violence, its falsehoods, and its blind spots. But I am also trying not to be ventriloquized by it. Art can pose problems in unique ways, allowing for other meaningful dialogues. It's not about imposing but about proposing. At its best, art is a conversation, a two-way street with the political.

There are dangers to this line of reasoning, of course. I don't like hiding behind the work or not having the courage to take a position of responsibility about a subject matter. When dealing with violence perpetrated against unarmed civilians or vulnerable groups, especially by armed and powerful state actors, I maintain it is wrong and that it needs to be countered. That's a line I draw and make no apologies for not crossing. So I am happy to defend this position. Like most people who believe their work is grounded by a utopian ethic, I am mindful that there are moments when the work needs to engage with questions of value and of relevance. And to be relevant certainly plays a major part in how I structure my thought process.

Do you see the artist therefore as having a crucial role in combating political amnesia and the erasure of certain oppressive histories?

There are a number of reasons why I am interested in recycling archival footage, music, artifacts, and narratives. Part of my project is to make explicit what is already happening in most societies: to reveal the coexistence of historical traces in the present and to draw attention to the alternative memories that exist in a coterminous relation to the present.

All moving images reference the past. There is always a present-tense commentary that historical images provide in the present. My ambition is always to draw out what I think is the value of that commentary in this present. In a broader sense, I am concerned with making work in which seemingly fixed boundaries between the two (the past and the present) are questioned and ultimately blurred.

For almost all of us, the boundaries that separate past and present are fictions. Why? Because the overlaps between the two are such that in most of our lives it's impossible to insist upon an absolute break between them. Narrative fictions insist on this separation but, in truth, most of us don't live our lives that way.

For instance, I am only able to speak to you as an artist because I have learned various ways of addressing you that are indelibly marked and stained by residues of the past. We are all, in that sense, quintessential products of memory and memory production. And so I try to make work which broadly tries to understand this cadence of temporality to our lives, especially the ways in which narratives of space (I'm American or British or Zimbabwean) rely on a sense of a shared communion with people across the overlapping time zones of nationality.

My parents were anticolonial activists, and one thing I learned from them is that lives are a messy and complicated mesh of always past and continuously present. So I am compelled to produce work that is against amnesia. Works that may not be consciously trying to remember "anything in particular" but instead privilege the importance of the memory as an organizing principle.

Another thing that I learned from their lives is this: when your mother leaves a country (England) in order to fight against that country elsewhere (colonial Ghana) and then ends up fleeing that country (postcolonial Ghana) to seek refuge in the country she started fighting against in the first place (England), the struggle for memory against a backdrop of confusing histories becomes important to you. And for me this is not simply about privileging any particular historic moment or narrative. On the contrary, what needs privileging instead is the idea that the fact of memory itself has a role to play in combating the epistemic violence of amnesia and forgetting.

We are living through a moment when the absurd threatens to colonize the real. Part of the dramaturgy of our present condition is the blurring of the lines between absurdity and reality. And part of this involves the commandeering of facts and fictions to peddle narratives that are patently untrue. It is an absurdity to claim that Great Britain was always "Great" for the vast majority of its Afro-Asian subjects, just as it is absurd to insist that Donald Trump was ever a successful businessman. In order to maintain such myths, there needs to be a selective appropriation of certain histories which then need dressing up in the language of an absurdist fiction to become "facts."

I am also interested in playing with the blurring of boundaries, but these "new developments" mean that I have to make a distinction between what I do and the muddle we currently find ourselves in vis-à-vis the "real." Yes, I am interested in blurring, but there is a difference between peddling myths as false narratives and using the fictional to open things up, to extend the narratives of possibility. My projects mix things up, but that is so that we might build connective tissue between characters, events, histories, and stories. It is basically a good old-fashioned attempt to open up avenues of veracity, turning creeks, if you will, into Panama Canals of meanings. But you need the creek to start. That is very different from the manufacturing or construction of the "real" from a purposefully deceitful position. I'm trying to broaden our affective grasp of moments, not shut them down.

Turning to your powerful and devastating installation Vertigo Sea, *which has been widely applauded, not least for bringing together the violent history of the transatlantic slave trade with the plight of contemporary refugees. Can you tell me about the inspiration behind this work? And what message did you hope the piece might convey?*

Artists often forget the detailed reasons why they started something, and that's natural: by the time you have to talk about something you made, you are usually already into making something else, trying once again "to mend the tear in the fabric of time," as Chris Marker eloquently put it. So you've already "migrated" elsewhere, as it were.

Interestingly, for me, however, with *Vertigo*, while I may not be able to note all its intended motives and ambitions, there is still this really powerful bond between us. And it's a bond that continues to hold strong even today.

Vertigo Sea is about a five-hundred-year history of deaths at sea. And those deaths connect continental histories with species genocide and the transatlantic trade, amongst others. I wanted to make something about the dramaturgy and solitude of suffering, especially of death at sea because it's such a major feature of the "migrant condition" at the moment. Thousands of young men and women from the global South have drowned trying to get to Europe in these rickety pirogues, for instance. And when that journey is one your parents made seventy years ago in the relative comfort of a ship, it seems to me that that you have an ethical responsibility to these lost lives, a need to make sense of their violent ends.

Often when people die as a result of a political narrative, they do so removed from others, removed from their very sense of belonging in this world. Such deaths often happen "alone," even though there may be countless others who die in a similar way with you. If you are one of three-hundred enslaved Africans, each individually tossed overboard from a slave ship, death is a solitary "becoming." Somebody wanted you to "disappear," and that is something they needed you to do alone. And those architects of your death wanted a sea of amnesia to wash over the memory of your disappearance.

The important thing for me was that there were hundreds of people like that who came to me during the research for the installation, from all over the world, a family of death, if you like. All "disappeared" into a watery space of oblivion: sub-Saharan Africans in the eighteenth and nineteenth centuries, Algerians in the 1960s, Argentinians and Vietnamese in the 1970s. And I remember feeling a very strong ethical obligation to try to exhume all of these dead people and memories together, to break the solitude by getting them to "talk" to each other. Art can do that; it can break the curse of solitude by getting them to coexist in the same discursive space. It can break the shackles of amnesia which had bound them, separately, to an eternity as condemned ghosts. It can release them from a forgotten and dehumanized fate, locked forever in different unmarked tombs across a watery planet.

That's what I meant by the "blurring." It's about this need to present narrative possibilities for forgotten lives, to talk about the memory of their suffering, to restore something more humane to their existence, to heal a tear in the fabric of time brought about by violence so that we might see the forgotten again as human beings who belong to our shared human family, despite the violence they have suffered.

Can you talk to me about the memory of the cultural theorist Stuart Hall, in particular the way his intellectual work helped shaped you as an artist?

The first thing to say [is] this wonderful man was a friend. He was initially a mentor, certainly a charismatic example and a figure who embodied all manner of possibilities for my generation. Many of us of that eighties generation of artists and activists gravitated towards Stuart because he seemed to possess this maverick combination of possibilities that we recognized in ourselves. He was a figure of multiple migrations and crossovers, and these seemed to say something directly to our then-present condition. And, what's even more important, since he uncannily seemed to sense this, the very textures of his life spoke to our experience. And this "standing" and "position" of necessity that he had for us was something he appreciated and responded to with remarkable generosity of his time, life, and ideas.

Stuart in this regard was not simply intellectually of value, and to be honest I don't think his "intellectualism" was the original draw for me. When you are sixteen or seventeen and you see this black man on the television, the attraction wasn't intellectual; it was an image of possibility and hope. What marked him was a difference: he wasn't an athlete, a pop star, or a performer. And that made you feel he represented something of considerable importance. It was only later that the intellectual magnitude of this thinking started to resonate and shape the way I saw the world.

I don't think the word "influence" best describes the impact his persona and work had on many of us. We absolutely were influenced, no question, but there is a broader cultural ecosystem which he became willingly and enthusiastically a part of that allowed for a considerable amount of

the collective work, the aesthetic struggle and cultural reflections we made in the eighties and nineties. This started
in the United Kingdom and then continued to spread across
the planet, including to the United States. Stuart embodied one of those alliances between the heart and mind that,
upon reflection, I can't imagine what our lives would have
been like without. And I mean that very seriously. There
were many desperate people in the 1970s with very desperate plans, so his example both as a figure and a thinker
proved invaluable to many of us.

*You have previously also mentioned your admiration for Andrei
Tarkovsky. What is it about his cinematic work, notably in the
context of tragedy and ruins, which you find most compelling and
influential?*

Like Stuart, Tarkovsky is one of those people who, for me,
the first encounter with proved fatal! I still feel like I have
never gotten over it. It proved fatal because it was so compelling and a true example of alterity. You couldn't get a better sense of the real potential of cinema, truly the invention
of unimaginable worlds. I remember my first viewing of his
brilliant film *Mirror*, which I watched when I was about sixteen. It just seemed like something had landed from some
alien planet. And that made it all the more compelling, even
though I am still trying to understand the nature of that
compulsion and genuine admiration.

At the heart of the Tarkovsky project is a kind of agnos-
ticism about the significance and importance of the visible,

the seen. And he comes at this in different ways, all of which serve to disrupt the notion that we are of central importance in all this, that we are the center of the universe. He offers a sort of pantheistic sense of our relationship with the elemental in his work, and that continues to stay with me. In this regard, I have always viewed him as an outlaw cynic who possessed the outside vision, which resonates and illustrates the importance of staying on the outside when it comes to questions of criticality and creativity. It also resonated personally. This outlaw status, being on the outside looking inward, depicted the reality I felt while growing up in England.

There is another lesson we can take from his cinema. Namely, when art is done well, it is able to move the border, aesthetically, discursively, and intellectually. It's possible to get people to believe they are part of something bigger, and that they should be open to new challenges and obligations as a worldly citizen. Through his work, Tarkovsky shows that art can have these magnificent protean qualities that disrupt familiar coordinates concerning the logics of space and time, transporting them literally to new lands of possibility and outlook.

Given the toxic political climate in the United States, the issue of race and its ongoing relevance seems as pressing as ever. What are your thoughts on the landscapes of racial prejudice you encounter?

When you encounter contemporary forms of racialization, it is both uncanny and deeply unsettling. It comes to me now with this aura of the eerie, the ghostly. It's one of those "forest of things" one genuinely felt we were seeing our way through. And so its contemporary intensity and durability, its staying power, feels genuinely eerie and otherworldly, like being stuck in an H.P. Lovecraft ghost story or something.

We can sense once again its "forcefulness," its durability across many landscapes of hatred. It is displaying a remarkably "viral" facility and capacity to transform, migrate, and return in multiple ways. So it is still a substantial, bodily presence that retains the ability to shock and devastate lives in the most appalling ways. But I cannot allow it to be so. It went out of my back door as a sick dog needing to be put down, and it's not coming back through the front door as a healthy puppy.

But undermining is a Janus-faced creature because it is also one of the protocols of racialization as well. Hands need to stay hands and not become human beings. And this involves rearranging the basis upon which claim of subjecthood can be made by the "outsider." An "inside" is needed, and racialization operates by rendering the existence of the outsider fragile, temporary, uncertain. Such that the very ground upon which the outsider walks violently moves with doubtful tremors that will continue until the "outsider" accepts the tautological logic of their enforced estrangement (I am an outsider and therefore should be outside) and decides that it's time to leave. Undermining as such is integral to the process of un-naming the outsider. It is also the starting point for the emergence of the "facile explanations" of race. You only have to think of the recent six-nation Muslim travel restriction to see what I mean.

How do you think society might resource the arts better in developing a critique of violence?

That's a very good question in the United States at the moment, isn't it? And it makes you understand why the threats to the National Endowment for the Arts are no mere coincidence. I see this long line of writers and thinkers who have been concerned with the links between politics and aesthetics, and one hopes that some of their charismatic examples might be of use here. It's a line that connects a range of disparate souls from the likes of Frederick Douglass to Virginia Woolf, W.E.B. Du Bois to Walter Benjamin, Emily Dickinson to Bertolt Brecht, Leo Tolstoy to Toni Morrison. Each of them understood and understands quite clearly the "political" importance of their work as art. Our task is perhaps first to try to understand why that importance has diminished over time. It is not that artists have necessarily been doing anything different, though it certainly benefits systems of power if the critical voice of the artist is marginalized.

Alongside this, we need to return something of this tradition, which maintains that we can rethink the world anew. That the creation of new worlds is not beyond us, and we have the ability to raise the issue about how the creative can be put to use in collectively answering the big questions. If someone was to say to me, "We really like your work and we hope it finds a home solely in the best gallery space on the planet," that would make me deeply unhappy. The hope is that it would reverberate and have resonance with people in their daily lives and contribute something to their daily struggles for dignity and in the fight for justice. Working with matters of the present, the production of art and its ability to change people's perceptions can and should be far-reaching. At least that is my hope looking forward in these uncertain times.

TWENTY

VIOLENCE TO THOUGHT

We have a responsibility to speak up to make the case for the possibility of a better, ethical, and just life for all.

When it comes to injustice, what is the role of the intellectual if not to ask the most difficult questions? Drawing upon his extensive work on the history of racial violence, David Theo Goldberg addresses the links between violence and the intellectual in the public arena, including personal stories about some of the threats he has received working within the academy. Speaking truth to power is often a dangerous affair. Recognizing this, Goldberg connects the relationships between violence and thought directly to the liberation of prejudice, and the anti-critical and anti-intellectual climate of the Trump era. He does this to emphasize the illusions of "post-raciality" and the denial of racism as a fundamental category of social structuring, and to emphasize that the need for critical scholars to remain committed to questions of justice and equality remains great.

Brad Evans interviews David Theo Goldberg

July 10, 2017

David Theo Goldberg is director of the University of California Humanities Research Institute. His books include *Are We Postracial Yet?* and *Between Humanities and the Digital.*

Brad Evans: I'd like to begin this discussion with a straightforward conceptual question. What do you understand the relationship to be between violence and intellectualism?

David Theo Goldberg: Violence is not in contradiction, nor is it necessarily even in opposition or contrast to intellectuality. It seems almost trite to say this. Intellectual intervention, theory too, can be violent in the operative senses of the term. Violence can disrupt, bring up short those at whom it is aimed. This disruptive sense of violence—what we might call the "violence of critique"—can be productive in some ways. It can get people to place into question the taken for granted, to strike off in a different direction, to unsettle the all too easily given and settled practices.

While the critique doesn't necessarily intend maliciously to harm, sometimes it may nevertheless end up, if inadvertently, doing so; for those in a position of received orthodoxy the critique may be taken as an attack upon their belief and value systems. But the violence of a dismissive attack can also be more destructive. It can prevent the enactment or achievement of worthwhile pursuits or goals or force people to abandon or defer compelling commitments. And it can do so through threat, veiled or explicit, humiliation or belittling, or refusal to take seriously, or indeed by willful misdirection.

Consider the broad, concerted, and enormously well-funded attack not only on the boycott, divestment and sanctions movement but on the person of anyone publicly supporting the movement, from undergraduate students and faculty to celebrity critics like Roger Waters. Tactics have included seeking to establish legislation and campus policies branding as anti-Semitic any critic of Israel's debilitating treatment of Palestinians or even pointing out disturbing characterizations of Palestinians by Israeli politicians, military personnel, or ordinary citizens.

There's another alternative but no less related sense in which intellectualism can enable or feed violence. Intellectualism can service violence by initiating, aiding, or advancing it instrumentally. It can calculate the odds that violent intervention will achieve the sought-after goals; it can calibrate the most "effective" measure of violence to bring about those ends; it can rationalize the violence already enacted; and so on. Think of the arguments, legal and political, made in the United States around the use of waterboarding or torture or to support building a border wall or the rounding up of the undocumented. Intellectualism and the credibility it gives to violence in these registers are hardly innocent.

There is, no doubt, the counter-consideration of intellectuality to all of this. Ethical and political arguments—transcendental or categorical or communitarian or, for that matter, utilitarian—seek to establish the just grounds for political relation and action. Here, in contrast to the violent uptake of ratiocination, thinking seeks to establish the grounds and means for reasonable living together, to treat all with dignity and decency, to curb if not eradicate the violent treatment of any and all.

Hannah Arendt contrasted a thinking praxis with thoughtlessness, the moral imperatives to engage others without violence against the instrumentalizing calculations that bring about violence without limit. Arendt is not signaling, as she is too often accused, that the likes of Eichmann [have] obliterated all thinking, that they have acted completely without the cunning of calculus. She is pointing to their evasion, itself almost calculated, of grappling with the humanity of the violated. To treat the radically violated as such requires their more or less complete dehumanization, what Fanon is the first to characterize as "racialization." It necessitates denuding themselves of their own capacity to be (potentially) thoughtful, feeling, caring—ethical—beings.

Picking up on this in the context of the dangerousness of thinking you allude to here (something Arendt understood all too well), like many academics who have a public profile in the humanities and social sciences, you have been subjected to a number of personal attacks and troubling threats to your physical well-being. How do you deal with these attempts to ultimately suffocate your work?

This has become all too often of late, alas. There's a difference, to be sure, between criticisms or dismissals of one's work that are the product of a failure, sometimes crude or silly, to understand what one is arguing or critical about, and ad hominems and threats to one's well-being. These personal threats may, of course, be in response to one's critique or attempts to get one to cease or (as you say) suffocate one's critical engagement. If the former at least acknowledges one has something worth responding to, the latter is far more insidious, if not sinister.

My responses in the latter such cases will vary by instance. After the initial surprise or shock or occasionally even disbelieving laughter at the crudity, there's a choice to be made. Does one simply dismiss it, putting it out of mind, and get on with one's day, one's critical life? Putting it completely aside is not necessarily easy, as it will niggle at the mind, prompting one to look out for other instances around the corner, over one's shoulder. Does one make it public, easily done in a more or less limited way through social media or more broadly by publishing about it in print media or a more formal publication?

This serves to warn others similarly engaged in such work while forcing the surreptitious out into the open. This too has an important social dimension, reminding one that you are not alone in facing up to these insidious attacks. That in working for justice one is part of a community. When I decide to go public in this way, I will try as best as the evidence allows naming the person or site from which the attack or threat is emanating, along with its nature. The effect of such a response has sometimes sent the attacker diving for cover, which can be quite satisfying. There is also the weighing up of whether one reports the instance to authorities, to institutional officers or even the police. The more personally intrusive the instance—a call to one's home, a demeaning message or death threat on one's personal voice-mail or (usually anonymous) email, ugly caricaturing posters with one's image plastered across one's workplace, that sort of thing—the more encouraged I am to report this to the police. This at least establishes a file, a paper trail, should things persist or ramp up.

In going public in this way, the response of colleagues invariably, though the institution only sometimes, has been terrifically supportive. It is important to know one is not alone in these cases. I have had people I barely know, who have heard about an instance, approach at public fora or a convention offering support, encouragement, solidarity. That sense of collegiality, of intellectual and political community, is enormously fortifying.

I have caught myself sometimes rewording expression in the wake of such attacks, seeking greater precision or clarity, sharpening the critique. Not a bad thing in itself, if not for the insidiousness giving rise to it. But in all, I must emphasize that my response, even if sometimes after a momentary stock-taking, is invariably to speak back, to extend the critique, to sustain the political pursuit, to insist on the critical scalpel. After all, that the attack is so crazed indicates its perpetrator must be unnerved to begin with. It signals a crack in their sense of dogmatic self-righteous absolution. The overriding response to the attempt to suffocate is to breathe deep and speak back with more cutting critique.

For many decades you have been mapping out the changing contours of racial violence and the intellectual conditions that naturalize divisions amongst people. What most perturbs you in the current political climate?

You make me sound so old! Unfortunately, while the expressions, forms, logics, and contours of racial violence have shifted across time, such violence persists. Racial violence waxes hard, wanes some, only to harden again. It does so in relation to shifting and interacting conditions of political economy, social, cultural, and legal considerations, not to mention the rhetorical opportunism of politicians.

What's most disturbing today is not just the resurrection of racism, or even its proliferation, as bad as these are. It is the license to say and act in blatantly racist ways with little restraint, magnified by a deafening lack of condemnation and constraint by those in a position to delimit the expression. Curiously, this renewal of racism without constraint or public condemnation operates in the name of "postraciality." The postracial insists that racial reference or classification is irrelevant, that structural racism is a thing of the past, no longer worthy of consideration, that the most disturbing racist expression is the charge of racism against white people. In the name of these claims the extension and renewal of historical racisms—racism proper—are being obscured. The force of the postracial today lies not in the claim to be beyond race, even in its aspirational sense. Rather, it is the subterfuge in the name of which the most violent and vile forms of racism are being recharged. The postracial, it turns out, is but the contemporary modality of racism's renewal and recharge. License is given, as a consequence, for those so inclined to express themselves publicly in blatantly racist ways with far less consequence than in the post–civil rights [movement] era past.

These expressions can take the form of words and deeds, sometimes with physical, and certainly invariably with expressive, violence. They obviously debilitate those at whom these expressions of violence are aimed, usually those in more vulnerable positions than the perpetrators. But in doing so they debilitate and delimit the society at large. And in that sense they issue an ethical and political challenge to all members of the society to insist "not us"! To remain silent, to insist on not assuming that responsibility, is to declare support for the injustice in question, if not enabling the perpetration. The choice to remain silent is to assume responsibility for enabling the persistence of racism in the name of its very denial. It is to erase the very grounds and terms for identifying the racist expressions and practices at work.

Situating this in the context of the struggles taking place in United States, from the Black Lives Matter Movement, to North Dakota pipeline Native resistance, what role and ethical responsibilities do you think academics and intellectuals have in this climate?

In the United States especially but more generally too there has been an active undertaking to undermine the capacity to think—fallacies are now abundant and unchecked—

as well as the authority of facticity. I call this the turn to "make-believe." Make-believe obviously centers the drive to fabricate both in the sense of falsifying whenever convenient and to fashion a narrative web designed to mislead and misdirect to realize political interests. But make-believe also involves compulsion, forcing belief on the polity, on threat of dire consequences, pain, or violence for any resisting. The anti-intellectualism of our times—consider as one instance among many the closing of Central European University by the Hungarian leadership—is at one with this prevailing culture. Trumpetarianism is a product of this confluence of forces.

Academics and intellectuals obviously have been targets of these contemporary developments. It is our work to know, to be in possession of the prevailing facts, to think clearly, compellingly, critically. So in the face of fact dismissal, "alternative realities," the political ignoring and outright rejection of scientific findings—in short, of the political recourse to pushing make-believe—we have a driving responsibility to speak up. To make a case for and from the facts, for and from critical thinking, for and from conscience, for and from the possibility of a better, ethical and just life for all.

Global pollution and climate change impact everyone, most notably the most vulnerable. Institutional violence, murderous practices, and unsubstantiated criminalization [of] people of color, immigrants, and refugees are effected in the name of all of us in society. This fabrication shapes how we live. Corruption, hypocrisy, and narrow self-interest undercut sociality to the demise of us all. Recall Thatcher's insistence that there is no such entity as society, only individuals and their families. Courageous citizens—often the youth—have been concerned to speak out against these rampant injustices. Academics especially have an institutional platform, resources, rhetorical skill, and domain expertise and so have special responsibility to speak out against these injustices and to support the critical work of those on the ground seeking to ensure a decent and dignified life for all, and especially for the most vulnerable.

To conclude, I'd like to return to an important phrase you used previously "working for justice." What do you understand justice to mean? And how might it help us rethink more ethical and peaceful relations amongst the world's peoples?

By justice, I mean minimally a commitment to the dignified and decent conditions for all to live fulfilled lives. It follows that a fulfilled life for one, whether individual, group, or state, should not be achieved at the expense or on the backs of others. That the world today is so thoroughly interconnected and codependent, that human life is one of deep relationality, entails that in fulfilling our own lives we are bound to enable the same possibility for all others. Each of us is defined by the same baseline that should acknowledge the human, economic, and political rights irrespective of individual or collective background. Individuals or groups might be fulfilled differently. But at a general level the pursuit of justice and peace will be measured in light of whether these baseline rights and the dignity and capacity to live decent lives, of people affected by one's actions, are fully respected. Which is to say are fully considered in and on their own and not imposed terms.

Given social conditions inherited historically and exacerbated today in both their local and global relations, any commitment to pursuing justice now must attend to considerations of repair. Reparation, as Achille Mbembe most notably has made clear, need not be narrowly construed to focus simply on a question of "returns." If we consider it rather in broader terms, repair has to do with remaking and reconstituting, a putting together and a making whole. Repair as return assumes that in some prior state things were as they should have been, that justice somehow prevailed, or, even if it did in part, that we could now somehow magically return to a disappeared state. Repair as remaking, as a reconstituting, is a commitment to establishing the grounds for making things together in a way in which the interests of all would have equal voice in the design and re-construction. Here the commitment is to remaking a world together, fully, where those hitherto set aside are re-centered in the reconstituting. It is this sense of justice that I see serving as a horizon for which to strive, to reach for a co-constituting world in which, in our complex of entanglements, we can all live dignified, peaceful lives together.

TWENTY-ONE

OPERATIC VIOLENCE

Opera has the ability to take us on a journey into the darkest and deepest recesses of human experience.

Despite its assumed elitism and evident gendered politics, opera provides a fascinating opening to discuss violence as cultural and political phenomena in an age of global witnessing. Concentrating our attentions in the most emotive and moving ways, opera allows questioning forms of violence from both the imperial past and the contemporary moment. In this conversation with the renowned operatic director Christopher Alden, the importance of opera is discussed in terms of thinking about the relationship between violence, performance, and witnessing; the problematic history of gendered violence and its beautification; and the challenges faced by the arts more generally in politically fraught times.

Brad Evans interviews Christopher Alden

September 11, 2017

Christopher Alden is a New York–born opera director who works regularly with the most distinguished companies. His

English National Opera production of Handel's *Partenope* was awarded the Olivier Award for Best UK opera production of 2008/09 as well as Australia's Helpmann Award for Best Opera in 2011. Alden's production of Britten's *Midsummer Night's Dream* won the Golden Mask Award for best Russian opera production in 2012.

Brad Evans: We live in an age when the arts are facing considerable financial and intellectual pressures. If we were to come at this negatively we could say that the issues the arts face is to present themselves as having political and social relevance beyond mere cultural pasttime. Yet the arts have always been a site for social commentary and imaginative resistance. What are your thoughts on this, given the current political climate?

Christopher Alden: Art is often at its most vibrant in times of political crisis, when the people at the top tend to exhibit a kind of nervousness about the arts as a result. Sometimes art needs to jab up against something in order for its relevance to become apparent. I have always felt that the visual arts, music, and theater are by nature intensely political. Maybe this is because I grew up as part of the 1960s generation. The flowering of protest witnessed during that time certainly revealed the importance of the arts in developing social and political consciousness, and we are starting to see similar developments in the fraught times in which we are currently living.

Being from the U.S., I have a strong feel for the edgy relationship between arts and politics, particularly when it comes to the issue of supporting the arts. In Europe, there is a solid tradition of public funding of the arts. In countries like Germany, the arts are heavily supported by public money, which frees artists up to create more openly provocative and confrontational work since they are not constrained by the fear of offending donors. I hope this does not change too much as Europe drifts to the right.

In the United States, however, there has always been an absurdly small level of government funding for the arts, and now there is the serious possibility of even that being diminished by the current administration's threat to abolish the National Endowment of the Arts and other publicly funded arts organizations like PBS. Consequently, artists in the U.S. have always been more dependent on support from private donors and corporations. Fortunately, in the current moment, it is clear that wealthy donors on the left are becoming more aware than ever that the arts are vitally important in maintaining a viable critique. The traumatic wake-up call which the Trump administration has precipitated isn't entirely a negative thing as it is galvanizing not only liberal-thinking artists but donors and corporate sponsors as well.

When we think about violence theoretically and conceptually, we are often drawn to theatrical questions such as its staging, the performativity, and the issue of forced witnessing. What do you think opera brings to this discussion?

Opera has always been a provocative, confrontational art form which asks difficult questions about the relationship between the individual and society, and it has always struggled to find the right balance between pushing the envelope and not going so far that it is rejected by the status quo.

When opera as we know it was born in seventeenth-century Italy, new pieces would be commissioned by the aristocracy and staged in the palaces of princes as private and socially exclusive events. Since then, the reputation of opera as an expensive and privileged kind of entertainment has clung to the art form. However, from its beginnings, there has always been another side to opera, which was created by musicians and poets who wanted to recapture the power of Greek theater to tell deeply meaningful stories through music. As with the Greek tragedies, whose performances were intensely communal events exerting a powerful influence on the politics of their era, such attempts continually blur the lines between art and politics and bring them together in novel ways. This is the subversive side to opera that seeks to challenge established ideas, norms, and assumptions.

There is something about opera that sets it apart from the other arts. The way in which it sings its stories can affect us in such a uniquely visceral way through the magical alchemy of its combination of text and music. It has the ability to take us on a journey into the darkest and deepest recesses of human experience. The power of music and the nonrational layers it evokes work on the spectator in ways which spoken theater cannot always achieve. Consequently, opera inspires a fanatical response from its devotees, many of whom have a strong sense of ownership of the great works from the past which they revere. This segment of the operatic public sometimes resents directors like me who are intent on interpreting these pieces from a modern perspective and stripping away the detritus of tradition to reveal the timeless truths, not always pretty, which these pieces sing about and which resonate down through time to our own moment.

As an operatic director whose work has been notably singled out for its engagement with violence, what ethical challenges (if any) do you think directors face or need to acknowledge when dealing with performances of violence?

This mad art form has a particular advantage when it comes to touching people. It taps into the raw energy of human emotion, which, of course, is also central in our attempts to understand violence and the pain and suffering of others. And what is ethics, especially when it comes to violence, if not the ability to feel some form of empathy, compassion, and connection with suffering?

How one depicts violence on stage is always a tricky question. In my work, I have usually tried to rob violence of its glamour by stressing its ugliness and brutality, unlike the more romantic theatrical/operatic tradition which was content to profit, uncritically, from the entertainment potential of violent acts portrayed on stage, often in a softened and prettied-up manner. I feel that my grittier approach has generally been successful in exposing dark layers in the music of operas, layers which had previously lain dormant in more soft-edged traditional stagings. I have to admit that, occasionally, the overtly nasty depiction of violence in my productions may have jutted up too abrasively against the music, preventing the opera in question from working its usual magic. There is always a delicate balancing act involved in bringing a modern sensibility into play when dealing with works of art from the past, and sometimes I may have crossed over the line.

One of the hallmarks of contemporary life is the speeding up of all social interactions. A notable casualty of this is the much-needed time for critical reflection. But arguably this is where opera truly has a critical advantage, as there is often a much slower temporality to the violence, which takes place in a more concentrated fashion. What lessons might we take from this?

The main reason I've been drawn to opera, a dreamlike, non-naturalistic art form with greater similarities to ritualistic Asian theater than to the Western kitchen-sink realism tradition, has been because of its poetic nature. It avoids presenting reality from a straight-on, literal point of view. Like nonrepresentational twentieth-century visual art styles, it attempts to get at the elusive nature of existence through more fragmented, abstract means. A prime example of this aspect of opera can be found in the works of Handel, one of the greatest music theater composers of any era. I am currently pleased to be working on a few different productions of Handel operas, both in the U.K. and the U.S., and Handel's genius in utilizing highly formalized eighteenth-century musical structures to bring to vivid life the full range of human experience never ceases to amaze and inspire me. His works are filled with exquisitely drawn-out arias where a singer will sing about a situation, a thought, or an emotion for an extended time, frozen in one moment as time stands still. The audience is invited to take the time to focus on that moment from many different angles, rather like the experience of looking at an abstract painting, which depicts a bowl of fruit from multiple perspectives simultaneously. This contemplative Kabuki theater-ish approach creates an atmosphere in which to dissect and ruminate on not only positive and creative human drives like love, empathy, and connection, but also the darker and, yes, more violent sides of human nature.

A potent example of this is my recent production of an early piece by Handel, *Acis, Galatea, and Polyphemus*, presented at the performance space in Brooklyn called National Sawdust, which transformed the mythical tale of the Cyclops in love with the sea nymph into a modern Trumpian pussy-grabbing parable of the sexual entitlement of powerful males it was set in a rich man's bathroom, [and] the sea nymph Galatea and her lover Acis were portrayed as two servants bathing their master, the Cyclops, whose threatening sexual harassment leads to the eventual suicide of one and the murder of the other. The timeless theme of bullying was reinforced by the fact that the Cyclops seemed to be driven as much by the thrill of humiliating Galatea in her lover's presence as by her actual seduction. Because of Handel's extraordinary ability to psychologize his characters through his music, the piece packs quite a punch and it did not take all that much tweaking to uncover strong parallels between this mythological tale and our current era defined by power, class, and the brutality of thwarted desire.

Returning to the question of sexual violence: Another criticism of opera is the way in which it can often beautify the death of its heroines. How are we to make sense of this politically? And does this perhaps tell us something more about the audience itself and what it desires when it comes to witnessing violence?

Opera's problematic relationship to women has been widely acknowledged for some time, especially in our current era, which is becoming increasingly more sensitized to feminist and gender issues. It began in the nineteenth century when the female soprano became the star of the show and replaced the dominance once afforded to the male castrato. The new focus on the plight of female heroines signaled a shift in the politics of opera. The great majority of operas premiered in the nineteenth century were written by male composers and librettists for the delectation of audiences sitting in opulent opera houses, watching stories often focused on beautiful, passive women suffering and dying for love.

Looking beneath the surface of these male-generated fantasies of female victimization reveals a fascinating side of opera, which speaks disturbingly about patriarchal societal structures. Men's complicated and conflicted feelings about women, ranging from idolatry to desire to fear to hatred, are taken extravagant advantage of in the eroticization of female disempowerment played out in an endless succession of scenes of operatic madness and suicide. The pornographic kick of opera as a kind of singing snuff film says a lot about the male need to take violent control of the power women exert over them, first celebrating it by putting it on a pedestal and worshipping it, then feeling dominant and victorious over it when the heroine is punished with madness and/or death.

Let's take the example of an early-twentieth-century piece, Puccini's *Madama Butterfly*, which tells the upsetting tale of a Japanese geisha who makes the mistake of falling in love with an American naval officer who considers her to be no more than his temporary concubine. After abandoning her and their child when his ship sails back home, he returns a couple of years later with his American wife, intending to take the child away. This leads directly to the suicide of the traumatized geisha. Puccini's opera is, clearly, a deeply political piece addressing head-on the dark side of imperialism, focused on a foreigner who buys into the American dream and is subsequently duped and victimized by it. But it is told through music of such seductive beauty and traditionally presented in picture-postcard productions which sugarcoat the story to make it palatable to bourgeois opera audiences who have probably come to hear the latest star soprano and tenor rather than to experience a harrowing evening in the theater. However, when the comforting layers of tradition are stripped away, the sadistic betrayal at the core of this story is revealed with devastating force, and, as in a Lars von Trier film, the audience is witness to the disillusioned heroine's painful downhill slide.

There is a terrible episode in Puccini's personal life involving his wife's hysterical jealousy of a servant who worked in their household. Knowing her husband's womanizing proclivities, she assumed the worst and hounded the servant relentlessly with her accusations of adultery to the point where the poor girl committed suicide. The subsequent post mortem revealed the dead girl to be a virgin, and, after being put on trial, Puccini's wife was sent to prison. This episode, which sounds a lot like the plot of a Puccini opera, illustrates the fact that Puccini can hardly be called a feminist, nevertheless he betrayed a certain ambivalent sensitivity to feminist issues by his choice to set to music a number of other stories, like Butterfly's, focused on woman's tenuous position in a patriarchal world. Of course, as in a Von Trier film, there is a very fine line in Puccini's operas between empathy for the victimized heroine and sadistic pleasure in witnessing her traumatic demise.

Turning to your adaptation of La Vida Breve, *the final scene featuring the savage cutting and suicide of the seemingly fated gypsy girl Salud is powerful and compelling. I was particularly drawn to the sacrificial element and its notable Catholic iconography, which resurrects images of the suffering of the cross. Do you think there is something about such theological traces which still resonates with audiences when coming to terms with violence?*

The operatic art form, with its focus on humanity's suffering and mortality, is often only a few steps away from the rituals of the Catholic Church. An excellent case in point is Manuel De Falla's *La Vida Breve*, yet another disturbing opera about the betrayal and eventual death of a credulous female, which takes place in the picturesque city of Granada and features gorgeous outpourings of folkloristic Spanish music. In my production for Opera North in the UK, I set the piece in the stark environment of a dress factory, where the heroine, Salud, is one of many women sitting at rows of sewing machines. I made this choice in order to stress the class conflict at the heart of the piece, as the plot is focused on Salud's relationship with a wealthy young man from the other side of the tracks who seduces and abandons the gypsy girl, then marries his well-to-do fiancée. The libretto never makes clear what Salud actually dies of after she learns of the betrayal, and, in traditional productions of the piece, she dies a rather generic operatic death, presumably of a broken heart. I replaced this sanitized death with an extremely upsetting, drawn-out scene where Salud takes a pair of scissors from her worktable and cuts her arms and face before fatally stabbing herself, as her fellow workers egg her on. The final scene was played as a frozen religious tableau, with Salud held aloft by her fellow workers, worshiping her as a kind of saint crucified on the cross of their powerlessness and disenfranchisement in a society which tacitly condones the entitled male's abandonment of the lower-class female. The darkly fatalistic Spanish Catholic imagery which dominates the libretto and the sensuous brutality of De Falla's passionate music inspired me to remove the piece from its naturalistic setting and instead play it out as a kind of religious passion play in which the shockingly violent act of Salud's self-martyrdom was the central and defining event.

To conclude, it seems that there is still a long way to go in any attempts to see opera as a political form of intervention on its own terms. How might critical thinkers resource opera better?

It is clearly problematic for plenty of people (among them, no doubt, some critical thinkers) to look beyond opera's reputation, in some quarters, as an elitist art form with its well-coiffed head in the clouds, divorced from the problems of the real world and extremely expensive to produce. But as somebody who has derived so much pleasure and inspiration from this challenging but rewarding art form, I hope that at least a segment of future generations will continue to be struck by opera's ability to communicate on so many different levels about the human experience. It is certainly encouraging that, during the past couple of decades, there has been a gratifying burst of interest, particularly in the United States in new works being produced by opera companies across the country. Audiences are connecting more and more with these pieces of musical theater created by composers and writers from our current moment, and this, more than anything else, points the way to the future of opera as a vital part of our cultural life.

TWENTY-TWO

THE VIOLENCE OF ART

Violence is the prime mover of human history and a discrete component of social self-modification.

How does art deal with the figurative in an age when violated bodies are so present in our visual media? Can we recover something from the figures of history to combat crude and essentialized representations? And how can we deal with the pessimism of tragedy and the nihilism of the modern condition without lamenting or wallowing in self-pity? British artist Jake Chapman addresses these questions by discussing art as a form of creative destruction. In doing so, he talks frankly about the aesthetic importance of engaging with violence for making sense of the human condition, the continued influence of Goya in his work, and his personal theoretical interests. The interview coincided with the launch of the Chapman Brothers' recent exhibition, "The Disasters of the Everyday," which offered another powerful engagement with Goya and his still all too resonant Disasters of War series.

Brad Evans interviews Jake Chapman

October 5, 2017

Jake Chapman is a visual artist renowned for his collaborations with brother Dinos—the Chapman Brothers.

Brad Evans: What do the terms "art" and "violence" actually mean to you? And can they ever be separated in practice?

Jake Chapman: While violence is presented as the excluded object of society, it is the prime mover of human history and a discrete component of social self-modification. Systemic violence ensures social stability through the imminent threat of superior force, enforcing the imperative that all violence is bad, whilst reserving exclusions—like "just" war or keeping the peace. And yet there is another form of violence that is creatively destructive. This is the violence I think we can talk about in the context of art, for while art offers a critique of the former, it engages in the latter.

In terms of thinking about art more broadly, within the most condensed history of human civilization there is an implicit disassociation between action and intention. What do I mean by this? Art appears to embody human intention in that it is crystalized in the form of civilized conduct. And yet the practical production of art itself works against this proposition by continuously disinheriting the conscious manipulation of materials for the purpose of some pre-inscribed intention or outcome.

Our interest in making art is not about producing some

object that reveals the essence of its maker, nor is it about offering up something autobiographically confessional. It is precisely the opposite. It is about demonstrating a certain refusal or at least critical disruption to the very idea of an authentic anthropomorphic self. And it seeks to unhinge intentionality and all the suffocating rationalities that art ostensibly confirms. So in that sense art offers a kind of ontological violence—an autonomously destructive energy, which comes alive in the creative process—a process that cannot be mastered by the author.

This is not about some avant-garde notion of destroying the past in order to bring about a linear future. It's more fundamentally internal to the process itself—within the mechanism itself. We are interested in the possible destruction of all instrumentalizing logic and any outcomes determined by the ambitions of intention. By intention we mean the assertion of human narratives that seek to dominate the outcome of the process. Such ideas do violence upon the notion that a work of art is necessarily communicative. Hence, whether it sets out to be violent or not, such a work of art will present itself as an assault upon the identity of any given viewer seeking the confirmation of their identity.

This reminds me of a quote you once gave when you said, "We can only denounce the violence we are condemned to repeat." Can you elaborate on this?

No great earthly change has been brought about by a moral imperative. I'm not saying ideas don't matter, but what seems quite obvious, to me at least, is the realization that war and violence have been the principle driver of history and demonstrate a remarkable capacity to modify and adapt morality in support of the civilization that violence apparently threatens. We are forever killing things off, but they never stay dead—and each transgression lacks fulfillment and thus requires endless repetition—the seasonal repetition and the wallowing in guilt as pleasure. We kill our gods over and over to justify our obligation in celebrating their eternal return, even if only in secularized form.

Your work is full of graphic references to the raw realities of mass violence and death. Why do these topics compel you as an artist?

Society measures civility by the self-reflexive understanding of finitude. We are civilized because we understand our cosmic insignificance. And yet the instruments we use to measure this analytics show themselves to be completely inadequate. When we say we comprehend death we seem simultaneously shy of comprehending the death of the species or planet, for instance. Its remarkable when you think of it, given that this is the only truth we face after birth. None of our reasoning helps us. Our ability to understand infinitude is itself finite.

There's a wonderful moment in Michel Foucault's *History of Sexuality* where he notes than when you exclude death it's all you end up talking about. The same we can say about violence. Like death, equally excluded, it's all we think about. This is certainly the case with art and artists who deal with forms of violence. As I mentioned, I think art deserves to disrupt the notion of the communicative model. Relinquish the idea that there is a universal truth or essence to be revealed!

How do you deal with criticism of your work in light of its politically fraught nature?

The artist is supposed to be preoccupied by a sense of inner personal rigor, and yet the work is made with a presumption of an eventual viewer. The artists can't fully experience the effect of their work on others, and in this sense cannot make finite claims over its meaning. Rather than providing the general autobiographical reason for a work, it would seem more pertinent to consider the work devoid of the artist and as an object amongst a history of objects.

Art suffers the obligations of its optical presence, and considerations of sight often eclipse thought. It is nevertheless interesting how some people actually receive our work. We experience the greatest ferocity from critics assuming a Pavlovian sense of disgust or outrage on the part of others who they never identify—the unknown people who they assume they represent by their melodramatic outrage.

The simple interpretive inaccuracies can be quite astonishing. For instance, in the sequence of works that allude to the industrial genocide of the twentieth centaury, often the work is reduced to the specificity of the Holocaust, despite the work containing anachronistic figures such as Steven Hawking or Ronald McDonald, Adam and Eve, skeletons, and ten-headed mutants. In fact, [given] the inversion that places Nazis in the subordination to violence, the work should really appear as a mirrored opposite to reality. We have, of course, encouraged misreadings in the work. For instance, in the series of "Siamese twin" sculptures, the permutational anomalies seem quite commonly to provoke an insistence above all else to ascribe features that are not appropriate to what is being presented—to ascribe gender (usually female), to describe them as monstrous (as compared to what?)—to assert that they are children (of exactly which parents?). We like to think of these works as Geiger counters for interpretive idiocy, a device for extorting vulgar Freudian assumptions about inhuman or nonhuman bodies.

What can art therefore offer to us in terms of rethinking what it means to be human?

Homo sapiens has evolved an ontology that allows each and every member of its species to believe that it is a monadic entity—an indivisible existential unit, unlike any other—a species of one. And in believing in such a rarefied ontology, it has merely caused a hideous social intimacy, resulting in the alienated angst of civilized being. Part of modern anxiety and the terror of modern life insists the only solution is to return to some natural order of things. But nature is not a useful horizon to compare technological anxiety against since human technology is absolutely synchronous with nature.

There's a nice linear analogue about the evolutionary relation of art and science. Once upon a time, in a dark and dank cave. Someone is furiously rubbing sticks together to make enough light for the purpose of someone else who is painting very elegant antelopes on the wall with charcoal from earlier-rubbed sticks. After the passing of a magnitude of time, the technological trajectory of rubbing sticks gives rise to the combustion engine, and all the earth's resources are eventually marshaled so that a rocket can be sent into space. A parallel evolution also occurs, such that the antelope paintings emerge from the cave into the world and at the apex of modernity are embodied in the paintings of Jackson Pollock. For science, human thought has reached the stars, but for art, the splashes of paint chucked on canvas on the floor betrays a break with linearity, a break with the assumption of pictorial representation—pictures that are literally "worse" than the elegant antelopes.

This represents something of the real genius of the trajectory of art. Even those who profess its linearity are forced to accept the failure of a stable communicative ideal. Imagine a Martian anthropologist coming to Earth to explore its excoriated ruins. They might gravitate to the ruins of places known to have symbolic importance like the Tate; they might wander across the rubble toppled by some extinction event, stepping over piles of loose bricks without ever knowing they were Carl Andres's sculpture.

As humans there is something we can certainly take from this. Or to put it more directly, how can we learn to live with the unrepresentable and the incommunicable as the most potent aspect of our creative expressions?

I know you have spoken at length about the influence Goya has had over your work, which resulted in your own adapted series In-sult to Injury. What is it about his work that continues to capture your attention?

Our engagement with Goya has been to amplify and tease out some of the truly monstrous elements of his work—the divine violence—that are routinely suppressed by the assertion that this is simply some humanist chronicle of atrocity. Goya understood better than anybody the seductive nature of violence and our social need to have its images continually reproduced. And yet he doesn't refrain from showing not only systemic violence but divine violence. Take *Great Deeds Against the Dead*, for example, from the Disasters of War series. This image is particularly heretic because it denies the idea that this sagging Newtonian flesh can be redeemed from the physics that will see it eventually melt into soil. The systemic murder of these three figures utilizes violence for the purpose of a warning to others, but the divine violence exhibits the heresy of gravity, acting upon their bodies indifferently, without purpose. Thus this image was a massive act of violence upon the world.

But Goya also understands the resonances which continue to carry over into the modern period. The cross becomes the tree, just as religious redemption becomes material redemption, so that it is still nonetheless symbolic and still charged with theological and erotic traces. Goya's brilliance then is about the materiality of the body overlaid arguably with even greater symbolic resonance and purpose.

The body that hangs, the body that drips, the body that is mutilated for the sake of it—it's not redemptive optimism that conveys meaning but the profound nihilism and self-doubt that characterizes the modern world. Goya grounds the metaphysics of sacrifice in full modern glory.

You have once talked about violence as being the absolutely neces-sary conditions of life. This reminded me of Nietzsche's earlier provocation that to live is to forever be in danger, such that we suffer into truth. How can we reflect upon this in light of contem-porary world events?

Let's take the example of Trump here. Not only has he dis-avowed truth, he's proved very adept at creating the condi-tions which continually deny his own truth. It's fully incapac-itating. Whatever he utters has no value. And yet it has been mobilized to devastating effect. That's its real genius. This is beyond crude Orwellianism, for it points to the production of a system of language that has no foundation in truth what-soever and purposefully dispenses with it. And yet there is a danger here that we lament some position of liberal purity, as if that period in history wasn't also full of violence. Indeed, it is precisely the neoliberals who are reducing politics to aesthetics and mere intuition, as if Trump and his followers don't aspire to the aesthetic model of puritanical liberalism.

I'm rewriting *1984* at the moment—my version is *1984.1.* If you think about Orwell's critique of freedom in the original text, it is ultimately posed in the form of free capitalist choice. Orwell has his enslaved populations to wear overalls, the food is bland, they are stuck in bureaucratic models of Stalinist non-production, and so forth. Orwell's disdain is that his fictional society is materially impoverished, and their desire has no correlation in the world for things that they could purchase as a voluntary choice. I'm interested that the greatest threat that one is supposed to imagine, certainly Orwell, is the subtraction of choice—this leads me back to the idea of the species of one, the construction of choice as the delirium of being but being a population nonetheless. In my version, Winston is a poet, struggling with the idea of a perfect liberal society—a man robbed not of choice but angst.

It is clear you ground your work in some complex philosophical debates. Which philosophers have come to inform your work?

I have always been interested in the works of Nietzsche, Bataille, and Deleuze and Guattari. Accelerationism is interesting, certainly because it describes a chaos of positions, contesting thought without squeamishness. Accelerationism is less a philosophical movement than it is the combination of all (antagonized and antagonistic) reactions to the gravitation pull of capitalism. I'm interested in an excruciating vivisection of the Enlightenment and the oppressive nature of the liberal instinct but not for the purpose of some fascistic feudal future. In fact, I'm quite tickled by the idea that capitalism might be accelerated until it collapses in favor of some new libertarian society—it's as if romantic idealism is just reconstituted at the end of history again—that the reward of chaos is some eventually ludicrous idyllic ideal.

We are, as you mentioned, living in turbulent and politically fraught times. What can the arts offer to us in coming to terms with the state of the world?

There is nothing more vicious than managerial capitalism. As for the arts, the notion of optimism has always troubled me. I'm not a fan of art becoming melancholic. Melancholia still holds out hope that its desires might or should be taken notice of and eventually met—or at least becomes an economy of pleasure in itself. Art can best abstain from culture within culture. The idea that we are now in a position where art feels like it has something to say merely misses the point, that this has always been the position—except the things it was always saying [were] supporting the doctrine of liberal humanism, which is exactly why we are where we are. Would I like art to say something—maybe—but not if it becomes a positivist vehicle for doing away with the tragic or the pessimistic. The danger for the art is in replicating its default position—to confront the right with dominant hegemonic liberal tyranny.

The call to arms against Trump—"we shall not be divided"—should not be a request to conglomerate, it also implies a political stability that has somehow been disrupted, which is even less than a trite Orwellian fantasy. Our aim should be to keep dividing ourselves until we are invisible. The aggregation of life into indivisible cultural monads is really terrifying to me. It's self-indulgent. It's narcissistic. And it should be resisted at all costs.

TWENTY-THREE

AFFECT, POWER, AND VIOLENCE: THE POLITICAL IS NOT PERSONAL

With affect, the political becomes directly felt. This has all kinds of implications for political practice. To act politically is to occupy potential.

To think is to feel, and to act means that truth can be felt in a variety of modes, including those that are prejudicial and uncritical. No author has rethought the importance of the concept of "affect" better than Brian Massumi. Discussing his continued fascination with the felt order of politics and why the visceral is integral to any critique of power and violence, Massumi reflects upon the continued importance of the concept in terms of providing more nuances in our conceptualizations, what he understands by the term "violence," his concerns with structural violence and its disempowering approach to questions of ontology and viable forms of political resistance, and why the political is not personal.

Brad Evans interviews Brian Massumi

November 13, 2017

Brian Massumi specializes in the philosophy of experience, art and media theory, and political philosophy. His recent books include *What Animals Teach Us about Politics*, *Politics of Affect*, and *99 Theses on the Revaluation of Value*.

Brad Evans: Amongst the many contributions you have made in your work, you are particularly known for innovatively developing the concept of affect. How do you understand this concept, and why is it relevant for understanding power?

Brian Massumi: I appreciate the question, because there tends to be a misunderstanding that affect is about only personal experience. Because of that supposed emphasis on the interiority of the individual, it is often thought that affect is by nature apolitical. For me, it has always been the exact opposite. I was attracted to the concept because of how directly political it is. It is a power concept through and through.

The basic definition that I keep coming back to comes from Spinoza, who spoke of "powers to affect and be affected" as what defines a body and a life. A power to affect and be affected is a potential to move, act, perceive, and think—in a word, powers of existence. The "to be affected" part of the definition says that a body's powers of existence are irreducibly relational. They can only be expressed in dynamic relation with other bodies and elements of the environment. The power to affect and the power to be affected are inseparable; they are two sides of the same coin. They are reciprocals, growing and shrinking as a function of each other. So, from the start, affect overspills the individual, tying its capacities to its relational entanglement with others and the outside. Affect is fundamentally trans-individual.

The word "power" here is in the first instance not power-over. It is power-to. Affect grasps life from the angle of its activity, its exuberance, its drive to express always more of a body's powers of existence or potential to be, in an always irreducibly relational way, in attunement with the affordances of the outside. It is an expansive concept and a concept of expression. Each act expresses powers of existence and varies them, affecting and being affected in a way unique to that circumstance, so that every act of being is also a modification that takes its place in an ongoing becoming. Power-to is the power to change. That is the starting point: a nonlimitative concept of power as life-enhancing and life-changing, through an openness onto the outside.

The problem then is to account for power-over, which limits power-to and curtails becoming through repression or the normative channeling of activity. By this account, power-over is emergent. It is not foundational. It is not a general, abstract force or Law with a capital L. It is a particular result, a kind of achievement. Like every achievement, it can come undone or be undone. It has to continually work to maintain itself. This means it is always manifesting its weaknesses, even as it exerts its sway. This is empowering politically because it makes change and the affirmation of powers of life primary and attributes them their own power—as a kind of directly affirmative, primary resistance.

Through this conceptualization of power, what you also seem to be proposing is a different concept of politics and the political.

This concept of power expands the realm of the political beyond its usual connotation of formations of domination, containment by institutions, and channeling by norms. It extends it to a level of emergence where positive powers of existence are stirring and vying to express themselves, laying claim to an autonomy of becoming. Power-to is a strange amalgam: it refers to a relational autonomy. This extension of the concept of power is often spoken of in terms of a distinction between "the political" (the autonomous expression of relational powers of existence as primary resistance) and "politics." Politics is the capture of powers of existence, turned against their own expansion and enhancement.

This might sound very abstract, but it's actually all about intensities of experience. There is a third part of the definition which says that a power to affect and be affected always manifests itself eventfully, in a transition, a passing of a threshold across which a body's powers of existence are either augmented or diminished. They are raised to a higher power or curtailed. This transition to a higher or lower power-to is felt as a shift in a body's intensity of existence, its capacity to be all that it can express, and express more of what it can do.

With affect, the political becomes directly felt. This has all kinds of implications for political practice. For one thing, it opens the way for a fundamentally aesthetic approach to politics, taking "aesthetic" in something close to its etymological meaning as pertaining to qualities of experience. But it also closes the door on the limiting idea that if you are talking about qualities and intensities of experience, you are talking about subjective interiority. Here you're talking about intensities of relation that register individually, while directly making a difference in the world. These pertain to the individual's autonomy of expression of its powers to be, but only to the extent that that expression is participatory, directly and dynamically entangled with the outside.

I'd like to bring this conceptual insight directly to the question of violence. What does the word "violence" mean to you from a political and philosophical perspective?

It is clear that the concept of violence cannot be reduced to direct, bodily violence. Violence is not only in the act. It also acts in potential. It operates even when it doesn't pass fully into action. This is widely acknowledged in political discourse concerned with "structural violence" and "microaggression." But from an affect philosophy perspective, the concept of structural violence is questionable. It is too broad. It makes violence into that kind of general, abstract force that underlies every situation and every act like an inescapable foundation.

This is a profoundly disempowering notion. It puts the individual at the mercy of forces that are not just circumstantially more powerful than it is by several orders of magnitude but are essentially so. It is hard to see how what is founded—the individual life—can escape or counteract its foundation—its formatting by power in that overpoweringly abstracts understanding of it.

The concept of affect offers two strategies here. The first is to define violence as power-over: the curtailment of the power-to. This acknowledges that violence is not reducible to the punctual acts that bring it to full expression in bodily aggression. It can act in and as its own potential. Violence can be as oppressive in the way it looms over us as an unspoken threat that is applied unequally, depending on the color of a body's skin, its gender, and other conventional markers that the exercise of power-over uses selectively to trigger itself into operation.

The second is to say that even though violence looms everywhere all the time, it never does so in a general way. Even as a threat, it is a particular operation. Or, more accurately, a particular way of being in pre-operation. To have any effect, the threat, as potential for violence, has to make itself felt in some way. To make itself felt, it has to introduce itself into each situation into which it moves. It has to make ingress, and it does this affectively. "Structural" violence is no less an event than the swing of a club. But it is a directly affective event which diminishes a body's expressive powers of existence even without actually lifting a finger. "Priming" is a way of talking about what kind of event this entering into pre-operation is.

Priming is the way in which the conditions set up for a situation implant certain tendencies in it. That is what I meant by pre-operation: being present in tendency. This conditioning-in of tendencies is contingent on signs, including but not limited to the bodily markers I just mentioned. Violence in the broader sense affectively "in-signs" itself into situations. The priming of the situation is the way it signposts that a conversion of the power-to into an exercise of power-over is imminent, looming over every action, on the brink of coming fully into act.

As I said, this in-signing is itself a kind of act or event. This means that it is possible to respond to the violence making potential ingress on the same plane on which it operates: that of live events. There may be an inkling of a potential to alter-prime the event toward a different set of conditions, activating different tendencies. This amounts to taking back potential. To act politically is to occupy potential.

Might we not also apply this logic of violence as potential to the concept of resistance?

Yes, violence is everywhere all the time, effectively in potential—but so is resistance. There is a primary resistance that is always churning, always vying, always pushing toward the augmentation of powers of life. And this can be performed. It can be enacted in a way that it is attuned to the ingression of violence in that particular situation, countering it head-on or clandestinely evading it. This brings things to a down-to-earth tactical level, which can save us from the paralysis that the over-arching general concept of structural violence can easily create. How can a mere part resist such a foundational whole? How can you fight a generality when your existence is always local?

The idea here is that the "general" violence has to make itself enter into each particular situation in which it wants to hold sway, but that ingression is always already met with primary resistance—and where there is resistance there is some degree of freedom in how a body is affected and can affect. The need to make ingression, rather than just being in place a priori, introduces a degree of play, in the sense in which we say a mechanism has play, which can potentially be exploited in situ to confound the operation of power-over. It opens the way for an affirmative "micro-politics" in response to the ever-renewed background conditions of micro-aggression and the punctual macro-explosions of outright violence that they hold in ready reserve.

The trick is to avoid responding on the same general level on which the violence seems to operate. Don't take it at face value. That only gives it more power. Always remember that power has to adapt itself to each situation, and that means that there is always a chance that resistance can counter-adapt itself on the fly—if it is affectively attuned to the singularity of each exercise of power. To do this, you have to live out the situational intensity of this experience, here and now, in all its complexities and sinuosities.

Principles are not enough. Critical judgment is not enough. Being "woke" is not enough. These are necessary, but they are raised to a higher power if they are used not as ends in themselves and not as general strategies but as avenues toward an affective attunement to the event in its singularity. That sets the conditions for more than a frontal response, in reaction to the threat of violence—which just weds you to the form of the aggression. When you think about it, reacting is just a contrary way of being constrained by what you are reacting against.

Affective attunement sets the conditions for a tactical power to improvise a response that is not dictated by the aggression as a reaction to it, in mirror-image form, but rather claims its own positivity, in eventful autonomy and relation, artfully playing to what is concretely being in-signed and enacted, refusing conversion by power-over while avoiding embodying its negative image. The emphasis then is on affirming counter-powers of moving, acting, perceiving, thinking that decide their own form as they enact themselves.

This gives resistance a plastic power-to in the face of power-over's ability to insinuate itself into every situation. It requires honing different modes of action, creating new sets of affective skills and tactics that are as aesthetic—because they are improvisational and affirm intensities of experience—as they are directly political because they are by nature relational and are all the more plastic and powerful the more relationally attuned they are and the more collectively they are mobilized.

So how does this notion of relationality relate back to your concerns with the personal?

Personalizing narratives actually occlude this affirmative power of resistance, because they are focused first on defining the present event in terms of the individual's past and only then look to opening the collective future in a break from narratives from the past. Yes, the personal is political. The personal is never untouched by the accumulated effects of power. It is never free of power effects and the traces of their violence. These are part and parcel of its very constitution. But precisely for that reason, the converse is not the case: the political is not personal.

The political is a collective break from the accumulating effects of power inherited from the past, claiming the right of ingress in the present. The political is what breaks through the personal, shattering the hold of the accumulated power effects that are part and parcel of its constitution, liberating self-affirming powers of primary resistance that co-occur with identity but do not belong to it, that are not contained in it but pass through and around it, that open instead onto the outside, onto new affective vistas of collective becoming. We live toward the future trans-individually, in excess over our personhood. The political is not coming home to a familiar face. The political is estrangingly intensive. It is rewilding. In its movement, we are strangers to ourselves. We meet ourselves anew as the animal we are just now becoming. The political acts in the name of a life we have not lived. It acts for the life we have yet to live.

Connecting this to the rise of Donald Trump in the United States, how can we make sense of this phenomenon, especially in terms of the liberation of prejudice?

Trump is an extreme example of the power of the personal and the personal as power. When I say that, I mean something very different than it might sound like. I don't mean that he embodies the "rugged individual" of American mythology or the old civic model of upright personhood, like the nineteenth-century ideal of the sovereign, self-governing individual as paragon of capitalist virtue providing a moral compass for entrepreneurial activity with which others identify and strive to emulate. This is the traditional theory of political leadership based on "identification" with a charismatic figure.

Nothing could be further from the Trump post-truth. There is nothing either particularly rugged or morally upright about him. His personality is not a bulwark against the excesses of capitalism. It's an opening of the floodgates. He does not stand in his person against capitalism's excesses—he flows with them. It is he who is identified with those excesses rather than others who are identified with him. He won election precisely because of his supposed capitalist prowess, in the one of the most corrupt sectors of the economy. He is the personification of capital.

This is precisely how neoliberalism strives to redefine the person: as "human capital" or what Foucault calls the "entrepreneur of himself." But what is this "himself"? It has no consistency. Trump says one thing one the day, something else the next. The center does not hold. There is no center. There is just an eddy of bluster on the roiling seas of social media. Trump personifies the deregulating tendencies of neoliberal capitalism. Through him, the "creative destruction" at the heart of capitalism's movements extend to the emotional composition of the person, now border-line, post-normative, trading in cartoonish exaggerations of the erstwhile norm, refracted through the distorting prism of a white hypermasculinity bloated to absurd dimensions. It is hard to take Trump seriously as a person. This is reflected in the colloquial use of his name as a common noun: the Donald.

The Donald embodies a certain hypercapitalist, overcoming of the person. His followers do not identify with him in the sense of recognizing themselves in him. Through his bluster, they identify themselves with capitalism's deregulated overspilling of the norms. They embrace the ideal of being "entrepreneurs of themselves," in "politically incorrect" excess over regulated norms of behavior. By what criterion is there an identity or sameness between a billionaire born into wealth and privilege and a middle American in the Rust Belt with the fear of God in them about falling into poverty (if they are not already in it)? Weirdly, it is less that Trumpians are recognizing themselves in his sameness than that they are *recognizing their own difference* in his distorted mirror. They are seeing what they experience as their own exceptionalism: what makes them special as Americans, vis-à-vis the hated "un-American Americans" ("liberal progressives," the "mainstream media," the "deep state" establishment, immigrant "job-stealers," "entitled" African Americans—the list is long).

This occurs not through Trump's person in any traditional sense but through his *persona*. His obsession with

Twitter and cable TV makes him a single-body media node. He lives for it. His life-form is inseparable from it. His person is an ongoing media irritation, an affective resonater, nodally positioned. He receives with a shudder waves of social and political static and no sooner sends them back out with a Twitter spasm, in a self-perpetuating cycle. This operates in a way that primes the social field for just the kind of ever-present threat and violence I was talking about earlier. The Trump figure is an *affective converter* of power-to into a contagion of power-over disseminating through the social field—a one-man epidemic of reaction-formation. But this is the strange phenomenon of a proactive reaction.

Here reactivity is affirmed as such. It is practiced as an offensive sport or, better, a war machine ever on the attack, rather than in self-defense. This is beyond "prejudice." It is a veritable mode of existence, affectively primed. There is no time left to go more into detail about this. The main point is that an affective approach to politics might offer some new conceptual tools for understanding the originality of the Trump phenomenon. We do ourselves no favors if we try to respond to it with obsolete conceptions about politics and persons. We are in uncharted, post-truth, deregulated territory, and we need new modes of understanding and resistance to be equal to the challenge of collectively reopening the potential of our quickly foreclosing future.

TWENTY-FOUR

THE INTIMATE LIFE OF VIOLENCE

Cognitive anarchy is something from which we can probably recover but only if we become capable of thinking symmetrically, if we relearn how to imagine the way the world looks from the perspective of an opponent, and if we practice reattaching words to their true referents.

Elaine Scarry's book *The Body in Pain* is a landmark text in terms of how we understand suffering and the victim. It addresses the intimate realities of violence and the ways personal injury are often revealing of much wider historical processes that mark the body with violent ascriptions. The body in pain is also a wounded and deeply violated social form. Reflecting upon the book's contemporary relevance, Scarry offers new insight into the question of trauma and victimhood in light of the changing nature of warfare and torture and the future role for the humanities in developing meaningful critique while reclaiming human dignity.

Brad Evans interviews Elaine Scarry

December 7, 2017

Elaine Scarry is an American essayist and professor of English and American literature and language. She is the Walter M. Cabot Professor of Aesthetics and the General Theory of Value at Harvard University. The author of many books, Elaine's work has been pioneering in rethinking the relationship between violence, the body, and trauma as a political and social category.

Brad Evans: Your earlier book The Body in Pain *was widely recognized for pushing forward our understanding of the intimate realities of violence as both a personal and political problem. Some twenty years after its initial publication, how has your understanding of human pain and suffering developed?*

Elaine Scarry: Some studies of suffering are historically specific; others are transcultural. Both kinds of studies are needed. My own approach in *The Body in Pain* was transcultural. The book gives a structural account of the place of pain and bodily injury in war and in torture and in doing so draws on instances of torture and war from many different geographies and, in the case of war, many different time periods.

It would have surprised me greatly if the practice of torture or war—following the publication of *The Body in Pain*—changed its form in the late twentieth and early twenty-first centuries, and as far as I can see it did not. (Had the book instead been looking at historically specific attributes of, say, World War II injuries, one might expect to see changes in these attributes.) Regimes use torture when they have lost legitimate forms of substantiation. True to that model, the United States began sanctioning torture after it suffered an unprecedented crisis of self-belief.

On 9/11, on a single morning, the population collectively witnessed the fact that the Pentagon could not defend the Pentagon, let alone the rest of the country. This stunning revelation might have led to a widespread debate about our capacity for defense and the way our military is trained for overseas wars of aggression but not for protection of the United States home ground (as I argued in *Who Defended the Country?* and later in *Rule of Law, Misrule of Man*). Instead of examining our defense and changing it, we quickly rebuilt the same Pentagon and switched to a shorthand form of demonstrating our prowess, namely torturing people at Abu Ghraib and alternative dark sites. Other severe moral and legal prohibitions—such as the army, navy, and air force handbook prohibitions on misusing the white flag and Red Cross, as well as the prohibitions on assassination—were abrogated by the United States during our wars in Iraq and Afghanistan in this same period.

The deeper the crisis of doubt and the higher the danger is [the more likely it is] that a country will rely on a grotesque mimesis of power such as torture or nuclear weapons. That's why when I see President Trump mocked and exposed for his untruths, I feel fear. His untruths should be rigorously and continually challenged and exposed, but the liberal press seems to have concluded—and perhaps they are not wrong—that this can only be done by every day humiliating him, every day scorning him. But this may put people elsewhere in the world in danger because constant belittlement may reinforce our president's own inclinations, acknowledged during the election campaign, to use magnified forms of compensatory power. When Nixon boasted, "I can go into the next room, pick up the phone, and in twenty-five minutes seventy million people will be dead," it is not coincidental that he was in the midst of an impeachment proceeding—that is, he was in the midst of being divested of legitimate forms of authority.

Can you elaborate more on the use of torture and its relationship between perpetrators and victims?

The phrase "compensatory drama" again calls attention to the continuity between the structural features visible in the historical events cited in *The Body in Pain* and the attributes of parallel events in our contemporary world. In Vietnam in the 1970s, the torture room was called "the cinema room"; in the Philippines, it was called "the production room"; in Chile, it was called "the blue-lit stage." The cruelty at Abu Ghraib was elaborately photographed; it was meant to be viewed by the prison guards and torturers (perhaps even for their pleasure, or their sense of triumph—hence the famous "thumbs up" picture). Because the events had been photographed, Joseph Darby—a twenty-first-century hero—was able to turn in the pictures to military authorities, inform the world, and document the wrongdoing. But the scenes, used as screensavers on prison computers, were not photographed in order to provide legal evidence of wrongdoing, just as the hours-upon-hours of CIA videotaping of "enhanced interrogations" at hidden detention sites were not meant to provide legal documentation. For whose eyes were those videotapes made? Not for any third-party review. The CIA destroyed their library of films, an act that led to the Senate's six thousand-page investigation into CIA torture.

In our own era, as in the past eras described in *The Body in Pain*, the torturer uses the interrogation not to get any valid information (the 2015 *Senate Report on CIA Torture* documents the total absence of useful information obtained through "enhanced interrogation") but to demonstrate how large-scale is his own world when juxtaposed to the tiny shreds of a world remaining to the prisoner. After waterboarding, the prisoner's voice is so small that in the case of Abu Zubaydah, when he tried to speak CIA memos record that he had only "bubbles rising through his open, full mouth"; in the case of Khalid Sbaykh Muhammad (waterboarded 183 times in fifteen sessions), he "expressed water when the abdomen was pressed." Vast, in comparison, is the voice of the torturer whose questions show that he is not just the valiant representative of his country but the noble representative of the whole earth, trying to find the location of the "ticking bomb." When two of the main CIA interrogators —psychologists Bruce Jessen and James Mitchell— wanted to cease their participation, the authorities under whom they served, [one of them said,] "kept telling me every day that a nuclear bomb was going to be exploded in the United States, and that because I had told them to stop . . . it was going to be my fault." I have written about the preposterous ticking-bomb pseudo-license for torture (in an essay called "Five Errors in the Reasoning of Alan Dershowitz") and here will only add one fact: 93 percent of the 14,900 active nuclear weapons currently in the world are in the hands of two persons, the American president and the Russian president. If we are trying to rid the world of ticking bombs we have a clear, question-free place to start.

A structural account of torture in any era reveals that interrogators seek, through the infliction of physical pain, to bring about a collapse of the contents of consciousness in the mind of the prisoner. In addition, they simultaneously enact this world-destroying power using the torture room itself. Even though an explicit instrument of torture will usually be present, the windows, doors, walls, and ceiling of the room will be enlisted into the torture in order to dramatize the world collapse. In the third quarter of the twentieth century, Basques imprisoned by Spanish suffered *el cerrojo*, the rapid and repeated bolting and unbolting of the door; in Portugal, gibberish was read at the door; in the Colonels' Regime in Greece, prisoners were punished for looking out the window, and were made to repeat the line, "make way, wall, that I may pass." The dark sites inhabited by twenty-first-century American interrogators show the same act of dismantling the basic unit of civilization. "Walling"—a form of torture in which prisoners are repeatedly bounced off a flexible wall—reappears throughout the 2015 *Senate Report*. So too does the closing-in of walls: Abu Zubaydah spent 266 hours in a large coffin; he spent twenty-nine hours in a small box that was twenty-one inches high, 2.5 feet long, and 2.5 feet wide.

In our own era, as in the past, the dismantling of civilization in the unmaking of the shelter is echoed in the importing of major institutions—medicine and law—into the torture room. Two physicians, Bruce Jessen and James Mitchell, are currently on trial for designing and overseeing the CIA interrogation experiments. Law was similarly dismantled: John Yoo, in the White House Office of Legal Counsel, sought to exonerate torture in a memorandum arguing that the infliction of suffering on prisoners did not count as torture unless it entailed the level of pain associated with physical injury so severe it would result in organ failure, death, or permanent loss of body function. Though the Justice Department later rescinded Yoo's memorandum—and though the Yoo standard has been almost universally disavowed—it should be noted that the infliction of suffering did in fact meet the Yoo standard, as evidenced by the organ failure and death of three prisoners—one by hyperthermia, one by heart failure, one by pulmonary embolism—each of whom was subjected to forms of pain equally suffered by many other prisoners.

Your work continually insists that any serious and meaningful critique of violence must deal with the question of trauma. But how are we to make sense of this when we seem to be living in terrifyingly normal times?

Are we living in terrifyingly normal times? I feel we are living in a time of cognitive anarchy. In the opening years of the twenty-first century, we collectively failed to keep a moral compass. We tortured and then, as a nation, shrugged off the question of whether officials who authorized the torture should be prosecuted (international law says prosecution is not discretionary in the case of torture). It felt better to forgive and forget. Leave it up to the executive branch; let each new president decide. Not surprisingly, polls by the International Committee of Red Cross/ Red Crescent show a decline in the percentage of people who recognize the prohibition on torture as an absolute. But torture, as Jeremy Waldron points out, is the line in the sand. The prohibition on torture is fundamental; it's the bedrock which if removed lets the structure of law (and the framework of thinking about right and wrong) waver. If we cease to be able to speak clear sentences about torture, then our ability to speak clear sentences about many other things erodes as well and . . . lo and behold, fifteen years later we wake up and find ourselves in the midst of blather.

Cognitive anarchy is something from which we can probably recover but only if we become capable of thinking symmetrically, if we relearn how to imagine the way the world looks from the perspective of an opponent, and if we practice reattaching words to their true referents. For example, when we use the words "nuclear weapon," instead of attaching the term (as we did between 2001 and 2016) exclusively to the names of countries that do not have nuclear weapons (e.g., Iraq, Iran) or to countries that have a tiny number (e.g., North Korea, which until last year had between two and ten), we could practice attaching the term to a country (United States) that actually has thousands and keeps them on alert round the clock and has them pre-assigned to cities all over the globe.

One of the real challenges we face today is holding on to the idea that the world can be changed for the better. This seems especially acute when confronting the almost daily attacks upon human dignity and selfhood. From a political and philosophical perspective, how might we better resource the arts and humanities better to counter the systematic negation of life?

Because certain aspects of the world are so starkly wrong, it is easy to see how the world can be changed for the better. (If the world were wrong in some intricate or obscure way, we would be in much less trouble, but it might be harder to sort out what needs to be changed.) For example, we have a gigantic nuclear architecture that is potentially planet-destroying. That destruction can, on a single afternoon, be set in motion by a handful of individual human beings, whether presidents or nonstate actors or hackers. Yet disassembling this nuclear architecture is comparatively easy. Scotland has shown us how to do it in a report—judged realistic by former members of our military—that shows some parts of the dismantling can be accomplished in hours (disassembling the nuclear triggers), other parts will take days, still other parts months, up to several years. Compare this to the difficulty of stopping global warming: the need to halt climate change is crystal clear but how to do it is not. The northern hemisphere (that currently contains all the nuclear states) can model itself on the southern hemisphere (almost totally blanketed with Nuclear Weapons-Free Treaties). We have a template of repair right in front of our eyes. And once the international ban on nuclear weapons is confirmed in the UN this September, the nuclear states will have an assembly of other countries encouraging them in their undertaking of disarmament.

Will the humanities provide the tool that is needed to disassemble the nuclear triggers? It's not impossible that the answer is yes. Over the past seventy years, the lynchpin of our nuclear architecture has been the arrangement for "presidential first use of a nuclear weapon"—the presidential launch of a weapon before any other country has fired one. This coming November, Harvard's Mahindra Humanities Center and its Office of the Dean of Arts and Humanities will be the lead cosponsors of a conference in Cambridge: "Presidential First Use: Is It Legal? Is It Constitutional? Is It Just?" The speakers include philosophers, constitutional theorists, a physicist, a mathematician, a former secretary of defense, a former missile launch officer, an anthropologist, a congressman. I believe this is the first public meeting or conference on the question, and if the question spreads across the country, if it comes to be asked by a large number of people, the tool that can be dissemble the triggers—an educated citizenry—will be close at hand.

While that outcome is very uncertain, what is not uncertain is the fact the six-thousand years of philosophy and literature have been addressing, and showing the concrete path of reversing, the human impulse toward totalizing destruction. You think you can shoot a nuclear missile and destroy the earth's forests? Read Gilgamesh, written in 4000 BCE, and learn what happens when you try to kill off the giant cedars. You want to melt the human form with nuclear weapons and napalm? Read the Iliad, written in 800 BCE, and see what happens when you hope to desecrate the human form by dragging corpses around the city. These writings are not just prohibitions on violence; they are cognitive maps for how to climb out of the pit of our own cruelty. When I addressed your question about *The Body in Pain*, I only referred to its opening on torture documents. The book goes on to an extended account of the way the Judeo-Christian scriptures and the philosophic writing of Marx show how the impulse toward annihilation is an aping of creation. Crucially, these books, step-by-step, disentangle that lethal confusion between invention and annihilation—the confusion we are in the midst of today. My recent book *Thermonuclear Monarchy* contains an extended account of the way Thomas Hobbes translated *The Iliad*. His word choices show how he foregrounded, credited, and celebrated the dissent of the individual soldier. And it is the dissent of individual citizen soldiers (missile launch officers, secretaries of defense, citizen soldiers) that can dismantle thermonuclear monarchy.

You may think—because humanities departments have had money taken away from them and because universities are currently in a period of self-sabotage by eliminating the professoriate and replacing them with barely paid adjunct positions—that the humanities will soon cease to be of help. We can put this on the list of easy-to-discern wrongs in need of repair. But, in the meantime, two observations.

While universities—and above all the humanities—appear to be greatly undervalued in the public media, there are many signs that they are instead an object of emulation and aspiration. Many tech companies are organized as "campuses." The TED talks are modeled on (and often draw on) faculty lectures. The fascinating intellectual website *Edge*—that each year asks thinkers to address a specific question—is a floating university. Cities, high-tech companies, and television stars all often urge their "followers" to read and discuss together a particular book.

Second, the humanities have deep civilization-shaping influence in spite of—perhaps even because of—the way they appear minimal, unobtrusive, unimportant. Take one example, the revolutionary new institution of gay marriage. If there is a single pivotal day and location to be credited, it is a Massachusetts court, presided over by Margaret Marshall, on May 17, 2004. But in the background are several decades of literature department courses on gay literature; cross-country university and city bookstores with sections dedicated to gay literature; nightly films and TV stories about same-sex partners.

When Shelley [says] poets are the "unacknowledged legislators of the world," we tend to place the emphasis on the word "legislators." And that is right: gay marriage isn't gay marriage until it stops being an airy nothing and becomes a matter of law. But the word "unacknowledged" may be equally important. Undervalued, under-credited, dismissed, the humanities quietly do their work and only now and then stand up to take a bow.

Even when the humanities do not appear to be in the midst of repairing civic wrongs, they are often surreptitiously carrying out that work. The objects residing at the center of inquiry—the visual arts, the verbal arts, great philosophic treatises—are objects of beauty. Like objects of beauty in the natural world, they increase our capacity for fairness by decentering us, enabling us to step outside ourselves and stand on the margins. They remind us what symmetry looks like at a time when our weapons, our money, and the size of the cars we drive are vastly out of proportion to the rest of the world. They affirm the life pact by bringing about in us higher levels of perceptual acuity and by, in turn, requiring that we treat them with care and protection, as though they were living entities. Themselves laden with the secrets of creating, they incite in viewers and readers acts of creation, which will then bring new art works and treatises—new objects of beauty—into the world.

TWENTY-FIVE

NEURO-DIVERSITY AND THE POLICING OF THE NORM

Isn't it at the germinal level that the political has the most potential for reorientation or even reinvention?

To place limits upon what it means to think and act in the world is a form of violence. This is especially acute when it comes to questions of "disability" and issues of perception regarding mental faculties for "reasonable" thought. Addressing the violence of policing neuro-diversity, critical philosopher and artist Erin Manning discusses the question of the neuro-political, especially how neoliberal societies produce violent forms of exclusion to those considered to differ from the neurotypical norm (notably autism) and what we might learn from autistic modes of perception.

Brad Evans interviews Erin Manning

January 2, 2018

Erin Manning holds a university research chair in relational art and philosophy at Concordia University. Director of the SenseLab, her recent books include *Always More than*

One: Individuation's Dance and *Relationscapes: Movement, Art, Philosophy.*

Brad Evans: Your work has for some time addressed fundamental questions around what it means to think and act in the world. This has invariably raised questions about limit conditions and forms of disavowal. Why are you interested in the neuro-political, and how does it speak directly to the problem of violence?

Erin Manning: I have never considered the concept of the "neuro-political" in relation to neuro-diversity. It's an interesting proposition, though, so let me think it through with you. Neuro-diversity is a movement that celebrates difference while remaining deeply nuanced on questions of medical facilitation and the necessity of rethinking the concept of accommodation against narratives of cure. The added emphasis on neurology has been necessary in order to challenge existing norms that form the baseline of existence. The "neuro" in neuro-diversity has opened up the conversation about the category of neurotypicality and the largely unspoken criteria that support and reinforce the definition of what it means to be human, to be intelligent, to be of value to society. This has been especially necessary for those folks who continue to be excluded from education [and] social and economic life, who are regarded as less than human, whose modes of relation continue to be deeply misunderstood, and who are cast as burdens to society.

"Classical" autistics fall within this category. As my work has sought to underscore (following the writings of autistics such as Tito Mukhopadhyay, DJ Savarese, Amelia Baggs, Melanie Yergeau, Ido Kedar, Lucy Blackman and many others), not only is the mainstream understanding of autism deeply flawed, autistics have a vital contribution to make precisely due to their neurology. One way in which neurological difference presents itself is through what I call "autistic perception." Autistic perception is a deep sensitivity to the coming-into-itself of form in experience. While all perception includes an edging-into-form, more neurotypically aligned perception in most cases occludes the process itself: objects and subjects are seen and not their process of coming-into-form. Autistic perception dwells in the intersticial, perceiving the process itself. Anne Corwin speaks of neurotypicals as those who "chunk" experience: neurotypicals perceive by categorizing. Autistic perception, on the other hand, troubles categories, feeling-seeing the world coming into itself. Autistic perception is the direct perception of the forming of experience. This has effects: activities which require parsing (crossing the street, finding the path in the forest) can be much more difficult. But there is no question that autistic perception experiences richness in a way the more neurotypically inclined perception rarely does.

As I've suggested at length in both *Always More than One (2013)* and *The Minor Gesture (2016)*, autistic perception is not a mode that should be reduced to autism. First, as every autistic will tell you, there is infinite difference amongst autistics. Second, autistic perception should be seen as a limit case of what accompanies all experience. Nonetheless, I think it's fair to say that this enhanced perceptual field is an aspect of much autistic experience and something neu-rotypicals could learn a lot from, not only with regard to perception itself but [also] as concerns the complexity of experience.

This has direct effects on what is considered a livable life. Much of life as it is organized in neoliberal capitalism works against autistic perception. This is not simply a ques-tion of speed: autistic perception is not necessarily slow. It is rhythmic, moving across relays of experience in-forming. This layering of experience is intense and often overwhelm-ing, particularly in circumstances that deaden complex rhythms, which is certainly the case in the forward-oriented tendencies of contemporary life. This includes education, which tends to be organized not in terms of what is lived but in terms of what needs to be parsed in advance as knowable.

I foreground all of this to underscore that there is a neurological difference, or a spectrum of neurology, that must be attended to. The movement for neuro-diversity is not interested in homogenizing experience. We are differ-ent, and we require different accommodations. On the other hand, my interest is not in the neural per se, which I find quickly loses its usefulness in such discussions, particularly in the ways it can be taken up in the humanities and the social sciences as an explanatory category. The neurological is only one point of departure for the question of autistic perception and of autism more broadly.

So I would say that the concept of the neuro-political is not particularly interesting to me. I want to support the movement for neuro-diversity because I find it exciting and deeply important in its foregrounding of complexity as the baseline. And I want to think about the ways in which an engagement with neuro-diversity affects how we think of the political and how we effect change. The political emphasis here is less on neurology than on the question of how normative modes of being subsumed under the unspoken category of the neurotypical organize experience, and how an engagement with neuro-diversity changes the questions we ask and the actions we support.

How does this concern with such diversity relate directly to the problem of violence?

Neurotypicality is a grounding narrative of exclusion. The neurotypical is the category to which our education systems aspire. It is the category to which our ideas of the nuclear family aspire. And it is the category on which the concept of the citizen (and by extension participation in the nation-state and the wider global economy) is based.

In the context of education, which is the one I am most knowledgeable about, the mechanisms for upholding the neurotypical standard are everywhere in force. Every classroom that penalizes students for distributed modes of attention organizes learning according to a neurotypical norm. Every classroom that sees the moving body as the distracted body is organized according to a neurotypical norm. Every classroom that teaches predominantly for one mode of perception is organizing its learning according to a norm. Every classroom that knows in advance what knowledge looks and sounds like is working to a norm.

Intelligence, understood as the performance of a certain kind of knowledge acquisition and presentation, is built on the scaffold of neurotypicality as the unspoken norm. To speak of the normative tendencies of education is not new. My concern is with what remains largely unspoken in that conversation. Having "special needs" classrooms upholds neurotypicality, for instance, as the dominant model of existence. Drugging our children because of their attention deficit is upholding a neurotypical norm. Sending our black and indigenous children to juvenile detention centers in disproportionate numbers is upholding a neurotypical norm which takes, as neurotypicality always does, whiteness as the standard.

To engage with neuro-diversity is to speak up about the extraordinary silence around neurotypicality and to acknowledge that we do not question ourselves enough as regards what kinds of bodies are welcomed and supported in education and in social life more broadly. It is still far too rare that we discuss neurotypicality as that which frames our ways of knowing, of presenting ourselves, of being bodies in the world.

In any classroom I've ever taught, I would say at least 50 percent of students don't work well with the norm. This may be clearer for me than for other professors because I teach in studio art, where students who have different modes of learning have already been funneled. But my experience is not limited to fine art students: it also includes students in the wider humanities and social sciences. Accommodations are not complicated: facilitating a classroom organization which is not completely frontal and allowing participation to occur in ways that don't privilege eye-contact or allowing for and even generating movement in the classroom are two simple techniques. The accommodations are not mine to make but ours to invent, and each class will do it differently depending on the needs of the participants. And, lest this be seen as an "unserious pursuit" (I wish I didn't have to underline this), these students I speak of are leaders in the field: brilliant writers and artists and philosophers and dancers, folks whose PhDs have become important books, whose teaching practices have deeply affected their students, whose thinking about what else knowledge can look like has altered their practices and continues to orient their politics.

The violence of the norm that is imposed without ever having to be spoken as such is debilitating. Not only does it normalize education, siphoning out difference of all kinds, it forces all bodies who want to be recognized as "knowledgeable" (and thus human) to be organized within an incredibly unimaginative matrix. This violence, of course, plays out far beyond the academic institution, affecting how bodies are considered to have value to society, even allowing certain bodies to be killed or altered to facilitate neurotypical existence (see Not Dead Yet for an account of how neurodiverse and disabled bodies tend not to be given the same life-saving medical treatment; see the Ashley Treatment for medical procedures that allow parents of disabled children to alter their bodies without their consent).

Connecting this more directly to the policing of thought, as you in-
dicate in your work, in order for thought to be recognized as being
meaningful, it needs to conform to pre-set ideas regarding authen-
tic thought processes. Can you elaborate more on this in terms of
the denial of alternative modes of thinking and expression?

I recently wrote an essay entitled "Me Lo Dijo un Pajarito:
Neurodiversity, Black Life and the University As We Know
It," where I engaged this question in detail. One path I
would like to highlight from that piece is the concept of the
free indirect. In *A Thousand Plateaus*, Deleuze and Guattari
write: "Language is not content to go from a first party to a
second party, from one who has seen to one who has not, but
necessarily goes from a second party to a third party, neither
of whom has seen."

Neurotypicality as mode of knowledge policing builds
on what it considers "direct" communication. But language,
as Deleuze and Guattari point out here, never comes directly.
It always moves through experience, altered by the detours it
has taken. Despite extraordinary work in studies of pedagogy, knowledge continues to be organized in most classrooms
as though language came directly, untethered, from a source
that can be named and sequestered. It is the order word that
makes this possible. Deleuze and Guattari explain:

> We call order-words, not a particular category of
> explicit statements (for example, in the impera-
> tive), but the relation of every word or every state-
> ment to implicit presuppositions, in other words,

to speech acts that are, and can only be, accomplished in the statement. . . . An order always and already concerns prior orders, which is why ordering is redundancy. . . . When the schoolmistress instructs her students on a rule of grammar or arithmetic, she is not informing them, any more than she is informing herself when she questions a student. She does not so much instruct as "insign," give orders or commands. A teacher's commands are not external or additional to what he or she teaches us.

Speaking in the free indirect, catching language in the making, the order-word is carried in the performance of what the instructor does not actually need to say. The school, its habits, the teaching expectation and pedagogical format enforce a certain organization of knowledge that moves through the free indirect to give it the form of a command, here, now. It is not language that constrains knowledge but the order-word that moves through it.

Because the order-word moves through language indirectly, pedagogies must be invented that are sensitive to how the order-word not only classifies knowledge but [also] organizes bodies. I am interested in pedagogical modes that open the way for the realization that there is no "individual subject" of enunciation. The "individual subject" is in fact what sustains the neurotypical norm: the belief that knowledge is sequestered and held by certain kinds of bodies allows us to police those bodies who learn differently.

What autistic perception teaches us is that things are not necessarily as they seem. Just because something can be categorized as an object or a subject does not necessarily mean [it is] more vital than other modes of welling experience. What is needed are not more categories but more sensitivity to difference and a more acute attunement to qualities of experience. This would allow us to see that knowledge circulates, and it is through this circulation that learning happens: language and other forms of expression move through us, and it is through this movement that we learn. Expression is social, and it is this sociality which most interests me. This is not to say that all enunciation happens "with" others. It is to underscore that language is social at its core, organized around the unsaid in the saying, oriented by the lapses and detours and reorientations of what we think of as direct communication. Our bodies, whether speaking or not, are alive with this sociality of expression.

To make this claim is to open language beyond linguistics, to value modes of expression that function across and beneath and in excess of words (including, of course, all that beyonding that takes place through the linguistic itself).

Deleuze and Guattari describe this interstitial modality of language in terms of "pass-words." These are modes of expression that activate a passage, that create circulation. Pass-words are the illicit carriers of a text's uneasiness: they undo language of its securing of reason as preestablished category. They make expression sparkle by moving it past the order-word, by freeing indirect language of the unspoken categories and imperatives that would shape it.

The challenge is that modes of passage, or pass-words, amplify the free indirect quality of expression: they make it felt that language moves us as much as we move it. This is why order-words tend to be more pervasive in the academic environment, where the detours of language tend to be excised from our work and from our bodies: we hold ourselves to the chairs in the same gesture that we delete lines of flight from our writing. To make apparent the flexibility of passage within expression would be to trouble the categories and methodologies that undergird our disciplines. It would also unsettle the linguistic bias of education—the notion that knowledge is expressed through a particular usage of language. Of course, there are plenty of examples of those who risk speaking across the lines. But the risk should not be underplayed: there are bodies, plenty of bodies, who are excluded from education because it is taken for granted that they cannot adhere to the order-words on which our educational systems are built and sustained.

New modes of knowing come with the danger of being "unrigorous," "unformed," "unclear." But we need to be careful in assuming that the order-word means rigor. The order-word is shorthand for knowing how to perform. Modes of passage that trouble existence as we know it will always feel uncertain: autistic perception lives in the quality of tendencies coming into themselves, not in already-rehearsed forms. Modes of knowing that take off from qualities informing will involve rethinking the very question of value.

If we take seriously Gilles Deleuze's idea that resistance is a

creative process, how might we revaluate the political importance
of those who society tries to pathologize and by that token effective-
ly disqualify from having a credible or authentic voice, on account
of what are badly perceived as neurological "deficiencies"?

Your question takes me in two directions. First, there is the
question of creativity, and then the question of how a creative
process activates a politics of resistance. Let me begin with
the first. Deleuze's provocation that there is no relationship
at all between art and communication is very important in
this regard. In *The Minor Gesture* I proposed the concept
of artfulness to allow us to move away from the concept of
art-as-object. Even with the proliferation, for at least the
last half-century, of more ephemeral works of art (including
performance, installation, et cetera), there tends to remain a
very strong association of art with an object, and thus with
form. If you add to that the current tendency to canalize art
toward a set of concerns or issues (as advanced by the now
ubiquitous artist statement), what we have is too strong a
tendency, I believe, to connect art to communication and,
by extension, to the order-word. I am much more interested
in the force of art for the invention of free indirect modes
of discourse. This is where the concept of the artful comes
in—a notion that what creates a shift or an opening in experience carries with it the quality of artfulness. This can
include an artwork but is not limited to it. Nor is it limited
to the human.

This leads us to the question of political resistance. Artfulness and autistic perception are deeply allied to the degree

that both engage with qualities of experience over category or form. In a world that foregrounds category at every turn, the tendency is to also see political change in terms of form: change is only change insofar as it has affected or altered the form. On the political spectrum, this situates change only in terms of what we might call macropolitics—politics that have a shape and a history and a preexisting orientation. But what about proto-politics—isn't it at the germinal level that the political has most potential for reorientation or even reinvention?

Creation as resistance begins here, I would say, where artfulness cleaves experience to produce not a recognizable set of frameworks but new modes of knowing, of feeling, of acting. There is no question that neuro-diversity opens the way to such practices, even if only by unsettling the norms through which objects and subjects come to be differentiated and "known."

This doesn't mean that resistance is a given within the field of neuro-diversity, however. Resistance is always to be crafted. The work must do its work, and, for that, the conditions of experience have to be recalibrated each time anew in relation to the ecologies of practices with which they compose. In Deleuze's vocabulary, artfulness always calls forth a people to come.

TWENTY-SIX

LIVING WITH DISAPPEARANCE

Cultural anesthesia preempts the capacity to publically circulate sensory experience along lines of race, class, gender, religion, and ethnicity.

We can often tell a great deal about violence by asking questions about its intended audience. But what becomes of symbolic violence when the body is rendered absent? And who suffers when the body of the victim vanishes without a trace? Allen Feldman, a professor of media, culture, and communications at New York University, discusses the unbearable trauma of living with forced disappearance and how state policies of denial impact public memory and the capacity for critical thought. To disappear a life is not only to deny any recourse to justice; it forces us beyond all political foundations to truth, knowledge, and agency.

Brad Evans interviews Allen Feldman

February 26, 2018

Allen Feldman is professor of media, culture, and communication at New York University. A pioneer in the ethnography of violence, the body, and the senses, his latest book is *Archives of the Insensible: Of War, Photopolitics and Dead Memory.*

Brad Evans: We know that violence is a complex problem that defies neat description. What is it about violence that commands your attention as a critical thinker?

Allen Feldman: The most cogent ethnographers of violence, which in my view include visual artists such as Berlin Dada in the aftermath of World War I, Juan Genovés engaging the Franco regime, and Gerhard Richter in the aftermath of the murder/suicide of imprisoned Baader-Meinhof members, were never in search of violence—rather violence found them. This encounter gave them no choice but to strive to depict state force in a manner that transgresses its culturally entrenched, visual, linguistic, and sonic vocabularies. This search for alternative grammars of violence is also my project, which is decisively mediated by narratives of inflicted and experienced violence by Irish Republican hunger strikers, black South African mothers in search of their disappeared, tortured ANC activists, and the AIDS-affected homeless in New York City.

Working with the sensory and anesthetizing nature of these grammars, in my recent book *Archives of the Insensible* I explore the emergent dematerialization of the consequences of violence described as a war against the critical witnessing of war. Consider the self-immunizing discourse of collateral damage, the juridical indemnification of racialized, preemptive police murder, and the spatially elongated kill chains of drone "crowd killings." I first encountered this type of state violence in 1993 when analyzing the transcripts of the trial of the police who beat Rodney King. I understood how the defense's editing of the video and police commentary aided and abetted the dematerialization of police violence by casting King as "aggressive" in being "drugged," hence bestial and, thus by inference, insensate. The defense's editing of the video choreographed King's dissected body into weaponized gestural fragments. In other words, King was bestial and drug-crazed to the extent that he could not feel and therefore could resist the baton blows enabling his impending assault on the police.

This racial tropology reappeared in the police characterization of Michael Brown in Ferguson as "bulking up" and as "demonic." King's animalistic anesthesia to pain retroactively established the sanitized and almost "humanitarian" application of "reasonable force" by the police. It was the fictionalized visual acuity of the police in retrospectively assessing the impact of their violence through a reedited version of the bystander's video that severed them from the material actuality of their assault. This positioned King as the auteur of violence as confirmed by the jury's exoneration of the police. The police inflicted cultural anesthesia on King, deleting his sensorial experience of pain and terror and *reincarnating their violence as his aggression* in a perverse minstrel show impersonation—the police played King playing them.

Cultural anesthesia stratifies and preempts the capacity to publicly circulate the sensory experience of violence along lines of race, class, gender, religion, and ethnicity. Such state practice prepares the sociocultural conditions of political apperception—the violence of politically blanking out violence and the collective capacity for its public witness and seditious de-justification. This pattern of deleting sensorial difference and the dissimulating planting of originary violence onto the Black, Muslim, or immigrant body informs the current structure of counterinsurgent governance linking Trump anti-immigrant rallies and torture at Abu Ghraib to the judicial murder of African Americans.

More recently you have been undertaking challenging research on political disappearance. How can we understand this phenomenon from the perspective of embodiment?

Political regimes of disappearance have become ubiquitous, traversing counterinsurgencies in South Africa, Chile, Argentina, Bosnia, Cambodia, Kashmir, Nepal, Sri Lanka, American extraordinary renditions, as well as the barely discernible elongated kill chains by which asylum seekers invisibly drown in murderous vessels in the Mediterranean—for they too are victims of structural disappearance that extends from their displacement by war to human trafficking to inhospitable EU borders. My interest in regimes of disappearance diverges from the legal and human rights discussion by asking what new forms of executive power emerge from this practice. I call the "embodied" and visual conditions of the politically disappeared "appearing under erasure." As Simone Weil describes:

It will surely kill, or it will possibly kill, or perhaps it merely hangs over the being it can kill at any and every moment . . . it turns man into stone. From the power of transforming a man into a thing precedes another power, otherwise prodigious, the power of turning a man into a thing while he is still alive. He is alive, he has a soul; and yet, he is a thing. . . . Still breathing, he is nothing but matter, still thinking he can think nothing.

Practices and campaigns of enforced or involuntary disappearance are historically linked to the spatial and visual logic of genocide. Following Hannah Arendt, I contend that enforced disappearance attacks the right of its victims to appear on the earth and classifies persons and populations as improper for cohabitation on the terrestrial surface of the planet. A nomos of the earth is advanced through enactments that void the diversity of cohabitation. In removing the disappeared from the terrestrial surface the executive power expansively virtualizes itself through the programmed immateriality of an absence—the deletion of the somatic materiality and biographical gravity of the vanished. Here the executive power delimits its dominion—not over the amassed corporeality of a body politic, nor even over the disfigured backs of the subjugated, but over the ephemeral historical dust and faded footprint of the absentee and deportee.

However, while genocidal operations can become public events through infrastructural mobilization and official manifestos of national cleansing, in contrast, enforced disappearance (in the state disavowal of these abductions) is frequently accidentalized, randomized, and rendered acausal by a power committed to the *disappearance of its disappearances*. Both the missing and the act of abduction are literally placed under erasure, not completely voided but subsumed under the quasi-opacity of a public retraction that can be re-scripted as a nondescript mishap inflicted upon those who henceforth will become nondescript.

Disappearance and its aftermaths can be designed to simulate the non-exemplary accident in order to inhibit the capacity of political and legal witness to catch its causality in the act. Disappearance provisions an alibi, in its sense of an elsewhere, by removing any terrestrial trace of the internal deportee and denying any rationality to their abrupt absence. The alibi is thus extended by the state's claim that the disappeared voluntarily abdicated their lives and their survivors for an elsewhere where they remain perpetually incommunicado—this is the utopia of the disappeared, the nonplace of their mostly wall-less confinement, a counter-geography of interminable displacement without end. The missing are suspended within the [interstices] of abduction, detention, decertified death, and the official denial as having actually occurred.

Too often the focus on disappearance attends to the body of the victim. But what does it mean to live with disappearance?

By instating a public secret, what we might term the regime of vanishment consciously simulates a structural indifference and anesthesiology that morbidly envelops the survivor families as much as the subtracted. The affective-sensorial experience of survivors of the disappeared is also excommunicated through a form of cultural anesthesia that I term the loss of loss—survivors of the disappeared frequently cannot speak publicly about their loss while a regime of vanishment is in power. The police, the public prosecutors, and the courts extend the stigma of culpability to the petitioning families, who are criminalized for recalling those who have become politically uninheritable.

In the exhumations performed by the South African Truth and Reconciliation Commission, the survivors of the disappeared grasped at any material fragment of usually incinerated remains as a fossil of the withdrawn persona as if they required not only proof of their abduction and execution but [also] of a prior life before the spirit was rendered bone, to paraphrase Hegel. In the documentary film *Nostalgia for the Light*, a Chilean woman whose brother was abducted by the Pinochet regime searches for decades through the Atacama Desert, where political prisoners were incarcerated, summarily executed, and secretly buried. She eventually recognizes, authenticates, and eulogizes a detached half-buried foot, preserved by desert aridity and encased in a recognizable sock, as belonging to her brother. The entire persona of the missing is reincarnated in [one's] ruined remnants. This investment in stranded fragments of history is not readily programmed into official and totalizing forms of commemoration by social institutions like transitional justice or museums of the disappeared.

I am taken by this powerful idea of the disappearance of disappearance. Can you explain this in more detail?

The disappearance of disappearance captures social torsions that Orlando Patterson associates with slavery, in particular social death and natal alienation (in this case cloaking both the disappeared and their affected peers, families, and related survivors). The disappeared and their affected families undergo a living death that, beyond any biological certainty, is a politically enforced de-animation of life without its documented termination as described earlier by Weil. Social death in Patterson is bound to *natal alienation* where the disappeared are forcefully estranged from their natality in all of its bio-symbolic nuances that have been explicated by Arendt. Natal alienation removes the disappeared from the locus of their birth as kin, subjects, and citizens, from their ascendants [and] descendants, and from the generic biopolitical condition of *natio* that constitutes the civil subject in the nation-state.

For Arendt, natality is not just biological, but [also] the ability to bring something new into the world, to initiate the unprecedented and the unrepeated, and this potentiality too is denied the disappeared and their stranded survivors. The missing are not only abducted and vanished for what they have done and said or for who they are (and many times not even that), but [also] for what they can politically become. If, as Judith Butler asserts, unwilled proximity and unchosen cohabitation are preconditions of our political existence, enforced and disavowed disappearance interdicts the possibility of the political through the banishment of present and future political interlocutors from the earth.

When we think about disappearance, we are drawn to the notion of absence. Under these conditions, the archive of the victim's life becomes important in the attempts to rehumanize the body that is no longer present. What aesthetic challenges does society face in this endeavor?

I cannot speak directly for the survivors of the disappeared as any generalization concerning the archival would run rough-shod over the heterogeneity of their desire for the disappeared who live on within and between the survivors in a time that is uniquely their own and which can never be completely so-cialized or ordered by institutions of justice, commemoration, and reconciliation. I can observe that in many post-conflict societies the survivors are repeatedly assaulted by the archi-val drive of the imperative for some form of closure, turning the page on a past that was not well lived. The cutting edge of "putting behind" this past is twofold, in that it both prescribes a futurity of certitude—reconciliation, post-conflict repara-tions, and other peace dividends—and also consigns the dis-appeared to a petrified and sealed yet never fully knowable past, now preemptively foreclosed by the rush to archive.

To memorialize, to archive, is to reduce the legacy and inheritance of enforced disappearance to pure readability. This is an attempt to reverse the loss of loss rather than to ethically learn from its irretrievability—a lesson the survi-vors coexist with daily. The legibility of victims promoted by memorialization and archivization insists on the convergence of the missing with a transmittable surplus—productivity, information, the control of space and time and moral calculability. For the archive, as a collectivizing monument, will inevitably betray the injured, the disappeared, and the dead in functioning like a machine that renders their unique suffering and that of their survivors exchangeable and commensurable. I would infer, without any empirical verification, that for their survivors the horror of collective commemoration of the disappeared is the leveling of the particularity and singular difference of their lost one and of the known particulars of their abduction, possible execution, and subsequent bodily disposal.

To homogenize the missing as a class, to make equivalence through monumentalization, is to reenact the reductive collective logic of enforced disappearance in its very condemnation. It could be likened to the inversion of the anonymized mass grave of the missing that turns it upside down and inside out, erecting a pyramidal structure of historical mummification. To memorialize the disappeared renders the missing, their survivors, and the perpetrators anachronisms. I would think that would be unacceptable for survivors who sustained over years and decades the "hauntology" of those under erasure in their search for accountability and an end to political impunity. For Derrida, "If the readability of a legacy were given, natural, transparent, univocal, if it did not call for and at the same time defy interpretation, we would never have anything to inherit from it. . . . One always inherits from a secret."

TWENTY-SEVEN

CRITIQUE OF VIOLENCE

Substituting productive ambiguities can encourage critical thinking rather than passive spectatorship.

The problem of violence cannot be studied within the confines of strict academic "disciplines." It disavows such crude reductions. No author has appreciated this more than Michael J. Shapiro, who has written extensively on the entrapments of academic thought so often tied to sovereign models and its hierarchical predilections. His work continually highlights the political importance of the arts in developing new angles of vision in the most pressing concerns. Such transdisciplinary mediations, for Shapiro, should not be reduced to acts of political or cultural appropriation but seen as viable forms of political intervention on their own terms. Discussing the importance of these pedagogical practices, Shapiro talks here about the need to take the arts seriously and what critique might mean in the twenty-first century.

Brad Evans interviews Michael J. Shapiro

April 2, 2018

Michael J. Shapiro is a professor of political science at the University of Hawai'i at Manoa. His books include *The Political Sublime* and *Politics and Time*.

Brad Evans: You have continuously pushed the boundaries of transdisciplinary engagements. Indeed, moving beyond more cultural appropriation in order to make a theoretical point, you have consistently argued the arts should be seen as a viable form of political intervention in their own right. What do you think the arts bring in terms of developing a critique of violence?

Michael J. Shapiro: On that question I share a lot with the Czech writer Milan Kundera, a position that is well captured by the title of one of his novels, *Slowness*. Near the beginning of the narrative he stages a media moment for a couple watching world news on television. The husband, recalling events of brutality and suffering he'd seen covered in recent television news broadcasts, says that violent events don't remain news for their whole duration and adds the ironic question, "The dying children of Somalia whom millions of spectators used to watch avidly, aren't they dying anymore?"

Similarly, in a review essay in which I analyzed a photographic exhibition entitled *Beautiful Suffering*, I was struck by a commentary in the exhibition brochure by the art historian Mieke Bal in which she extolled the value of "slow looking." Noting her observation about the alternative durations offered by visual media, I suggested that in contrast with mass media, especially television news, for which events are commodities oriented toward quick sales (their visuals are aimed at capturing one's momentary attention as they compete for viewers with other news services), artistic genres summon a more critically detailed yet all too human reaction, not only because of their subject matter but also because of their form.

Exhibitions (and their catalogs) have longer durations so that what has disappeared from mass media is resurrected and made available for us to renegotiate continually an event's significance. As I have argued in my recent book on politics and time (which focuses mainly on documentaries), what artistic genres offer political thinking is best captured grammatically by the future anterior, the will-have-been. So, for example, as we witness the effects of contemporary episodes of slaughter, depicted in a documentary that familiarizes us with the innocence of specific victims of drone attacks in Pakistan—Robert Greenwald's *Unmanned: America's Drone War*—we are sent back to prior violent events with innocent victims involved. Among the past events we're encouraged to rethink is the Hiroshima atomic bombing. Thanks to the alerts delivered by artistic media, Hiroshima as an event always "will-have-been." Moreover, unlike the mass media, whose discursive currency reinforces structures of power by rehearsing what is always already intelligible (i.e., immediately spendable as interpretive capital), when artistic genres intervene in events (here I am paraphrasing Krzysztof Ziarek, who has concerned himself with the "force of art") they alter their significance and thus liberate them from the hold of power. This precisely affirms the liberating, hence political, importance of the arts.

Can you elaborate here more on the importance of temporality in terms of developing viable critiques?

In addition to working with slowness as a critical aspect of artistic genres, I have evoked the concepts of mediation to assess the way the arts contest the mass media's way of nar-rativizing violent events. After working on two mediations of the 9/11 event that included Don DeLillo's novel *Falling Man* and Art Spiegelman's cartoon version, *In the Shadow of No Towers*, I discovered Johan Grimonprez's film, *Dial H-I-S-T-O-R-Y*, a video assemblage that pre-mediates the 9/11 event by assembling the history of airplane hijackings as portrayed by television media. Given that, before the 9/11 event, televisual and other mass media had prepared the public for interpreting it, in Grimonprez we observe what is effectively a challenge to the way such media *will have* nar-rativized the catastrophe in its more linear fashion.

As Grimonprez argues, "every technology invents its own catastrophe." He singles out television news, which he says has reinvented a way to look at the world and think about death. His response is to challenge television jour-nalism's commanding position by bringing the journalists into his videos, showing how they turn an event into a com-modity for consumption. He then goes on to decenter their role by juxtaposing a mixed-media narrative that confounds receptive comprehension. His film opposes the way main-stream television has imposed the interpretation of events by substituting productive ambiguities that encourage criti-cal thinking rather than passive reception.

I want to point out that the artistic strategy at work here is one of repetition. When artistic repetition mimics an event within an altered moment and with different angles of vision, it encourages political reflection by revealing the contingencies of experience. It provokes critical thinking that interrupts the more passive stance of recognition and thereby imperils what the philosopher Gilles Deleuze identifies as "opinion . . . a thought that is closely molded on the form of recognition [a form of thought mired in] orthodoxy."

A notable feature of your work has been to stress the importance of cinema as a critical medium for interrogating pressing issues in world politics. What does cinema offer to us in the rather troubling contemporary moment? And which films or feature productions stand out for you in this regard?

I'll put it simply first. Cinema has the capacity to restore what perception tends to evacuate. Rather than working with a singular and centered viewing subject, it provides a multiplicity of viewing positions (Robert Altman's camera work is especially notable in this regard). Moreover, it often displaces perceiving subjects by making its field of production (e.g., the land or cityscape), its protagonist. The more critically oriented films, which Deleuze has famously referred to as a "cinema of seeing," grab our attention in a critical way because unlike a "cinema of action" (in which we are asking ourselves what will happen next), we are asking ourselves what we are seeing.

That said, there are many films that have helped me with my inquiries into issues of violence. I'll rehearse here aspects of my analysis of David Cronenberg's *A History of Violence*. Mainstream entertainment reviews emphasized the film's dramatic action, which begins when two violent visitors enter Tom Stall's (Viggo Mortensen) diner in the small town of Millbrook, Indiana. After Tom, with surprising agility, disarms one of them and shoots them both, the media coverage alerts his mobster brother, Richie (William Hurt), in Philadelphia, who sends three thugs to bring Tom back because in a former life, as Joey Cusack, his violent antics had compramised his brother's Mafia career. Tom/Joey's long-suppressed capacity for sudden effective violence surfaces again as he kills two of the thugs, while his son shoots their leader. The Joey persona surfaces again near the end of the film when, after driving to Philadelphia to try and reconcile with his brother, he extricates himself from Richie's attempt to have an associate garrote him and summons his violent self again to kill Richie and his mobster associates in the household before he returns home as Tom to join a family dinner underway.

As we witness the transformations of Tom into Joey and back again—managed with Mortensen's amazing ability to display different personalities with different facial expressions—and see, as well, moments of suppressed otherness in his wife Edie (Maria Bello) and son, Jack (Ashton Holmes), a major dimension of the film title becomes apparent. Beneath the surface personalities of three of the protagonists is another, violent self (which in Tom's case involves a hidden history).

If we heed the film's transformations in personality, we can see them as lessons in the divided subjectivities of individuals, all of them embodying suppressed capacities for violence. However, that reading neglects what I regard as the film's more significant political pedagogy, which is about *collective* rather than individual identity, managed with the film's images as well as its spatial narrative. To access that dimension of the film we have to summon the figure of the allegory and ask, "Why Philadelphia?" The answer emerges when we recognize first of all that "Philadelphia" (from the Greek) means brotherly love. Importantly, we are alerted to a strange "Philadelphia" when, instead of visiting the iconic Independence Hall, we are invited into Richie's home, which resembles a Gothic mansion. Thus, finally and crucially, the film's politics of (a Gothic) aesthetic emerges if we see Richie's Gothic mansion as an allegory of the history of Philadelphia's violent otherness.

Thinking allegorically, we can discern a similar ambiguous legacy in the history of Philadelphia, a city that has never lived up to its name. Without going into elaborate detail, one can point to the unseen infrastructure of slavery (the unfreedom hidden within the freedom-seeking moment) in Independence Hall's painting of the signing of the Declaration of Independence. That unfreedom is highlighted in a commentary on the painting by the writer Jamaica Kincaid (whose angle of vision is doubtless affected by the fact that she entered the United States as a bonded servant). Discerning what I have called a "racial Gothic," she wonders who exerted the labor involved in preparing the signer's clothes and managing their wigs so that they could enjoy their thinking, "the luxury of it," and "have time to examine that thing they called their conscience and act on it."

The legacy of the paradoxical unfreedom within the freedom-making moment remains in a contemporary Philadelphia that is a "mosaic of paradoxes" (as its put in a critical reading of John Edgar Wideman's novel *Philadelphia Fire*, inspired by a policing moment that took many African American lives). The paradoxes that characterize the city are the juxtapositions between "extraordinary wealth and grinding Third World poverty, racial tolerance and black ghettoes, urban renewal and urban decay, social mobility and social stasis," i.e., Philadelphia is as paradoxical as the simultaneous brotherly love and brotherly hatred between Richie and Joey, acted out in a Gothic mansion that is suffused in bright lights and dark shadows.

More recently you have turned your attention to the importance of music. Can you explain what interests you here and how it relates to the problem of violence?

That turn has a long and humbling intellectual trajectory from which I will offer brief excerpts. Once I became interested in the philosophy of language and the politics of discourse (a radical shift from my early quantitative work on decision-making), I began to recognize that intelligibility is an ambiguous achievement and that my inquiries should be aimed less at clarifying issues than at uncovering their ambiguities. That epiphany was inspired in part by my reading of

Jean-Paul Sartre's biography of Gustave Flaubert (entitled in English *The Idiot of the Family*), in which he attributes Flaubert's literary creativity to a childhood during which he was slow learning language and as a result was not "robbed early on of his native poetry."

Committed to the position that the reigning structures of intelligibility have the effect of imposing passive acceptance of dominant realities and as a result of continually legitimating structures of power and authority, I moved on from the philosophy of language to analyses of genres that challenge entrenched forms of intelligibility, reinvent the rules for textual formation within genres, and create the conditions of possibility for critical thinking. In the process of turning toward cultural and artistic texts as my field of analysis, I was edified by studies that compared challenges to literary and musical intelligibility—for example, one that compared the parallel challenges to traditional forms of intelligibility of Richard Wagner and Stéphane Mallarmé, who (re)punctuated music and poetry respectively. Wagner's challenge is issued through a "fracturing of the musical period" (by departing from symphonic music's traditional quadratic form), while Mallarmé's challenge operates through obfuscation of "the syntactic hierarchy of the poetic line."

Looking for contemporary musical examples, I turned to the compositional strategies of the jazz-musician-composers John Coltrane and Thelonious Monk. Their innovations can be understood within a linguistic frame, one of which is what Houston A. Baker Jr. has called the "Deformation of Mastery," which is the approach through which some African American writers have enacted what he calls a "go(ue)rilla action in the face of acknowledged adversaries" (i.e., a mode of writing that reinflects language to challenge the discourses that have aided and abetted white dominance and violence).

I want to refer to some recent work in which I return to Coltrane's and Monk's music to treat the way jazz thinks the political. In one case, a jazz composition has responded to violence by fusing form and content to deliver explicit political meaning—John Coltrane's "Alabama," a piece with musical resonances that capture the rhythms of Martin Luther King Jr.'s eulogy at the funeral of the two young African American girls who died when "dynamite Bob" blew up a black church in Alabama. In contrast, Thelonious Monk's music makes no direct political statements that can be discerned in, for example, his riffs on such popular songs as George Gershwin's "Nice Work If You Can Get It" and Al Dubin and Harry Warren's "Lulu's Back in Town." However, one can recognize the political sensibility inherent in his musical compositions, which like African American language (mis)use, "Black talk," offers a counter-intelligibility (or what George Lipsitz famously calls a "strategic anti-essentialism"), which emerged among a people who faced attitudinal and structural inhibitions that stood in the way of freedom of civic expression.

Finally, I want to conclude my riff on the jazz-violence connection by referring to the observations of Christopher Small, who has concerned himself with the resistant, oppositional impetus of African American jazz. As jazz performers compose as they play, they are involved in what he calls a "struggle between freedom and order," for their performances constitute "a movement back and forth between the spaces of black vernacular orality and the values and assumptions of the white social order."

In a similar vein to the position consciously taken by Hannah Arendt, I have always seen your work as being on the "outside" of the narrow confines of academic disciplines. What advice would you offer to junior scholars in this regard as the pressure to conform to positivist standards is more pernicious than ever?

As a senior scholar with job security I have had the luxury of operating outside of the confines of disciplinary protocols, i.e., a freedom to practice what Jacques Rancière calls indisciplinarity, a transdisciplinary approach that breaks disciplines instead of merging them into one or another interdisciplinary mode of thinking. However, as I have been aware that junior scholars are in a more precarious situation and have accordingly wanted to articulate the rationales for transdisciplinary methods for myself as well as those who are more vulnerable, I wrote a text on the subject. In that monograph I develop and illustrate, in a series of studies, a method that foregrounds "aesthetic subjects" who are protagonists in artistic texts. Their movements in the spaces those texts articulate map and at times alter politically relevant terrains.

In contrast with psychological subjects, who as objects of investigation are treated in social science investigations as people whose attitudes, beliefs, and values can be measured and correlated with actions or decisions, artistic texts are focused on the implications of events rather than on their causes. They contain staged encounters that help us interpret the multiple ways that events are experienced (for example, there is no better analysis of the continuing effects of the 9/11 attack on the World Trade Center than Don DeLillo's novel *Falling Man*, whose diverse characters experience incommensurate aftereffects). Similarly, more interesting than what it is that causes a minister to lose her/his faith are its consequences, which are powerfully addressed in Ingmar Bergman's film *Winter Light* (1963). In an telling encounter with a fearful parishioner who has learned from the print media that China, once it develops a nuclear weapon, will blow up the world, Bergman's protagonist, Tomas Ericsson (Gunnar Björnstrand), obsessed with his own anxieties, cannot provide solace for his parishioner, Jonas (Max von Sydow), who in despair commits suicide after leaving the church.

Among what we learn from the film is the importance of paternal authority. The pastor, who is no longer able to take his role seriously, cannot function as an adequate father because *he* has experienced an inadequate father. He has faced what Michel Foucault refers to as "the father's no"; "God the father" does not function as father for him, because of "his" silence. A relay for that virtual father, the pastor-as-father is undone and is no match for the print media's fear-mongering. However one might warrant my reading of the film (it's merely an illustration), I have intended my "method" of turning to artistic texts and focusing on aesthetic subjects as a source of solace for those who want to stray from mainstream social science explanatory methods.

Stylistically, I prefer to let my approach (which is akin the way Walter Benjamin identified his method—"literary montage"—with which one shows rather than tells) speak for itself. However, I don't recommend that avoidance to junior scholars in the social sciences. In light of the institutionalized method-obsessed expectation that scholars must justify knowledge claims with resort to a methods commentary, I recommend capitulation and thus explication within the text. At the same time, I also recommend that the junior scholars, faced with social science disciplines that remain in a pre-Kantian philosophical slumber, seek to edify their readers by articulating the philosophical frames (which are largely delivered by post-Kantian philosophers) that help direct the methods through which the artistic and cultural texts with which they work can serve as the objects of investigation.

Thus my methodological advice is to heed texts rather than stand-alone objects. A text can be seen (in the words of John Mowitt) as "an antidisciplinary field" rather than as an intra-disciplinary object. As such, a text can open the spaces that the discursive practices of disciplinary orthodoxies have closed. As the semiotician Roland Barthes (whose perspective has inspired Mowitt) pointed out decades ago, a "text" (as opposed to a mere "work") is a "methodological field" worthy of elaborate analysis. Moreover, in addition to semiology, there is an abundance of critically oriented, politically relevant modes of analysis that uncover the way texts (literary, architectural, musical, visual, et cetera) think in politically perspicuous ways.

TWENTY-EIGHT

VIOLENCE IN PORN: IT'S NOT WHAT YOU THINK!

It is through our consent, and the intimacy created by that consent, that we present a dialogue about boundaries.

Pornography is perhaps the medium that, despite its vast heterogeneity, gets treated as a blanket category and has been historically labeled as uniformly and inherently violent. Through this, pornographers have themselves faced the violence of marginalization and criminalization. In more recent years, different and better narratives about porn and sex work in general have emerged, but the violences of anti-sex worker legislation and scant worker rights persist in force. Adult performer, filmmaker, and activist Mickey Mod discusses where it is correct to locate sites of violence in the industry, such as the use of racist, ableist, ageist, transphobic, and sexist tropes. As a black performer, Mod has experienced firsthand the grim taxonomies into which mainstream porn organizes actors of color. He has also seen crucial sites of resistance against this, exploring how pornography can produce a visual field prompting and serving more ethical sexual relationality that can challenge and subvert our conceptions of violence itself.

Natasha Lennard interviews Mickey Mod

Mickey Mod is an adult performer, erotic filmmaker, and the vice president of the Adult Performer Advocacy Committee.

Natasha Lennard: Can you tell us about your entry into the porn industry, the impetus for it, and the sort of work you have tended and choose to do?

Mickey Mod: My situation was pretty unique. I was twenty-eight, living in San Francisco surrounded by people who wanted to create sexual performance art. I enjoy a lot of different types of sex, and I had always had exhibitionist fantasies. I saw an ad on Craigslist looking for male performers. I wasn't in a relationship at the time, and as I read the details of the posting looking for male extras for a BDSM group scene, I thought it was an opportunity to enact a fantasy that I didn't know how to access in my personal life in a controlled environment. Performing in porn gave me a financial stability that I didn't have working restaurant and bartending jobs after college. It gave me access to a community of sex-positive people who wanted to create content. In the ten years since then I have worked throughout the U.S. and Europe as a performer and director in a number of different genres of pornography, from mainstream to BDSM and fetish content.

The conversation around porn and violence has changed dramatically in the last decades. In the early days of online porn, the broad (and conservative) contention was that porn was oppressive to its workers and psychologically damaging to its viewers. Porn gets treated as a homogenous category of "bad," and critics call to ban and criminalize the entire industry, even though millions of people watch some form of pornography.

Porn gets a blanket treatment that no other medium does. When we see violent, potentially damaging and oppressive content in mainstream cinema, we don't call for the end of movies or the criminalization of Hollywood, we call for improvement. What are the effects of treating porn as one big violent category?

When pornography is treated as a monolith, the workers involved in any area of the industry lose the ability to talk about their own experiences, but they are simultaneously held responsible for any incident of abuse or misconduct anywhere it may occur. Adult entertainment is made by many companies and individuals, each with their own policies and beliefs about how to best make a product and profit.

Yes, some porn companies have bad and unethical practices, however, I don't hold HBO accountable for the mistakes of PBS because both of them are television networks. Owing to societal stigmas around sex, public discourse does not accord porn its rightful status as a heterogenous, varied industry. This stigma is so great that it stymies discussion about improving working conditions or making a better product. When you treat something as per se "evil," you pave the way for stereotypes to continue, issues to get ignored, for victims to get blamed. You deny the possibility of change.

Listening to performers about their own experiences is a task that few seem to be able to handle. Often the popular discourse centers on the latest mainstream documentary on porn with a narrow agenda. Or I've noticed people refer to some unnamed cousin's friend, who did one scene [and] had a bad experience; suddenly this character gets to be the projected example, the received wisdom, for all people in the industry. When discussions of porn and sex work are reduced to moral arguments alone, it stops being recognized as work. We need to discuss the economic choices that workers, consumers, and corporations are making with regards to policies and products—the same way you would with any other form of entertainment.

In a pushback against resolute, anti–sex work second-wave feminism, we saw a lot of pro–sex-work, pro-porn arguments focusing on how much the workers loved their work. It was an understandable and often true response to criticisms insisting that all sex workers were necessarily without choice or liberty. But this counter-argument landed us in a tricky place. It meant that in order to defend sex work as a choice, the workers had to profess to love their work. The "happy hooker" narrative, I believe it's called. We're seeing a useful corrective now, in which we don't demand that sex workers love their work for it to be respected as work—and therefore in need of workers' protections and rights.

It's not just a sex work problem—the eroticization of labor under late capitalism ("love your job!") infects all parts of the economy, especially service work; the affective demand on sex workers seems higher, though. I'm curious how, in your years of work, these sorts of issues have played out for you. Do you feel you have to defend your work to skeptics by saying that you love it? And do you think working in porn should in fact be treated as just another job?

There is such a pervasive narrative that sex workers can't enjoy their work, either as a result of coercion or some form of trauma that leads us to sex work in the first place. Yet it is utterly insane to demand that someone enjoy or love their job every single time they go to work. It is equally insane to tell some they need to quit their job any time they're having a bad day or need support. I would love to discuss working porn just as any other job. I would love to for people to think that because my job involves sex that I'm not damaged, unintelligent, or incapable of being in a relationship. Most importantly, I would love for people to actually listen to the experiences of sex workers and understand that there is a range of experiences.

Many discussions about porn and violence focus solely on content and what images and messages are transmitted to (especially young) viewers. But this focus often misses some of the sites of real violence in porn: namely, the way the so-called "tube sites" of free online porn (most of which are owned by one leviathan company, MindGeek) have come to systematically shape the entire industry, often to the detriment of workers. Many people don't have any idea about this business model. We ask for ethical porn and don't always consider ethical consumption. Could you explain a little bit about how that works, how it impacts performers, workers, and industry ethics?

Tube sites like *Pornhub.com* have built their business models on stolen content. This content is uploaded by people who do not have any legal right to the content and often edit out the legal information required by producers in order to let the viewer know that the product was made lawfully. For example, 2257 information, which is the statement that appears before adult entertainment to inform the viewer that all participants are over the age of eighteen, is removed. Interviews with performers conducted before rough and BDSM scenes, during which performers actively set their boundaries and discuss the acts in which they will and will not engage, are removed. Titles of productions are renamed in ways that may be offensive and include hate speech and racist and misogynist search terms and tags, over which the performers featured and the original production companies have no control.

When porn is delivered in these ways, it doesn't show the viewer that the original product followed basic legal guidelines. It obscures the fact that performers are able to make decisions about the content they are creating.

Oftentimes scenes and entire films are posted for free, with very little recourse for performers or production companies to make a profit. Companies thus make less money, make less content, and offer low rates. They take fewer risks in developing new content or expanding into the sort of different genres that might challenge some of the more problematic stereotypes in porn.

Tube sites and many production companies regularly use search terms, titles, and tag categories which rely on some of porn's more problematic stereotypes. The performers featured under these categories and titles on a tube site have no control over that and may find those terms derogatory to themselves or the communities to which they belong. Such categorizations can reinforce violence committed on those communities. It's a conservative business model insofar as the major content providers would argue that these porn stereotypes are simply "what people want," without considering that consumers only learn to want and choose from what has been made available to them—it's a cycle inscribed into the back end of the tube site model, which is hard to break.

When content is produced that dehumanizes and nonconsensually objectifies its participants, we create violence. When we fail to provide transparency about a product's intent or the process of its production and limit the performer is and viewer's ability to participate based on accurate information, we produce a kind of violence. Failing to discuss issues around representation of marginalized communities with members of those communities—I don't see this as specific to porn.

We've talked in the past about how categorization in porn reproduces and reasserts some of the worst racist, sexist, transphobic

*and ageist tropes. "Thug, MILF, Shemale," et cetera. The massive
porn tube sites are organized around these categories, maintaining
a cycle in which the very porn that gets made is made to then fit
in with this grim taxonomy. Can you tell us about some of your
experiences navigating this as a black performer?*

There are limited opportunities for performers of color to
perform in a way that's not tied to or predicated on their
identities as such. You're a black performer, first and foremost. And there's an expectation that this category of performance live up to certain stereotypes—this will be explicitly
a thematic element of the film and its presentation. For example, the "cheating wife with black man" trope. It's important to note that these narratives are almost always placing
the black man and his sexuality as something that happens
to white people. The presumption is a white audience with a
fear of people of color. Another problem, as I said before, is
a performer doesn't always know how the final product will
be packaged, even after filming—production companies can
rename and reframe content, and this is even before the tube
sites get to it.

Consider the fact that an "interracial" scene, as they
are called, almost always means a black man with a white
woman. White female performers can negotiate exclusivity
agreements and higher pay for "interracial" scenes; this isn't
accorded to black performer on whom the scene also relies.
And this is certainly never a choice given to women of color.

When a white female performer says "I don't do interracial," it might be a business decision, it might be on

her agent's advice, or it might be because she's a racist—I have no way of knowing. Of course, every performer is entitled, and must be, to choose with whom they will or will not perform. No one should have to do any "type" of scene. But as it stands, white fragility and discrimination are over-determinant in shaping the industry for performers of color. And since, in general, adult performers tend to stay in the industry for a very short time and don't necessarily feel invested in or identified with it, it's a challenge to organize and advocate for long-term change.

The expectations of porn to evolve are extremely low because of the shame around sex. That low expectation allows for a tolerance for behavior and categorization common with so many forms dehumanization. It's easy to be transphobic, racist, homophobic when dialogue around the medium of porn sex isn't accepted. Shame recognize shame. Being a minority in America is exhausting and can lead to insanity because of the compromises you have to make in order for your survival. Porn is no different. It holds up a fun-house mirror to the ugliness we would rather not discuss. Porn is a theater of shame. It can be transgressive and subversive but only if the audience and performers acknowledge that a performance has taken place.

You do a lot of BDSM work. This is perhaps the most intense site for teasing out distinctions between violence, physical pain, and harm—things which are presumed to collapse together in most other areas of life. BDSM dynamics also often satirize, play with and highlight societal hierarchies and power structures that are under-examined in "normal life." How has BDSM informed your understanding of the term "violent"? Production companies focused on ethical BDSM often include "before and after" scenes to stress the necessity of consent and care. The risk with free online porn, where scenes are stolen, spliced, and shortened, is that the scenes stressing consent can get cut. What are your thoughts and concerns with regards to this and how your body and acts might be contextualized in this way?

Among the many reasons I had for choosing to do BDSM performance work, what stands out to me to be the most important was my ability to be a collaborator in the scene based on my limits. Both as a submissive and a dominant, I was able to discuss my boundaries about the dynamics involved and the environment within which my scene partners and I felt the most safe. Violence doesn't usually come with a discussion about safety—there are no trigger warnings; there are no safe words. But with BDSM performance, I'm exploring physical pain and my reaction around processing that pain while knowing at any time that if anyone feels uncomfortable, we can stop.

As a society, we don't respect the choices of most individuals, and we certainly don't respect the right of women to consent to anything. The discussions around the morality of BDSM are almost always centered around whether a temporary choice of submission is acceptable in a society of constant oppression.

I view BDSM as a way of discussing the power dynamics that surround us. We use physical acts and language that mirror those dynamics, but it is through our consent and the intimacy created by that consent that we present a dialogue about boundaries. Establishing limits and having those limits respected is not a luxury that we have in most areas of our lives.

We look at boxing and mixed martial arts as sports that are modeled on techniques for harming one another. We respect an athlete's choice to engage in these activities because we understand that when the final bell rings they will walk away. The fight is real, but when sex is real we can't handle it. We are far more comfortable with actions that remind of destruction than those that remind us of creation.

Adult entertainment can be an important site creatively for addressing power, hierarchy, and oppression. Race play can produce intense and cathartic discussion. When people are ready to be offended, as is often the case with porn, sometimes they're also ready to challenge and be challenged. When sites remove the parts of scenes featuring negotiation around consent and boundaries, they throw away this most crucial aspect of BDSM. This editing then reinforces the harmful stereotypes about BDSM and sex workers, which doesn't move us forward in our understanding of the needs of others and what sort of conversations BDSM can productively bring forth.

TWENTY-NINE

AGAINST VIOLENCE, QUEER FAILURE

Can an art of failure create places of connection and solidarity not based on identity and likeness but on a willingness to change the world?

The renowned queer theorist Jack Halberstam was interviewed some months before the Trump administration's decision to ban most transgender individuals from the military—a move prompted, it seems, by one of the president's blustering tweets and grounded in nothing more than bigotry. But here Halberstam stresses the necessity to question why the state and corporate interests might find benefit in supporting LGBTQ communities (such as revenue streams from formerly excluded communities) and when it benefits them to oppose those same communities (to, for example, garner conservative votes). Halberstam insists that we look at the intersection of racist and class violence when we address violence against LGBTQ communities and individuals. To treat "anti-trans violence" as a banner term in order to gather statistics overlooks the fact that the majority of victims are also poor and black. Here questions of triggering and trauma and how we might problematize the current debate about "trigger warnings" on campus without playing into the rhetoric of the vile far right are discussed.

Natasha Lennard interviews J. Jack Halberstam

Jack Halberstam is professor of American studies, ethnicity, gender studies, and comparative literature at the University of Southern California. His books include *Gaga Feminism: Sex, Gender and the End of Normal* and *The Queer Art of Failure.*

Natasha Lennard: For a number of years you have spoken about the issue of "triggering"—the idea that certain cultural or political content could be unbearably traumatic for a person (usually a student in these conversations). You have criticized the way a rhetoric of trauma gets established, presuming every subject is somehow always damaged and ready to be triggered. These discussions have only become more and more prominent and have been weaponized by the far right to call everyone from centrist liberals to antifascist leftists "triggered snowflakes." Can you tell us a bit about the dangers you see in current debates over "triggers," both in and outside of academia?

J. Jack Halberstam: It is true that as this debate about triggering has played out in the last year or so, the right has certainly latched on to the idea of whiny lefty liberals and the futility of a certain brand of identity politics. I think, however, one does not want to cede the terms of important debates to right-wing nuts. Anything we say, after all, can and will be used against us in these shouty and polarized times.

So if we believe that there might be some difference between professors who refuse to give trigger warnings, and even express concern about them, and right-wingers who complain about "triggered snowflakes," then the next question is how might we navigate this complex terrain. First, professors need to understand why students have latched on to the demand for trigger warnings; second, students might want to think about the implications of insisting upon them; and, finally, we might all think about the meaning of "safe space" in an era preoccupied with security and surveillance.

I realized from some of the responses [to my essay on triggering] that the anger and upset about content warnings, triggers, and demands for safe space is a kind of misplaced outrage about the legacy of debt, ruination, and political mayhem that we are passing on. When students ask for safe space, in a way they are expressing a really righteous fury about the loss of public spheres of conversation, the escalation of even banal debates online and in the media, the diminishing influence of academia and the humanities in particular, and the end of utopian thinking in an era of a rapidly disintegrating sense of futurity. Student debt, climate change, racial capitalism, social inequality—these are the truly triggering topics, but since they cannot be resolved the energy they generate drifts elsewhere.

Long before the issue of gendered bathrooms in schools came to the national political stage, you wrote about "the bathroom problem."

You noted the potential violence that trans and even those with gender ambiguous appearances face if deemed to have used the "wrong" bathroom. Writing in the 1990s, you highlighted the spurious arguments behind the enforcement of strict gender-seg-regated bathrooms. The Trump administration was swift to with-draw Obama-era federal guidelines, which had protected trans kids' ability to use bathrooms and facilities corresponding with their gender identity. It's telling that this seemed such an urgent intervention for Trump in the first month of his presidency—why do you think this is?

Well, this issue is a bit more complicated in the sense that Trump has not specifically targeted LGBT issues in his first few months as president. Instead, he has pointedly made war on immigrants, Muslims, and poor people while ensur-ing that more money will pour into the coffers of the rich, less education will be available to the children of the poor, and he and his cronies will continue to benefit massively, now and for generations, from unfettered corporate theft. While those details are being worked out, in many ways his decision not to fight gay marriage or target bathroom bills federally (he tends to leave those up to the states to enforce or deny) is designed to make him seem modern and toler-ant. Of course, Pence is another matter. I think the larger question is why states and corporate interests have become so supportive suddenly around LGBT issues. What kind of revenue can LGBT communities generate for conservative corporate interests? When does it benefit states to oppose their LGBT communities, [and] when does it benefit them to support them?

I can speak personally and say that the last two years have really changed for me in terms of bathroom policing. Even though I have become more ambiguously gendered after getting top surgery, I am challenged far less in women's bathrooms precisely because we have had public conversations about bathrooms, and people have heard that they should not be challenging others about their basic rights to use public facilities. That said, I was challenged last week in a bathroom in an LGBT center in Toronto for godsake, right before an event on "gender fluidity" at which I was speaking!

You choose, as you put it, a "floating" approach to your gender pronouns. "I prefer not to help people out in their gender quandaries and yet, I appreciate you asking," you wrote in a blog post, referencing Herman Melville's Bartleby the Scrivener, that beloved recalcitrant character who would "prefer not to." Is "preferring not to" somewhat predicated on a privilege, i.e., knowing that in your position, your preference (or non-preference) might not invoke violence against you that many queer folks seek to avoid through "passing" as male or female?

I appreciate the question, but I have to say that living in a gender-ambiguous body has very few privileges. In fact, being gender-ambiguous is often the precondition for violent punishment given that your gender ambiguity has raised flags for your tormentors that would not go up if you were seamlessly passing. Also, lots of trans people cannot pass—

they might be too short, too tall; they might not tolerate hormones or be able to afford surgery; they may look ambiguous even after transitioning. Saying I prefer not to enforce gender pronouns is not a statement about freedom but a verdict on the vocabularies available to us to tell each other who we are.

Also, a word on violence against trans people—the vast majority of violent incidents directed against transgender people are experienced by poor people of color. So when we offer up statistics as part of a generalized narrative about transgender vulnerability to violence, we are not really noting that way that class and race markers are far more important in assessing vulnerability than cisgender versus transgender might be. If we sorted for class and race difference, we might discover, for example, that white trans men experience less violence than white cis-women. I think the grouping of all trans people under one banner for the purposes of gathering statistics about violence is inherently flawed. Similarly, to claim much higher suicide rates for trans youth or queer youth in general requires us to know how many straight young people commit suicide because they are heterosexual. It is not far-fetched to say that a young person may be suicidal because of the pressures of heterosexuality, but when non-gay and non-trans young person kills themselves, we never see this reported as "heterosexual suicide." If we do not report on heterosexual suicide, how can we know whether rates of suicide for queers and trans people are higher or lower?

Finally, many young trans people will report suicidal

ideation to their therapists because it is a surefire way to access hormones and surgery. Sandy Stone in her classic "Posttranssexual Manifesto" talked about how transsexuals, in the early days of gender clinics, would tell the therapist whatever it [was] the therapist needed to hear in order to get treatment and hormones. This meant that transsexual stories were all remarkably uniform, and in a way they were authored by and for the therapist rather than by and for the transsexual "patient." Stone tells of how closely transsexual autobiographies mirrored the account of the transsexual profile provided by psychiatrist Harry Benjamin: "It took a surprisingly long time—several years—for the researchers to realize that the reason the candidates' behavioral profiles matched Benjamin's so well was that the candidates too had read Benjamin's book, which was passed from hand to hand within the transsexual community, and they were only too happy to provide the behavior that led to acceptance for surgery." Something along these lines happens today through *YouTube* videos where young people record their transitions and upload them for others to watch and learn from. The kids who watch these videos learn what to say and to whom.

I am not saying that trans people are not victims of violence, but in a contemporary context there is certainly much less bullying, pathologizing, and physical violence directed at middle-class white trans people than in the past. Trans men and women of color remain subject to the violations that are meted out systematically under systems of white supremacy.

Famously, you've advocated for an embrace of failure from a queer perspective, as an enterprise against capitalism's taxonomy of success (profit) and failure (inability to accrue profit). Right now we have a president who can't stop using the term "winning," who gained support based on the idea of his business "success," but who many see as having failed upwards to the highest seat of power— a violent form of failure and success combined. How do narratives of success produce violences which embraces of failure might stop? How might taking up the idea of failing queerly be of use to the messy and scrambling attempts we're seeing at building some sort of "resistance"—a resistance movement that is framed around a rhetoric of seeking coherent left alternatives, with an eye to "winning"?

I think Trump's endless claims to be winning and to be "tremendously successful" and to have the biggest this and the best that only intensify the need for a queer art of failure. I have noticed lots of new work on failure in the mainstream recently that notices how failure becomes a kind of low-level resistance to the streams of braggadocio issuing forth from the White House even as we watch presidential crime happen on a daily basis.

I agree that failure harbors some hope for resistance. With no functional model of socialism available to us and only a few global intellectuals like Judith Butler, Angela Davis, Fred Moten, Lisa Lowe, Saidiya Hartman, and Paul Preciado willing and able to think about crafting alternatives, we certainly have to turn to the counterintuitive logic of failure to think about new forms of alliance and action.

I personally love the poetic reach of Moten and Harney's concept of "the undercommons," which represents a fugitive force of intellectual refusal and opens onto the closest thing we have to utopia—an imagined landscape in which we embrace each other in what they call "our mutual debt" on behalf of tearing down the system that is an impediment to building a world in which we can thrive. "We owe each other everything," they write, suggesting that we should honor our debts to each other rather than digging into models of economic indebtedness produced by the state to maintain systems of radical inequality. Moten and Harney propose "study" as an activity to be cultivated on behalf of learning to fail at making profit while succeeding at making new forms of connection and new futures for us all. I hope that the art of failure participates in imagining and creating an under-commons—a place of connection and solidarity not based on identity and likeness but on a willingness to change the world.

ACKNOWLEDGMENTS

This anthology is the outcome of many enriching and challenging conversations with inspiring critical thinkers, artists, and cultural producers. We remain humbled by the opportunity to have discussed these pressing issues in such respectful and stimulating company. None of this, however, would have been possible were it not for the initial foresight of Peter Catapano and Simon Critchley of the *New York Times* forum "The Stone." It is our hope that we repaid their initial belief in this project. We are also extremely thankful to Taylor Adams for his meticulous editing and patience, Tom Lutz, Boris Dralyuk, and Cord Brooks from the *Los Angeles Review of Books*, whose support and contributions have also been integral to the development of these timely yet tragically timeless conversations, along with City Lights for its dedication to the radical voice. It has been a pleasure to work with these committed people.

Brad Evans would also like to acknowledge all the support of friends, family, and colleagues (who are too numerous to mention here). You know who you are! He is continually amazed by the spirit of his beautiful daughter Amelie, and he cherishes every moment they share together. And most of all, he is thankful every single day for the love and support of Chantal Meza. She has encouraged him to see the world for all its beauty and pain, and has made him realize the true meaning of "home."

We don't like to speak about "debt" because that is a form of violence itself. We are, however, thankful and grateful for those who engage in this ongoing fight for justice, dignity, and a world where nobody is disposable.

ABOUT BRAD EVANS AND NATASHA LENNARD

Brad Evans is a political philosopher, critical theorist, and writer, whose work specializes on the problem of violence. The author of many books, edited volumes, and articles, he serves as Professor of Political Violence and Aesthetics at the University of Bath, UK. He is currently the lead editor for a dedicated section on violence, arts, and critical theory with *The Los Angeles Review of Books*. He is also founder and director of the Histories of Violence Project: www.historiesofviolence.com

Brad's books have received prestigious international awards and have been translated into many languages, including Spanish, Turkish, Korean and German. His latest books include *Histories of Violence: Post-War Critical Thought* (with Terrell Carver); *Portraits of Violence: An Illustrated History of Radical Thinking* (with Sean Michael Wilson) *Disposable Futures: The Seduction of Violence in the Age of the Spectacle* (with Henry Giroux), *Resilient Life: The Art of Living Dangerously* (with Julian Reid), *Liberal Terror*, and *Deleuze & Fascism: Security: War: Aesthetics* (with Julian Reid). Brad's web site: www.brad-evans.co.uk.

Natasha Lennard is a journalist, essayist and columnist. She is a contributing writer for *The Intercept* and her work has appeared regularly in *The Nation, Esquire, The New York Times*, and *The New Inquiry*, among others. She teaches critical journalism at the New School For Social Research in New York. She is author of *Being Numerous: Essays on Non-Fascist Life*.

NEW AND RECENT IN THE OPEN MEDIA SERIES

American Nightmare:
Facing the Challenge of Fascism
By Henry A. Giroux with a foreword by George Yancy

Have Black Lives Ever Mattered?
By Mumia Abu-Jamal

Loaded:
A Disarming History of the Second Amendment
By Roxanne Dunbar-Ortiz

Torn from the World:
A Guerrilla's Escape from a Secret Prison in Mexico
By John Gibler

I Couldn't Even Imagine That They Would Kill Us:
An Oral History of the Attacks Against the Students of Ayotzinapa
By John Gibler with a foreword by Ariel Dorfman

Storming the Wall:
Climate Change, Migration, and Homeland Security
By Todd Miller

Narrative of the Life of Frederick Douglass, an American Slave,
Written by Himself: A New Critical Edition
By Angela Y. Davis

CITY LIGHTS BOOKS | OPEN MEDIA SERIES
ARM YOURSELF WITH INFORMATION